김희민 교수의
정치학 연구

김희민 지음

HeeMin Kim's Political
Science Research

박영사

지난 **40**년 동안 항상 곁에 있으면서 최고의 지지자로
머물러 준 나의 아내, 서윤경에게 바친다.

◆◆◆◆◆

For Yun Gyeong·Seo Kim,
who has been my number one supporter
for the past 40 years.

목차

‖ 비교정치 ‖

‖ 기타 (한국정치/국제정치/이론/교육) ‖

필자는 지난 2019년 여러 실력 있는 후배교수들과 함께 한국 보수정부의 부침이라는 책을 펴냈다. 그때도 박영사에서 책을 출판해 주셨다. 이명박·박근혜 정부의 여러 결정들을 보면서 "왜?" 하는 질문을 국내 정책과 외교정책에 묻는 그런 연구들을 모았다. 또 촛불 혁명에 대해서도 분석을 해보려 하였고 촛불 이후의 정국도 예측해 보려고도 하였다.

2019년은 저자가 1989년에 미국 플로리다 주립대학교에서 강의를 시작한 지 30년이 되는 해여서 제자, 후배교수들과의 출판은 더욱 의미가 있었다. 마침 나이도 회갑에서 1년을 넘긴 시점이어서 뭐 회갑 기념 그런 의미도 부여했다. 하지만 그 책은 필자의 30년 기념이나 회갑에 맞추어서 제자들이 기획했던 것은 아니고, 당시 급변하는 한국 정치상황에서 해외 학술회의와 국내 학술회의 등에서 발표된 논문들을 모아서 출판한 것이다. 편집도 필자가 직접 맡아서 했다.

그 책의 머리말에 필자는 다음과 같이 적었다.

"이제 100세 시대라고는 하나 언제까지 본인이 연구를 '잘'할 수 있을지는 모르겠다. 한국의 경우 교수들에게 정년이라는 인위적인 종착점이 있고, 그로 인해 은퇴 시기가 연구 종료 시점이 되는 경우가 많은 것이 안타깝다. 본인의 경우 육체적으로 또 정신적으로 언제까지 좋은 연구를 할 수 있을지는 알 수 없지만, 그날이 올 때까지는 최선을 다해 연구하고 싶다."

그때가 2019년 8월이었다. 말이 씨가 된다고 했던가? 필자는 같은 해 11월부터 유전성 망막 질환이 갑자기 발현하면서, 빠른 속도로 시력과 시야를 잃었다. 2020년 여름에는 정부로부터 중증 시각 장애인 판정을 받게 된다. 물론 너무 놀랍고 두려운 시간을 보냈다. 2020년 후반에는 관악구에 소재한 실로암 시각장애인 복지관이란 곳에서 시각장애인 기초 재활 교육과정을 반년 동안 이수했다. 내 경우에는 눈으로 보지 않고 귀로 들어가며 타자를 칠 수 있는 소프트웨어의 발견이 너무나 큰 도움이 되었다. 물론 이런 소프트웨어가 있어도

모든 게 다 쉽게 되는 것은 아니다. 먼저 컴퓨터의 포인터가 어디 있는지가 안 보이니, 마우스는 더 이상 쓸 수가 없었다. 또 어떤 기능을 사용하더라도 자판의 여러 개의 키들을 동시에 눌러야하고, 그를 위해서 수도 없는 자판 키들의 조합을 외워야 했다. 그리고 이 소프트웨어가 글자는 읽어줄 수 있지만, 표·그림·사진 등을 읽을 수 없으니, 특히 인터넷에 들어가면 제대로 된 정보의 수집이 쉽지 않았다.

2021년 여름에는 서울대학교를 조기 은퇴하였다. 약간 남은 시력과 복지관에서 배운 스킬들로 강의와 연구가 전혀 불가능한 것은 아니었으나, 불과 2년 남은 정년까지 버티기 위해서 완벽하지 않은 강의로 고객(학생)들을 대하고 싶지는 않았다.

반면에 연구는 아직 내 머릿속에 넘쳐나는 연구주제와 하고 싶은 말들을 어떻게 하든 지금까지 해오던 것 같이 연구논문의 형태로 계속 써대고 싶었다. 그런데 지금부터 나의 역할에 대해 나와 내제자들 사이의 의견이 좀 달랐다. 제자들은 이미 선생님의 연구력은 다 아는데, 새로운 논문 몇 개 더 적는 것에 너무 큰 의미를 두지 말란다. 공통적으로 그들은 내가 해 온 연구를 한국의 정치학자들과 학생들에게 의미 있는 모습으로 남겨주는 것이 더 가치가 있을 것 같다고 했다. 아마도 내가 평소에 그들에게 이야기했던 어떤 안타까운 심정들을 그들이 먼저 기억했던 것 같다.

미국에서 22년 대학 강의 후 귀국을 하여 나와 내 주변을 돌아보았을 때, 정말 안타까운 점이 있었다. 먼저 재정이 감당 안 되고 미래의 사회과학자를 꿈꾸는 학생들은 이미 모두 북미 혹은 유럽으로 유학을 가고 없다. 그럼에도 불구하고 한국의 대학들은 또 다 그들만의 대학원 과정이 있다. 사실 사회과학에서 새로운 분야의 개척과 기존 분야의 첨단연구가 한국에서 나오는 경우는 별로 없다. 물론 한국학은 예외다. 한국에서 학위를 하는 학생들은 어느 대학에 진학을 하고, 지도교수가 누군가에 따라 배우는 것과 쓰는 논문이 너무나 다를 수 있다. 그래서 지난 10년간 필자는 '연구란 무엇인가?', '과학 철학이란 무엇인가?', '정치학에서는 어떤 질문에 답을 하는 것이 옳은가?', '어떻게 주장을 표현할 것인가?', '또 이론이란 무엇인가?', '자기 이론에 대한 증거는 어떻게 제시하는 것이 옳은가?', '연구 설계는 어떻게 하는 것인가?', '분석을 할 때 어디까지 자기의 이론을 증명하였다고 주장하는 것이 옳은가?' 등등 정치"학'의 가장 기초적인 문제부터 학생들의 머릿속에 넣어주려고 노력했다.

제자들은 평소 나의 그런 우려를 상기시켜 주었고, 나는 그 맥락에서, 본인이 앞으로 학생들을 직접 가르치지 않아도 도움이 되는 방법이 없을까에 대해 고민하였다. 장고 끝에 한국에서 네 권 정도의 서적을 출판하는 장기 계획을 세웠다. 지금의 시력으로 네 권을 다 마칠 수 있다는 보장은 물론 없다. 그래서 나름대로 우선순위도 정했다. 그중에 첫 번째가 바로 이 책이다. 이 책은 필자가 평생한 연구 중에 (필자가 보기에) 가장 창의적이고 좋은 논문을 추린 결과이다.

많은 사람이 본인이 한국 민주주의의 전문가라고 알고 있는데, 사실 필자는 그렇게 생각 하지 않는다. 굳이 나의 가장 직접적인 전문 분야를 이야기하라면, 비교정치와 정치이론이 라고 말하고 싶다. 한국 정치의 경우도 특정 이벤트(선거, 합당 등)을 따로 설명하는 것이 나의 목표가 아니고, 수십 년 동안 계속 이어져 오는 논쟁, 즉 합리적 선택이론 (Rational-Choice Theory)이 비서구 사회에 적용 가능한 가의이론적 논쟁에 기여하는 것이 다. 지난 수십 년 간 많은 동,서양의 학자들이 합리적 선택이론은 시장 경제로 출발한 서구 사회에만 적용할 수 있다는 주장을 폈다. 나의 입장은 비서구권 국가에서도 "적용가능하다" 는 것이다. 이 논쟁에 관한 필자의 연구 중 필자의 판단에 수작(秀作)으로 여겨지는 것들은 이미 『Korean Democracy in Transition: A Rational Blueprint for Developing Societies』 (University of Kentucky Press)와 『게임이론으로 푸는 한국의 민주주의』(서울대학교 출판 부) 등 두 서적에 모아서 출판이 되었다.

위에서 말한 한국 연구 외에, 어찌보면 본인의 1번 분야라고 볼 수 있는 비교정치이론 등의 분야에서 잘 썼다고 생각하는 논문 14편을 모은 것이 이 책이다. "14"라는 숫자는 별 의미가 없고, 책을 만드는 데 적절한 분량이 그 정도라고 하여 14편을 골랐다. 그래서 이 책은 비교 정치를 주로 하면서 이론, 교육 합리적 선택이론과 관계가 없는 한국 정치 분석 등에 관한 연구도 담고 있다. 그러니까 누군가 나의 연구가 궁금하다면, 위에서 언급한 한국 정치 책 두 권 중에 하나와 이 책을 읽으면 나라는 사람이 평생 한 연구의 핵심을 파악하는 것이 된다.

위에서 말한 것처럼 이 책의 목적은 해외에서 사회과학이 어떻게 진화하고 있는가에 대한 정보의 access가 부족한 사람들에게 도움이 되는 것이다. 하여 이 논문들을 적을 때 필자의 느 낌을 남겨놓기 위해 번역을 하지 않고 영문 그대로 출판한다. 해외 학술지 출판에 대한 이해를 증진하고, 또 아래에서 이야기하는 이 책의 효율적인 사용을 위해서도 이 논문들을 원문 그대로 읽는 것이 더 도움이 될 것이다.

외국에서 정치학을 공부하는 이들(한국 유학생 포함)은 어차피 나의 글을 읽을 기회가 있을 것이다. 비교정부론, 합리적 선택이론, 아시아 정치 등의 과목에서 나의 글들이 이미 읽히고 있다. 하여 영문으로 하는 출판이지만, 해외 출판의 필요성은 느끼지 못하여서 한국에서만 출판하는 것으로 하였다.

두 번째로, 이 책에 실린 논문들을 통해, 한국에서 성장한 사람이 해외 학계에서 어떤 논문을 쓰면 살아남을 수 있는가에 대한 지침서로 생각할 수도 있겠다. 해외 박사의 적체로 정치학을 공부한 사람들이 직장을 구하는 것이 아주 어려워지고 있다. 이들 중 일부가 해외로 눈을 돌린다면, 한국 사람이 한국 정치 외의 분야에서 무엇을 얼마큼하면 인정을 받는가에 대한 정보를 얻을 수 있을 것이다.

마지막으로 이 시장성이 별로 없는 책을 만들어주신 박영사에 감사드린다. 이 책의 아이디어 처음부터 끝까지 함께한 손준호 선생과 편집부의 양수정 선생께도 깊은 감사의 마음을 전한다. 또한 pdf 형태로 있던 논문들을 hwp 형태로 바꾸는 것을 도와주신 서울대학교 규장각 한국학 연구원의 이숙인 박사님, 정치교육연구원의 김영기 선생께도 감사드린다. 앞에서 본인이 한국에서 네 권의 책을 출판하는 장기 계획을 가지고 있다고 말했는데, 두 번째 책의 머리말도 쓸 수 있는 기회가 꼭 왔으면 좋겠다.

2022년 5월 서해 바닷가에서,
김희민

01.

Voter Ideology in Western Democracies, 1946-1989

Heemin Kim[*] & Richard C. Fording[**]

* Department of Political Science Florida State University, Tallahassee, Florida, USA

** Department of Political Science, University of Kentucky, Lexington, Kentucky, USA

Abstract. We propose a measure of voter ideology which combines party manifesto data compiled by Budge, Robertson, Heari, Klingemann, and Volkens (1992) and updated by Volkens (1995), with election return data. Assuming the comparability and relevance of left-right ideology, we estimate the median voter position in 15 Western democracies throughout most of the postwar period. The plausibility of our assumptions, and therefore the validity of our measure, is supported by the results of several validity tests. With this new measure we are able to make cross-national comparisons of voter ideology among these countries as well as cross-time comparisons within individual countries. We discuss the potential application of our measure to various debates in political science.

Introduction

The term "ideology" has been used in the social science literature for some time. In part, this is due to the fact that many political events are either known or assumed to have been driven by ideological differences between groups, political parties, or even countries. As a result, many political scientists have tried to describe the ideological tendencies of political parties or the electorate within countries during various historical periods.

Since it is ideological differences that seem to drive many political phenom-ena, political scientists often want to compare ideological positions among different political parties or voters. Too often, however, we are forced to do so in a more or less subjective fashion. Ironically, given the importance of ideology in our theories of political behavior and change, there has been little systematic effort put forth to construct a measure of ideology that is comparable both across time and across countries.

In the case of political parties, most research has either focused on comparing parties and party movement within countries (e.g., Budge, Robertson & Hearl 1987), or comparing parties across countries at one relatively short period in time (e.g., Castles&Mair 1984; Janda 1980).[1] As for voter ideology, due to some methodological problems (mainly data-related), comparativists have had difficulty as well. Though some research does address the nature of ideology across countries and time (e.g., Inglehart 1977, 1990), the reliance of comparativists on survey data necessarily limits the number of countries that can be studied and the period of time for which they can be observed. In this paper we develop measures which we feel allow meaningful comparisons of party and voter ideology across different countries as well as across different time periods. Although we develop measures of both party and voter ideology, the emphasis in this paper is primarily on the latter. Since it is not feasible to describe the exact shape of the voter distribution on an ideological dimension in all Western democracies, we estimate the median voter position in these countries as our indicator of voter ideology. The choice of the median voter position is well justified not only because it indicates the central tendency among voters, but also due to the amount of attention paid to the median voter in the (formal) theoretic literature. We develop a measure of party positions using party manifesto data compiled by Budge, Robertson, Hearl, Klingemann, and Volkens (1992) and updated by Volkens (1995). We then estimate the median voter position by combining our party ideology measure with election return data for each country.

In the first section of the paper, we review possible methods of measuring voter ideology and argue that to date, no method exists which is adequate for cross-national research. In the following section, we then describe how we operationalize the concept of ideology. Upon testing the validity of our measure, we present cross-national and cross-time comparisons of voter ideology in 15 Western democracies. In the final section, we discuss the relevance of our findings to ongoing debates in political science.

Alternative Measures of Voter Ideology

The most obvious source of data for measuring mass ideology is survey data. Despite its potential advantages, however, survey data are inherently limited for a number of reasons. First, and perhaps most significantly, representative survey data are not readily available for most countries prior to the 1970s. For example, one of the most popular survey series used in comparative political research, the Eurobarometer, did not begin until 1971. As a result, any measure of ideology developed with such data would be restricted in the sense that it could only be employed in cross-sectional analyses, or only for a limited number of time points.

Second, even if survey data were readily available prior to the 1970s, and therefore were amenable to longitudinal as well as cross-sectional methods of analysis, there may be insurmountable problems in using these data for comparative research. The sensitivity of survey responses to quest if wording demands that survey results be based onmore or less identical questions if they are to be meaningfully compared. Unfortunately, it is doubtful that enough identical questions could be found in various surveys across enough countries to provide a reasonable basis for a survey-based measure of ideology.

Finally, even the one survey series which is identical across countries, the Eurobarometer, is inadequate in this respect. Of the few ideologically relevant policy questions that exist throughout the series, none are consistently available over any extended period of time. In addition, the left-right selfplacement scale, which is included in nearly every Eurobarometer survey, is just as limited. Since the 'left' and 'right' only exist in the mind of the respondent with respect to the location of the 'middle', self-placement scores can only be compared across countries and time periods if the location of the middle can be assumed to be the same in some absolute sense. Because it is likely that this is not the case, aggregate country measures of left-right self-placement are likely to be very inadequate measures of ideology.[2]

An alternative approach to measuring voter ideology is to infer ideology based on its (presumed) relationship to other variables for which data exist. Ironically, this approach has been taken by a limited number of studies in the area where one might expect to observe the least diversity in ideology, American politics. This approach has generally taken two forms. One method of measuring ideology among American states has relied on the assumption that state policies should reflect the overall ideological tendency within a state (e.g., Klingman & Lammers 1984). In one respect, these policy-based measures are superior to any survey-based measure in that they should be observable for all periods of interest. The disadvantage of a policy-based measure, however, is that since it is policy that we are often trying to explain, we are left without a measure of the dependent variable.

A second approach in the American state politics literature rests on the assumption that the elected representatives of a state at the federal level should mirror the ideology of their district, and as a whole, their state. State ideology is thus inferred based on various interest group ratings of members of congress (e.g., Rabinowitz et al. 1984). Although this measure does appear to perform adequately, it has disadvantages as well. Since this measure may be tapping elite ideology as well as voter ideology, its use precludes the inclusion of elite ideology into the model at hand. More importantly, however, this approach to measuring ideology cannot be easily applied to cross-national research due to the lack of common political institutions among Western democracies.

Measurement of Voter Ideology: An Operationalization

Assumptions

In the absence of an adequate technique for measuring voter ideology, we propose an alternative. Our measure of ideology rests on three basic assumptions about how voters think and behave when making voting decisions. First, we assume that a left-right ideological dimension can be found in most industrialized democracies. Survey research has repeatedly shown that the majority of voters in most (if not all) Western democracies conceive of politics in such a fashion, and can readily place themselves on some type of left-right scale (e.g., Inglehart & Klingemann 1976). Even in the USA, where early research seemed to demonstrate an absence of ideological thinking, more recent research has found ideology to be an important organizing framework for political attitudes for a significant portion of the electorate (Achen 1975; Jacoby 1995; Nie, Verba & Petrocik 1976).

A second assumption inherent in our approach is that left-right ideology is an important, and often primary determinant of vote choice in Western democracies, and that it has been so for the entire postwar period. Few would dispute the importance of the left-right dimension in influencing vote choice in these countries.[3] There is the perception, however, that the salience of this ideological cleavage has diminished over time, and particularly since WWII.

Such a view is fueled by evidence of the diminishing importance of social class in predicting vote choice (e.g., Franklin 1985). It does not necessarily follow, however, that the importance of left-right ideology has diminished based on this trend. Indeed, recent evidence suggests that although ideological cleavages are not as strongly related to class position as they once were, the left-right dimension remains a most significant, if not dominant cleavage in Western democracies (Blais et al. 1993; Budge & Robertson 1987; Knutsen 1988; Lijphart 1984; Morgan 1976; Warwick 1992).[4]

Finally, we assume that the left-right dimension is comparable across countries. Though little direct evidence exists to evaluate this claim, there is reason to believe this assumption is more or less plausible. Over the years, a large literature has developed which confirms that there is a common ideological dimension with which one can compare party ideology across different countries (Browne et al. 1984; Budge & Robertson 1987; Castles & Mair 1984; Cusack & Garrett 1993; Dodd 1976; Gross & Sigelman 1984; Janda 1980; Laver & Budge 1993; Laver and Schofield 1990: 248; Morgan 1976; Warwick 1992). From these results, along with the common perception that in many countries, left-right ideological orientations serve as a basic reference point for voters' choices of candidates/parties (Fuchs & Klingemann 1990; Inglehart & Klingemann 1976; Lancaster & LewisBeck 1986; Langford 1991; Laponce 1981; Lewis-Beck 1988; Percheron & Jennings 1981), it logically follows that there is a common ideological dimension with which one can compare voter ideology across different countries.

Assuming the comparability, continuity, and relevance of the left-right dimension, it is then possible to develop a measure of the ideological position of a particular electorate that is comparable across countries and across time.

To do so, one must first begin to conceive of elections as large-scale opinion polls. In this sense one might think of ballots as questionnaires which instruct the 'respondent' to choose the party that is closest to him or her on a left-right ideological scale. Assuming we have accurate, comparable, interval-scale measures of party ideology for each party in an election, we can then treat election results, along with the corresponding measures of party ideology, as a grouped frequency distribution and calculate fairly reliable estimates of measures of central tendency such as the median and the mean. In other words, we infer ideological tendencies based on the rational choices of ideological voters.

Measuring party ideology

Such a strategy requires the completion of two major estimation tasks. First, it is necessary to develop a reliable, interval-level measure of party ideology that is comparable across countries and time. We construct such a measure based on manifestos (platforms) issued by parties at the time of each election.

One objection to using manifesto statements to construct a measure of party ideology is likely to be that voters rarely, if ever, read them. Although this is undoubtedly true, this does not necessarily mean that manifesto statements are poor indicators of ideology if manifestos are representative of party behavior that is observable to voters. Recent evidence concerning this question indicates that this may indeed be the case. Contrary to the expectations of many political scientists, evidence from the USA, the UK and former West Germany indicates that parties do indeed fulfill the vast majority of their pledges (Budge & Hofferbert 1990; also see Robertson 1987 for a review of research in this area). As a result, though manifesto statements may not affect voter perceptions of parties in any direct way, a measure of party ideology based on manifesto statements is likely to be highly correlated with voter perceptions due to their common relationship with party ideology.

Our measure of party ideology is based on manifesto data collected by Budge et al. (1992) and updated by Volkens (1995). The manifesto data set, which includes twenty major democracies and spans most of the postwar period, is based on an exhaustive content analysis of manifestos (platforms) issued by all significant parties competing in each postwar election. The data set employs a total of 56 common categories, including external relations categories (e.g., antiimperialism), freedom and democracy categories (e.g., human rights), political system categories (e.g., governmental and administrative efficiency), economic categories (e.g., nationalization), welfare and quality of life categories (e.g., environmental protection), fabric of society categories (e.g., multiculturalism), and social group categories (e.g., underprivileged minority groups). For each document the data represent the percentage of all statements comprised by each category. In effect, this standardizes the data with respect to document length, yielding a measure of party emphasis that is comparable.

We develop a measure of ideology for each party in each election, for a total of 15 countries.[5] The first task in measuring party ideology is to define left-right ideology and to choose an appropriate set of categories which capture the left-right dimension. Ideology is a set of ideas that relate to the social/political world and that provide a general guideline for some action (Mahler 1995: 36–37). As such "ideology provides politicians with a broad conceptual map of politics into which political events, current problems, electors" preferences and other parties" policies can be fitted" (Budge 1994: 446) and thus incorporates a broad range of political, economic, and social issues.

There have been a few recent attempts to identify a left-right dimension utilizing party manifesto data. Each of these studies uses a correlation-based statistical technique, such as factor analysis or principal components analysis, to identify a common left-right dimension from an analysis of manifesto data (Bowler 1990; Budge & Robertson 1987; Laver & Budge 1993; Warwick 1992). The most comprehensive measure is that of Laver and Budge (1993) in that they analyze all countries and the entire period in the data set. They use a series of exploratory factor analyses to identify potential combinations of categories to build a left-right scale. From these analyses, they identify 13 categories as comprising left ideology and another 13 as comprising right ideology. These 26 ideological categories consistently loaded together in their factor analyses (pp. 24–27). Based on their analyses of the entire data set, we use the same 26 categories in our attempt to build a measure of party ideology in 15 industrialized democracies during the postwar period.[6] The data in the manifesto set are collected such that statements in each of these 26 categories demonstrate either pro-left or pro-right tendencies. Based on these 26 categories, we first develop separate measures of left and right ideology for each party in each election for these countries in the following manner:

$$IDLeft = Pro\text{-}Left\ Categories$$
$$IDRight = Pro\text{-}Right\ Categories$$

In other words, IDLeft represents the percentage of all party statements that advocate left-wing positions, and IDRight represents the corresponding per-centage of all party statements that represent right-wing positions. We then compute our measure of party ideology (IDParty) as follows:

$$IDParty = (IDLeft - IDRight) / (IDLeft + IDRight)$$

We assume that voters evaluate parties on their net ideological position (scores) with respect to the left-right dimension. The measure is thus computed by subtracting the rightist score from the leftist score (% leftist statements − % rightist statements), dividing by the total percentage of leftist and rightist statements. This procedure yields a measure of voter ideology that ranges from −1 to 1 where the larger score indicates greater support for leftist policies. For ease of presentation and interpretation, we transform this measure so that it takes on a possible range of 0 to 100.[7]

Measuring voter ideology

Having developed a measure of party ideology, our second major estimation task is to estimate the median ideological position within the electorate of each country, at each election. We proceed in a series of three steps. First, for each election, we obtain ideology scores for each party in that election and place the parties on an ideological dimension by their score.

Second, for each party, we find an interval on this dimension where its supporters are located. This was done in the following manner: for each party we calculate the midpoint between this party and the one immediately left of it and another midpoint between this party and the one immediately right of it. We assume that those who vote for this party fall into this interval between these two midpoints on the left-right ideological dimension. In other words, this is a simple application of the Euclidean preference relations: simply put, voters choose the candidates/parties that are closest to them. Voters on the left side of this interval will vote for the party on the left of this party and the ones on the right side of this interval will vote for the party on the right of it.

Third, for each election, we find the percentage of the vote received by each party.[8] At this point, we now have the percentage of the electorate that fall into each interval that we have created. Having now transformed the data to a grouped frequency distribution, we estimate the median position by using a formula outlined in almost any introductory statistics text (we use Bohrnstedt & Knoke 1988: 52). The particular variant of this formula that we use is as follows:

$$M = L + \{(50 - C) / F\} * W,$$

where

M = Median voter position (ideological score);

L = The lower end (ideological score) of the interval containing the median;

C = The cumulative frequency (vote share) up to but not including the interval containing the median;

F = The frequency (vote share) in the interval containing the median;

W = The width of the interval containing the median.[9]

Having created a measure of voter ideology for each country for each election year, we then compute a yearly series of voter ideology scores within each country. We estimate missing (non-election) years by using linear interpolation, which assumes steady change in ideology between elections. While we realize that ideology is not likely to change this steadily in every case, we feel that in general this approach is reasonable since it is likely that ideology is relatively stable in the short run. More importantly, estimation of missing years facilitates comparisons across countries, which would otherwise be biased due to the irregularity of the timing of elections across countries.[10]

Tests of Validity

Although several of the assumptions we make in constructing measures of party and voter ideology are supported by related empirical research, it is unlikely that any of these assumptions holds perfectly. Recognizing this, we examine the validity of our measures in a series of tests below. If our measures of party and voter ideology conform to conventional wisdom regarding ideological differences across countries and time periods (face validity), and if they correlate with other indicators of ideology constructed or used in past research (convergent validity), we can be reasonably confident that the assumptions are accurate enough to produce valid and reliable measures of party and voter ideology.

Party ideology

We test the validity of our final party ideology measure in two ways. First, we compare our ideological scores with those reported by Castles and Mair (1984),who computed left-right ideology scores by polling political scientists in a number of democratic countries. In each case, the authors asked these 'experts' to place the parties in their country on an eleven-point ideological scale (0–10), with a score of 0 being ultra-left.

The authors then averaged the scores given by each expert, and reported this figure as the party's final ideological score. The measure is comparable across countries, they argue, since the frame of reference for these political scientists likely extends beyond their native country.

Since the measure reported by Castles and Mair is based on information collected in the early 1980s, it is likely that the respondents' temporal frame of reference encompassed a period prior to that time as well. We therefore compare the experts' measure to our measure averaged over all elections since 1974. The results of this comparison support the validity of our measure, as the two are highly correlated ($r = -0.85$, $n = 67$).[11]

Although our measure appears to correspond with the judgments of political scientists, it is mass ideology that we are interested in, and therefore it is mass perceptions of party ideology that ultimately count. To compare our measure to the perceptions of voters, we use Eurobarometer data from 1979, 1983, and 1987 to estimate voter perceptions of party ideology by averaging the left-right self-placement scores of party identifiers for each year in nine Eurobarometer countries.[12] The result is a measure of party ideology which represents the average self-placement scores of a party's supporters.[13] We then compare this measure to our manifesto-based measure of party ideology from the election closest to each year.

Unlike the measure reported by Castles and Mair, however, this measure cannot be assumed to be readily comparable across countries, since voters are likely to base their self-placement scores on the location of the 'center' in their own country. In other words, the Eurobarometer measure would only be comparable if it could be assumed that the center, in an absolute sense, is the same across countries. Rejecting this possibility, we standardize the manifesto-based measure by subtracting country means from each party score. Another problem with constructing a survey-based measure is that for smaller parties, Eurobarometer sample sizes are often extremely small. We therefore omit parties with less than fifty identifiers in the country sample.

Although one could not reasonably expect our manifesto-based measure to be as highly correlated with mass perceptions as it was with the measure based on highly informed expert judgments, the correlation between the mass perception measure and our measure is strong ($r = -0.74$, $n = 87$), and thus provides reasonable assurance that a measure of ideology based on party manifestos does indeed correspond with mass perceptions. These results are graphically displayed in Figure 1.

Median voter ideology

In order to examine the validity of our measure of voter ideology, we proceed with two 'tests'. First, we examine the longitudinal validity of our measure with respect to two cases where sufficient survey data are available, and where it is generally agreed that significant ideological change has occurred over the period for which we have data. We first examine ideological change in the USA. In a recent book, Stimson (1991) constructs a measure of mass support for leftist policies, which he calls 'policy mood', based on a rather sophisticated and exhaustive analysis of similar policy items contained in surveys conducted in the USA since the early 1950s. Stimson's measure, though not exactly the same as ours, is still close enough to our conceptualization of the left-right dimension to warrant comparison. Both measures of ideology are presented below in the top panel of Figure 2.[14] While the nature of our data does not allow actual year by year comparisons, we can compare some general features of the two measures. Most notably, both measures find the most left-leaning period in recent American history to have been the early to mid1960s.

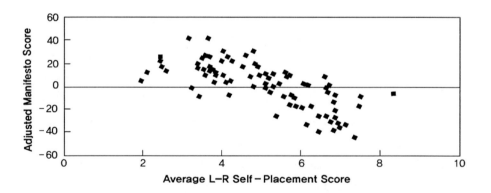

Figure 1. Voter perceptions of party ideology and manifesto scores

In addition, both measures find that there was a steady movement to the right until the early to mid1980s.

We next examine longitudinal variation in ideology in the UK. We compare our voter ideology measure in this case to a measure of ideology constructed from Eurobarometer data from 1973 to 1988.[15] The specific item from the Eurobarometer is the 'left-right partisan support index', which combines party preference data with a dichotomous measure of party ideology (left-right) created by the authors of the survey. When aggregated to the national level, the measure represents the percentage of respondents who support a leftist party. As can be seen in the bottom panel of Figure 2, both indicators of ideology display a steady and significant shift to the right during the 16year period. Again, this is consistent with conventional wisdom as well as more systematic research (Castles 1990).

A second test of our voter ideology measure utilizes data from other countries. This test is based on the presumption that the ideological tendencies of countries with respect to the left-right dimension should be reflected in the specific policies that they pursue. We rely on a measure of leftist policies created by EspingAnderson for the year 1980 (1990: 52, see Table 2.2). Briefly, this measure attempts to capture the 'decommodifying potential' of welfare policies in various democratic states, or in other words, the extent to which a country's welfare policies might contribute to the 'emancipation from market dependency' (see Chapter 2). The correlation between our manifesto-based measure of ideology for 1980 and the decommodification scores once again supports the validity of our measure ($r = 0{:}77$ $n = 16$. See Figure 3).[16]

Considered together, the results of these tests demonstrate the validity, and hence potential usefulness of our measures of party and voter ideology. While it is undoubtedly true that our left-right dimension is not exactly comparable across all countries or totally dominant in voting decisions, the consistency of the results suggests that these assumptions are valid enough in each case to result in a fairly accurate indicator of ideology. This is significant, we feel, since these same assumptions are continually made in empirical research which attempts to look at the effects of ideology on policy (e.g., Hibbs 1977; Hicks & Swank 1992).

United States 1952–1989

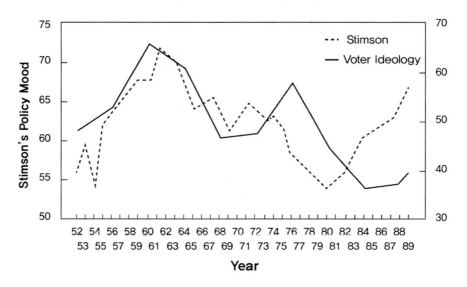

United Kingdom 1973–1988

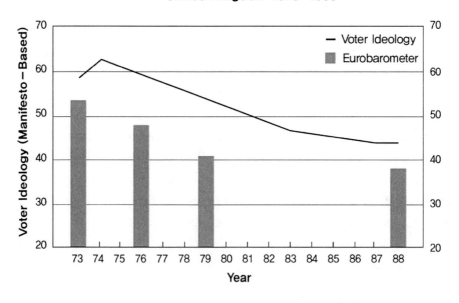

Figure 2. Alternative measures of voter ideology

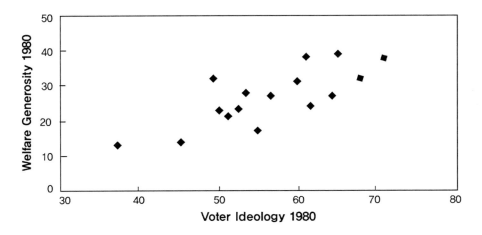

Figure 3. Voter ideology and welfare policies

Voter Ideology: Cross-national and Cross-time Comparisons

In Figure 4 we present a Cross-national comparison of the average ideological scores of 15Western democracies during the entire period of 1946–1989.[17] In short, Figure 4 presents a snapshot describing the entire period of analysis. During this period, it is clear that Norway, Sweden, and Luxembourg have been the most left-leaning states, while Ireland, Australia, and the USA have been at the opposite end of the ideological spectrum of Western democracies.

Next, we examine aggregate movement in ideology among our panel of countries during the years 1946–1989. The results of this analysis can be found in Figure 5, which displays ideology scores averaged across all countries (n = 15) over the entire period 1946–1989. Consistent with conventional wisdom, Figure 5 indicates that the period of the 1960s and early 1970s was indeed a relatively left-leaning period among these democracies.[18]

Though Figure 5 displays ideological movement among all countries in our sample, there is no reason to believe that all of these countries have followed this identical pattern during this period. Indeed, though the majority of countries we examine do show some type of movement toward the left during the 1960s, in general there are significant differences across countries in the magni

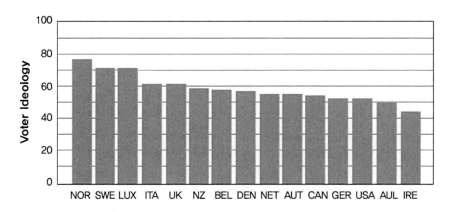

Figure 4. Voter ideology in Western democracies 1946–1989.
Average median voter position

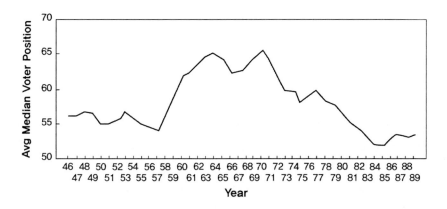

Figure 5. Voter ideology in Western democracies

tude of such ideological shifts, not only during the 1960s, but throughout the entire period of analysis. Although a presentation of all 15 countries is beyond the scope of this presentation, we present two examples of different patterns of ideological movement in Figure 6. In Figure 6, which displays ideological movement in both Norway and Denmark, we can see that although there have been some shifts, voter ideology in Norway has been consistently left-leaning, and hence relatively stable, as it has stayed above the ideological score of 60 throughout the period of analysis. Voter ideology in Denmark, however, displays a different pattern with greater short-term fluctuations.

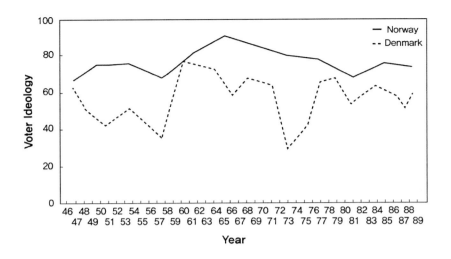

Figure 6. Examples of ideological stability and volatility

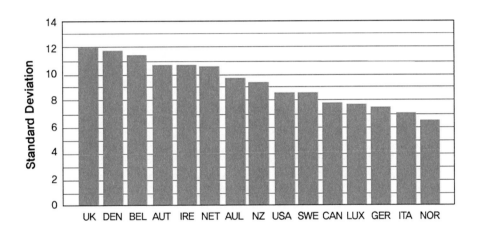

Figure 7. Ideological volatility, 1946–1989

Although space does not permit a presentation of each individual country, we can get some idea of the relative ideological volatility across countries during this time period by computing the standard deviation for each country series. Since our measure of voter ideology is comparable across countries, such a measure of ideological volatility is comparable as well. Figure 7 presents such a comparison. During this period, Norway, Italy, and former West Germany have maintained relatively stable ideological trends, while voter ideology in the UK, Denmark, and Belgium has exhibited significant variation over the years 1946–1989.

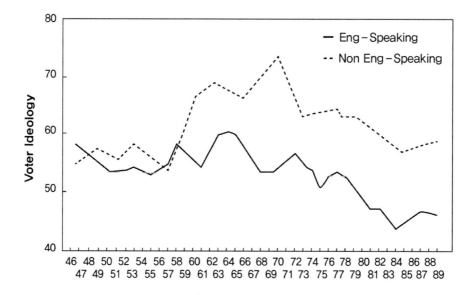

Figure 8. Voter ideology in Western democracies

One of the more interesting features of the aggregate movement in ideology displayed in Figure 5 is the movement toward the right which begins in the 1970s and extends into the 1980s. Although such a trend is perhaps not unexpected, there is some reason to suspect that this rightward movement is not common to all the countries in our sample, and that it is either most pronounced, or even entirely driven by a movement toward the right among the English-speaking democracies. Such a possibility is suggested by Francis Castles (1990), who argues that in recent years, a movement toward the right has been strongest in these countries, as evidenced by the economic policies of these countries. We investigate this possibility by examining ideological trends among the English-speaking nations (Australia, Canada, Ireland, New Zealand, UK, and USA) and the other Western democracies separately. The results of this comparison, which are presented in Figure 8, offer a couple of interesting findings.

First, though a divergence in ideology can be seen among the two sets of countries, the real departure between the ideologies of the English-speaking and other Western countries occurred in the late 1950s rather than the 1980s.

Since then, these two groups of countries have maintained a fairly substantial distance in ideology, with non-English-speaking countries substantially more left-leaning than English-speaking countries. Second, and more important-ly for the question at hand, these two groups of countries have displayed strikingly similar trends in voter ideology. Generally speaking, both groups experienced a general shift to the left during the 1960s, as we might expect given the fact that this was a period of relative economic prosperity throughout the West. We also find that both groups began to shift back to the right during the early 1970s, which also coincided with the first oil shock and the subsequent downturn in most Western economies. The fact that these trends were at least to some extent a common experience among Western democracies contradicts evidence presented by Host and Paldam (1990) which suggests that 'international opinion swings' do not exist among Western nations. With regard to Castles' argument that the shift toward the right in the 1980s has been stronger in English-speaking countries, we need to note that he is talking about a policy shift to the right in these countries. Since the magnitudes of shifts to the right in voter ideology in the 1980s are quite similar in these two groups of countries, this suggests a non-ideological explanation for the differences Castles finds between the two sets of countries.

Discussion

In this paper, we have developed a measure with which one can compare voter ideology across different countries and across different time periods. Our measure passes several validity tests and provides many interesting insights concerning voter ideology in Western democracies. The trends in ideology in these countries themselves are important findings, but there are many other ways to use these measures either to study political phenomena which previously was not feasible, or to improve (or revitalize) existing research in comparative politics. The research presented in this paper should therefore be considered as the beginning point of a larger body of research concerning the origin of voter ideology, its impact on government and public policy, and the development of theories of democracy. We conclude this paper by pointing out just a few areas of research in comparative politics in which our measure of voter ideology can be used.

First, as we saw above, voter ideology in Western democracies exhibits significant variation across different countries and across different time periods.

At the same time, Figure 8 reveals a common pattern of ideological movement among the English-speaking countries and the other Western democracies.

This warrants a future investigation into the sources of ideological change and covariation among these countries. This is now possible by utilizing our measure of voter ideology, and looking at the role that culture and geography might play in patterns of ideological diffusion, the possible significance of international events such as the cold war, and the importance of economic conditions in explaining differences in ideology across countries and within countries over time. By looking at the importance of these factors, it may be possible for us not only to make intelligent judgements about why certain shifts in voter ideology occurred in the past, but also to make predictions about when and where similar shifts are likely to occur. Research in this direction has already begun (Kim & Fording 1997b).

Second, let us go back to the cross-national comparisons displayed in Figure 4 above, where some may find a few 'unexpected' results with respect to the relative placement of certain countries. If this is the case, it is most likely due to the fact that we generally form our perception of the ideological tendencies of countries based on our observation of the parties in power, and policy outcomes in those countries. To the extent that our results are valid, they demonstrate that the linkage between citizen ideology and government/policy is weak in some countries. In many cases, this is probably due to the characteristics of the party system, the electoral system, or the process of forming coalition governments in those countries. As a result, what our measure makes possible in this context is to examine the linkage between voter ideology and the ideology of parties in power, or policy outputs under different institutional devices of the party and electoral system. In other words, it is thus possible to identify an institutional design that best translates voter preferences into government policy.

A third implication of our results reported above (especially Figures 4 and 5) cautions against the use of formal models as theoretical grounds for certain empirical studies. Take the so-called 'Do Parties Matter?' debate as an example. In short, this debate refers to the question of whether government partisanship makes a difference in economic policy outcomes and performance.

Those who believe that the parties in power do not make much of a difference in economic policies often present the 'policy convergence thesis' in majoritarian systems by citing the median voter theorem (Downs 1957) and its subsequent refinements such as Riker and Ordeshook (1973), Enelow and Hinich (1984), and Calvert (1985) (e.g., Jackman 1987, 1989). Those who believe that the parties in power do make a difference often try to show why the median voter theorem does not hold in the real world by citing Palfrey(1984), Aldrich and McGinnis (1987), and Tsebelis (1989) (e.g., Garrett & Lange 1989; Korpi 1989; Lange & Garrett 1987).

Based on these theoretical grounds, some scholars have conducted cross-national and cross-time empirical analyses to study whether the parties in power actually make a difference in economic policy outcomes. What we need to remember, however, is that most of the formal models cited above, including the median voter model, are static models describing candidate behavior in a single hypothetical society. This being the case, the theoretical grounds for these empirical analyses, regardless of whether they are for or against the median voter theorem, are valid only when the median voter position is constant across different countries (with majoritarian systems) and across different time periods. Though this assumption has never been plausible, our measure of voter ideology reported above clearly shows that this is not the case.[19] The lesson here is that one needs to be cautious about using formal models as theoretical grounds for any kind of comparative research.

Finally, although our focus in this paper is clearly voter ideology, our measure of party ideology can also serve useful purposes. Specifically, our party ideology scores, along with other existing measures of party positions constructed from the manifesto data (e.g., Budge, Robertson & Hearl 1987; Laver & Budge 1993), can be used to reassess the findings of several of the above-mentioned studies that look at the effect of governmental partisanship on economic policy outcomes (such as the level of government spending and monetary policy) and economic performance (such as level of inflation, unemployment, and economic growth). Over the years, various measures of government partisanship have been developed to answer these questions.

In some studies, government partisanship has been considered either left or right (Alt 1985; Hibbs 1977; Rose 1980; Williams 1990). Some studies use the weighted mean of the leftist and rightist parties in the government, weighted by the number of votes that leftist and rightist parties received (e.g., Cameron 1978). Probably the most popular measure of government partisanship has been the percentage of cabinet portfolios held by left or right parties (Alvarez et al. 1991; Cameron 1984; Hicks 1988; Jackman 1987; Korpi 1989; Lange & Garrett 1987). Despite what appear to be differences in these measures, all of these measures of government ideology share one common characteristic: party ideology is dichotomous, that is, either right or left, and is constant over time. Clearly, the findings of Budge, Robertson, and Hearl (1987) demonstrate that such a conceptualization of party ideology is quite a distortion of reality, both in longitudinal and cross-sectional terms. As a result, measures of government ideology based on dichotomous measures of party ideology are likely subject to measurement error.

Recently, some ordinal measures of government partisanship have been developed (e.g., Budge & Keman 1990; Crepaz 1992; Schmidt 1982) which employ more than two categories. These measures, however, are likely to suffer from similar problems due to the limited number of categories. With an interval measure of party ideology, as we have developed in this paper, one can build an interval measure of government partisanship by computing a weighted average of government ideology, based on the party ideology scoresof the parties in power, and weighted by, for example, the percentage of cabinet portfolios held by each party.[20] Using our measure of party ideology, this new measure of government partisanship can presently be built for 15 countries for most of the postwar period. Incorporating this improved measure, we may indeed find that government ideology plays a different role in policy making than we have so far been able to detect.[21]

Acknowledgments

An earlier version of this article was presented at the annual convention of the American Political Science Association, 1995. We thank William Berry, Ian Budge, William Clagget, Mike Lusztig, Erik Plutzer, Evan Ringquist, Duane Swank, and the anonymous reviewers of the European Journal of Political Research for their valuable comments on various versions of this article. We also benefitted from the suggestions and information provided by Shaun Bowler, Russ Dalton, Neal Jesse, George Tsebelis, and Guy Whitten. We thank the Economic and Social Research Council at the University of Essex and Zentralarchiv f´ur Empirische Sozialforschung an der Universit" at zu Koln for providing the ECPR Party Manifesto Data to us.

Notes

1. Budge and Robertson (1987) do compare parties across countries for a prolonged period of time, but they do so for a limited number of parties. Recently, Laver and Budge (1993) have developed a more comprehensive measure of party ideology which incorporates most postwar European parties.

2. Although we do not know of any empirical studies to support this criticism in a comparative context, there is some evidence from the USA which supports the sensitivity of self-placement to context. Examining survey responses over time, Miller (1992, 1994) has found that the meaning of the labels 'liberal' and 'conservative'(the American equivalent for 'left' and 'right') has changed significantly over time, and is influenced by one's social network.

3. While the role of ideology has often been ignored in the American voting literature, both experimental (e.g., McKelvey & Ordeshook 1990) and survey-based studies (e.g., Levitan & Miller 1979) find ideology to be an important determinant of vote choice in the USA.

4. Using party manifesto data, Laver and Budge (1993) convincingly show that the left-right dimension not only exists but is essential in the party programs in Western democracies.

5. Out of 20 countries in the manifesto data set, we include 15 in our study. The countries we include are Australia, Austria, Belgium, Canada, Denmark, Ireland, Italy, Luxembourg, the Netherlands, New Zealand, Norway, Sweden, the UK, the USA, and the former West Germany. We exclude Northern Ireland because it is not an independent country. We also exclude Israel and Sri Lanka since our focus in this paper is restricted to industrialized democracies. Japan is excluded since manifesto data are not available prior to 1960. We also exclude France due to the exclusion of certain parties from the manifesto data set for recent elections, however we include both France and Japan in various validity tests (when possible) presented in the next section. All political parties included in the data set for these countries are listed in the codebook accompanying the manifesto data.

6. The specific categories, as listed in the codebook, are as follows. Leftist categories are: Regulation of capitalism, Economic planning, Protectionism: positive, Controlled economy, Nationalization, Decolonization, Military: negative, Peace, Internationalism: positive, Democracy, Social services expansion: positive, Education: positive, and Labor groups: positive. Rightist categories are: Free enterprise, Incentives, Protectionism: negative, Economic orthodoxy and efficiency, Social services expansion: negative, Constitutionalism: positive, Government effectiveness and authority, National way of life: positive, Traditional morality: positive, Law and order, National effort and social harmony, Military: positive, and Freedom and domestic human rights. Detailed definitions of these categories are listed in the codebook as well as in Laver and Budge (1993: 20–24). The salience of the left-right dimension is indicated by the frequency with which ideologically relevant statements appear in party manifestos. Overall, left-right statements comprise about half (47%; sd = 13.9%) of all statements in the entire sample of documents ($n = 1009$). The salience of left-right statements is also consistent over time.

Since 1966, the percentage of left-right statements averages 45% ($n = 567$), only slightly lower than the average for the entire period.

7. Although we use the same manifesto categories as Laver and Budge (1993), we construct our measure of party ideology somewhat differently. Their measure is equivalent

to the numerator of our measure, or in other words, the difference of IDLeft and IDRight as a percentage of all statements in the document. We believe that the denominator of our measure should be restricted to the total number of left-right statements only, since we necessarily assume that voters evaluate parties strictly with respect to the left-right dimension. Regardless of this difference in the two measures, the two are nearly identical in empirical terms as they are correlated at 0.95.

8. For election data, we primarily relied on Mackie and Rose (1990). In some cases we supplemented these data with election results reported annually in the European Journal of Political Research.

9. In this paper, we assume sincere voting by assuming that voters choose the candidates/parties that are closest to them. It has been argued, however, that voters may not always vote for their most preferred candidates (in our case, ideologically closest candidates).

This is known as tactical voting. We feel comfortable ignoring the possibility of tactical voting in computing our final voter ideology measure for the following reasons.

First, for a majority of the countries for which we construct voter ideology scores, the possible bias introduced by tactical voting is minimal. Tactical voting, as it is usually described in the literature, primarily takes place under single-member district plurality electoral systems and takes the form of third party supporters voting for one of the major parties (Duverger 1963; Riker 1982). Tactical voting may also be expected in some non-PR countries as well, in particular those with electoral systems with an ordinal ballot structure where vote transfer is possible. This means that of the 15 countries for which we construct voter ideology scores, only six might be affected in any meaningful way. For countries with ordinal ballot structures (Ireland and the Australian House), since the incentive to vote tactically is minimal for the first preference vote (Jesse 1995), we only use election results from the first preference votes (and not the transfers). In constructing voter ideology scores for the former West Germany, we only use election data from the list-PR (Zweitstimme), where it is expected that tactical voting is minimal (Barnes et al. 1962; Fisher 1973), and not the results from the Erststimme, which employs an election system that may induce tactical voting. This leaves three countries with a multiparty system whose electoral system is characterized by single-member district plurality rule: Canada, New Zealand, and the UK. Our initial strategy was to control for the effect of tactical voting in these three countries by building a model which predicts the level of tactical voting in each election in these countries. In building this model, we incorporated factors that are known to affect the level of tactical voting which we can measure using available data: the closeness of the race between the two top parties (Cain 1978; Niemi, Whitten & Franklin 1992; Tsebelis 1986), a small party's distance from contention (Niemi, Whitten&Franklin 1992), and the distance between party positions (see Black 1978). After estimating the relationship between these variables and observed rates of tactical voting (based on the limited number of elections for which levels of tactical voting have actually been measured), we then generated predicted levels of tactical voting for all minor parties in all elections in Canada, New Zealand, and the UK, and adjusted election results accordingly. It turns out that tactical voting does not affect our estimate of the median voter position in a significant way as our original measures of voter ideology and the tactical voting-adjusted measures are correlated at 0.99 in Canada, New Zealand, and the UK. This being the case, we report our original measure in this paper for simplicity and clarity of presentation. Our model of tactical voting, along with our estimates of tactical voting for all relevant elections in these three countries is reported in another paper (Kim & Fording 1997a). Those interested in the details of this model can obtain a copy from the authors.

10. Because of the irregularity of the timing of elections across countries, the first and last years for which we have manifesto data vary somewhat across countries. The first election year for which data are available among these countries ranges from 1945 to 1949, while the last year for which data exist varies from 1986 to 1988. Because of the need to impose a common beginning and ending year for these countries in the analyses of voter ideology that follow, we employ the following strategy. For the first observation, we chose 1946 as the common beginning year. For 5 of the 15 countries in our study this required extrapolating backward for one to three years. For the last observation, we chose 1989 as the common ending year. We accomplish this by extrapolating party scores one election forward, and using these party scores along with the appropriate election results to compute additional median scores. By doing this, we are able to extend the data into the early 1990s for a few cases, and to at least 1989 in every case. This strategy has the advantage of utilizing nearly all of the information contained in the manifesto data set while only requiring a minimal amount of extrapolation.

11. Several tests of validity reported in this paper rely on correlation levels between our measure and other indicators of party or voter ideology. It is difficult to determine, a priori, a minimum level of correlation that would demonstrate validity. This is due to the fact that those variables with which we correlate our measure are themselves only indicators of the concept we wish to measure (ideology), and in some cases likely subject to as much or more measurement error than our own measure. We leave it up to the reader to evaluate the strength of the correlations reported in this paper, but we feel that correlations in excess of 0.70 (which indicate at least 50% shared variation) with a range of different indicators are strong support for validity.

12. Countries that we are able to include in this test are: Belgium, Denmark, France, Italy, Ireland, Luxembourg, the Netherlands, the UK, and the former West Germany. Due to the lack of manifesto data, we exclude the remaining Eurobarometer countries of Greece, Northern Ireland, Portugal, and Spain. The choice of 1979, 1983, and 1987 was essentially arbitrary. Our primary concern was to make sure our analysis was based on a sufficient number of cases over a period of several years.

13. This approach to measuring party ideology was first used by Inglehart and Klingemann (1976).

14. Values for the manifesto-based series include observed ideological scores in election years, and estimates based on linear interpolation in non-election years. Data for the 'policy mood' series are revised estimates, reported in Stimson (1994). The first year of Stimson's series was 1952.

15. The selection of years for this analysiswas limited by the availability of the Eurobarometer data and the frequency with which the particular item was included in the survey.

16. We include median voter estimates for both France and Japan in this test, and exclude Luxembourg due to the fact that a decommodification score is not reported by Epsing-Anderson. This yields an N of 16.

17. The average scores reported in Figure 4, as well as the subsequent analyses, are based on observed and interpolated scores for each country (see p. 80).

18. Readers should be aware that the range of ideology displayed on the Y axis varies across figures displaying longitudinal data, thus giving the initial impression that ideological movement across time is greater (or less) in some figures than it is in others.

Since our purpose in displaying the data in the various longitudinal figures is not to compare across figures, but rather to make longitudinal comparisons within each series, we felt this could best be achieved by minimizing the range of the Y axis in each figure so that variation is more easily observed within each series.

19. In the case of non-majoritarian multiparty systems, other formal models are cited to support arguments made by each side (e.g., AustenSmith & Banks 1988). Nevertheless, the same problem exists in that singlesociety, static models (static in the sense that they do not model more than one election cycle) are being used as theoretical grounds for comparative, dynamic analyses.

20. It has come to our attention that Cusack and Garrett (1993) build a similar type of interval level government partisanship measure, a weighted-mean index of cabinet seats held by parties arrayed on a left-right continuum, by updating and extending the party ideology measure developed by Castles and Mair (1984).

21. The first step in this direction has been taken by Klingemann et al. (1994) who examine the link between party ideology and various policy outputs.

02.

Voter Ideology, the Economy, and the International Environment in Western Democracies, 1952–1989

Heemin Kim[*] & Richard C. Fording[**]

* HeeMin Kim, Associate Professor, Department of Political Science, Florida State University

** Tallahassee, Florida3 2306-2230 (hkim@garnet.acns.fsu.edu) RichardC. Fording, Assistant Professor, Department of Political Science, University of Kentucky, (rford@pop.uky.edu).

Source: Political Behavior, Vol. 23, No. 1, Special Issue on Comparative Political Behavior (Mar, 2001), pp. 53-73

Abstract. Although it is commonly assumed that voters shift on an ideological spectrum over time, there has been relatively little scientific inquiry into the reasons for shifts in voter ideology. In this article, we attempt to explain why voter ideological shifts occur utilizing an interval measure of voter ideology recently developed by Kim and Fording. A pooled time-series analysis of 13 Western democracies for the period of 1952-1989 identifies several internal and external factors causing shifts in voter ideology. With respect to domestic influences, the state of the country's national economy, primarily inflation, seems to drive movement in voter ideology in a most significant way, but we find that the direction of this relationship is dependent on the ideological disposition of the incumbent government. With respect to international influences, we find significant ideological diffusion across neighboring countries of Western democracies. The effects of ideological diffusion are strongest within countries that are small relative to their neighbors. We also find that ideology is influenced by the international political environment, especially the level of East-West tension during the Cold War.

Introduction

We frequently hear that voters in a certain country "shifted" to the right or left during a certain time period. For example, not many people would dispute the assertion that American voters, as a whole, moved to the right in the 1980s.

In addition, it is often asserted that common ideological trends can be observed among groups of countries. For example, many commentators have suggested that the United States was not alone in its movement to the right during the 1980s. Likewise, most people would agree that the 1960s was a relatively liberal period in all Western democracies. Given these seemingly similar trends in voter ideology across Western democracies, we are left to ask: What common experiences and traditions do these countries share that might cause them to follow similar ideological paths? To the extent that they do not, what causes the differences in these countries? Obviously, these are questions of great interest for candidates, policymakers, and political scientists alike. Nevertheless, no scientific inquiry into the reasons for shifts in voter ideology has been possible since political scientists have not had a measure of voter ideology that is readily comparable across different time periods within a country, let alone across different countries. This is unfortunate, given the importance of ideology in our theories of political behavior and change.

Recently Kim and Fording (1998) developed a measure of voter ideology for 15 Western democracies for the period of 1946 through 1989. In constructing this measure of voter ideology they first build an interval level measure of party ideology based on manifesto data collected by Budge (1992) and updated by Volkens (1995). Combining this measure of party ideology and election return data, Kim and Fording estimate the median voter position in all elections for these countries for a 44-year period. Based on the results of several validity tests, they argue that their measure allows a meaningful comparison of voter ideology across different countries as well as across different time periods.

Utilizing the Kim-Fording measure of voter ideology, in this article, we explain why voter ideological shifts occur in Western democracies. In the first section, we review variation in voter ideology reported in Kim and Fording

(1998). Based on our theoretical expectations as well as variation in voter ideology in Western democracies reported in the previous section, we then develop several hypotheses concerning the sources of shifts in voter ideology in these countries. Upon describing individual measures and methods utilized for our analysis, we present the results of a pooled time-series analysis of ideological change. We summarize our findings in the final section.

Variation in Voter Ideology: An Overview

Assumptions of the Kim-Fording Approach

The Kim-Fording (1998) measure of ideology rests on three basic assumptions about how voters think and behave when making voting decisions. First, Kim and Fording assume that a left-right ideological dimension can be found in most industrialized democracies. Survey research has repeatedly shown that the majority of voters in most (if not all) Western democracies conceive of politics in such a fashion and can readily place themselves on some type of left-right scale (e.g., Inglehart and Klingemann, 1976). Even in the United States, where early research seemed to demonstrate an absence of ideological thinking, more recent research has found ideology to be an important organizing framework for political attitudes for a significant portion of the electorate (Achen, 1975; Jacoby, 1995; Nie, Verba, and Petrocik, 1976).

A second assumption inherent in the Kim-Fording approach is that left-right ideology is an important, and often primary determinant of vote choice in Western democracies, and that it has been so for the entire postwar period.

Few would dispute the importance of the left-right dimension in influencing vote choice in these countries.[1] There is the perception, however, that the salience of this ideological cleavage has diminished over time, particularly since WWII. Such a view is fueled by evidence of the diminishing importance of social class in predicting vote choice (e.g., Franklin, 1985). It does not necessarily follow, however, that the importance of left-right ideology has diminished based on this trend. Indeed, recent evidence suggests that although ideological cleavages are not as strongly related to class position as they once were, the left-right dimension remains a most significant, if not dominant cleavage in Western democracies (Blais, Blake, and Dion, 1993; Budge and Robertson, 1987; Knutsen, 1988; Lijphart, 1984; Morgan, 1976; Warwick, 1992).[2]

Finally, Kim and Fording (1998) assume that the left-right dimension is comparable across countries. Although little direct evidence exists to evaluate this claim, there is reason to believe this assumption is more or less plausible.

Over the years, a large literature has developed that confirms that there is a common ideological dimension with which one can compare party ideology across different countries (Browne, Gleiber, and Mashoba, 1984; Budge and Robertson, 1987; Castles and Mair, 1984; Cusack and Garrett, 1993; Dodd, 1976; Gross and Sigelman, 1984; Huber, 1989; Huber and Inglehart, 1995; Janda, 1980; Laver and Budge, 1993; Laver and Schofield, 1990; Morgan, 1976; Warwick, 1992). From these results, along with the common perception that in many countries, left-right ideological orientations serve as a basic reference point for voters' choices of candidates/parties (Fuchs and Klingemann, 1990; Inglehart and Klingemann, 1976; Lancaster and Lewis-Beck, 1986; Langford, 1991; Laponce, 1981; Lewis-Beck, 1988; Percheron and Jennings, 1981), it logically follows that there is a common ideological dimension with which one can compare voter ideology across different countries.

Assuming the comparability, continuity, and relevance of the left-right dimension, it is then possible to develop a measure of the ideological position of a particular electorate that is comparable across countries and across time. To do so, one must first begin to conceive of elections as large-scale opinion polls. In this sense one might think of ballots as questionnaires that instruct the "respondent" to choose the party that is closest to him or her on a left-right ideological scale. Assuming we have accurate, comparable, interval-scale measures of party ideology for each party in an election, we can then treat election results, along with the corresponding measures of party ideology, as a grouped frequency distribution and calculate fairly reliable estimates of measures of central tendency such as the median and the mean. In other words, we infer ideological tendencies based on the rational choices of ideological voters.

Constructing an Interval Level Measure of Voter Ideology

To construct a measure of voter ideology, Kim and Fording (1998) first develop an interval level measure of party ideology based on manifesto data collected by Budge (1992), and updated by Volkens (1995). The manifesto data set, which includes 20 major democracies and spans most of the postwar period, is based on an exhaustive content analysis of manifestos (platforms) issued by all significant parties competing in each postwar election. The data set employs a total of 56 common categories, including external relations categories (e.g., anti-imperialism), freedom and democracy categories (e.g., human rights), political system categories (e.g., governmental and administrative efficiency), economic categories (e.g., nationalization), welfare and quality of life categories (e.g., environmental protection), fabric of society categories (e.g., multiculturalism), and social group categories (e.g., underprivileged minority groups). For each document, the data represent the percentage of all statements comprised by each category. In effect, this standardizes the data with respect to document length, yielding a measure of party emphasis that is comparable.

Kim and Fording (1998) develop a measure of ideology for each party in each election for a total of 15 countries.[3] The first task in measuring party ideology is to define left-right ideology and to choose an appropriate set of categories that captures the left-right dimension. Ideology is a set of ideas that relate to the social/political world and that provides a general guideline for some action (Mahler, 1995, 36-37). As such, "ideology provides politicians with a broad conceptual map of politics into which political events, current problems, electors' preferences and other parties' policies can be fitted" (Budge, 1994, 446) and thus incorporates a broad range of political, economic, and social issues.

There have been a few recent attempts to identify a left-right dimension utilizing party manifesto data. Each of these studies uses a correlation-based statistical technique, such as factor analysis or principal components analysis, to identify a common left-right dimension from an analysis of manifesto data (Bowler, 1990; Budge and Robertson, 1987; Laver and Budge, 1993; Warwick, 1992). The most comprehensive measure is that of Laver and Budge in that they analyze all countries and the entire period in the data set. They use a series of exploratory factor analyses to identify potential combinations of categories to build a left-right scale. From these analyses, they identify 13 categories as comprising left ideology and another 13 as comprising right ideology. These26 ideological categories consistently loaded together in their factor analyses (pp. 24-27). Based on their analyses of the entire data set, Kim and Fording (1998) use the same 26 categories in their attempt to build a measure of party ideology in 15 industrialized democracies during the postwar period.[4] The final measure of party ideology is computed by subtracting the percentage of all party statements advocating right-wing positions from the corresponding percentage of all party statements representing left-wing positions, and dividing the difference by the total percentage of all leftist and rightist statements. The result is a party ideology measure of relative liberalism, taking on a possible range of 0 to 100.[5] To create a measure of voter ideology, Kim and Fording (1998) then estimate the median ideological position within the electorate of each country at the time of each election by combining ideology scores for each party with the relative vote shares received by these parties in the election. As a result, the Kim-Fording measure of voter ideology is, like their measure of party ideology, a measure of relative liberalism, taking on a possible range of 0 to 100.[6]

The Dynamics of Voter Ideology: Individual Country and Aggregate Trends

Figure 1 displays ideological movement in the United States.[7] Most notably, the most liberal period in recent U.S. history has been the early to mid 1960s. Figure 1 also shows that there was a steady movement to the right until the early to mid 1980s.

There is no reason to believe that all Western democracies have followed the same pattern as the United States. Indeed, although the majority of countries examined do show some type of movement toward the left during the 1960s, in general there are significant differences across countries in the magnitude of such ideological shifts not only during the 1960s but throughout the entire period of analysis. In Figure 2, which displays ideological movement in both Norway and Denmark, we can see that although there have been some shifts, voter ideology in Norway has been consistently left-leaning, and hence relatively stable, as it has stayed above the ideological score of 60 throughout the period of analysis. Voter ideology in Denmark, however, displays a different pattern with greater short-term fluctuations.

Although there is a common perception that the 1980s was a period of conservatism in Western democracies, there is some reason to suspect that this rightward movement is not common to all Western countries and that it is either most pronounced, or even entirely driven by a movement toward the right, among the English-speaking democracies. Such a possibility is suggested by the comparison of the Figures 1 and 2 above and also by Francis Castles (1990), who argues that in recent years, a movement toward the right has been strongest in these countries as evidenced by the economic policies of these countries. We investigate this possibility by examining ideological trends among the English-speaking nations (Australia, Canada, Ireland, New Zealand, the U.K., and the United States) and the other Western democracies separately. The results of this comparison, which are presented in Figure 3, offer interesting findings strongest in these countries as evidenced by the economic policies of these countries.

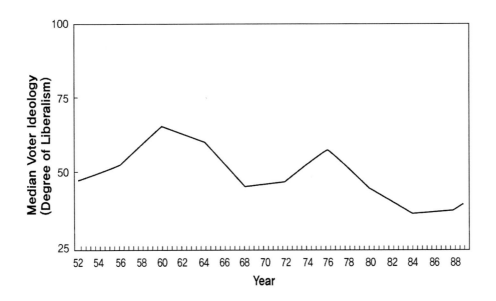

Figure 1. Voter ideology in United States, 1952–1989

Although a divergence in ideology can be seen between the two sets of countries, the real departure between the ideologies of the English-speaking and other Western countries occurred in the late 1950s rather than 1980s. Since then, these two groups of countries have maintained a fairly substantial distance in ideology, with non-English-speaking countries substantially more left-leaning than English-speaking ones. Although both groups experienced a general shift to the left during the 1960s, as we might expect given the fact that this was a period of relative economic prosperity throughout the West, the leftward movement was much more pronounced in non-English-speaking countries. We also find that both groups began to shift back to the right during the early 1970s, which also coincided with the first oil shock and the subsequent downturn in most Western economies. The fact that these trends were at least to some extent a common experience among Western democracies contradicts evidence presented by Host and Paldam (1990) that suggests that "international opinion swings" do not exist among Western nations.

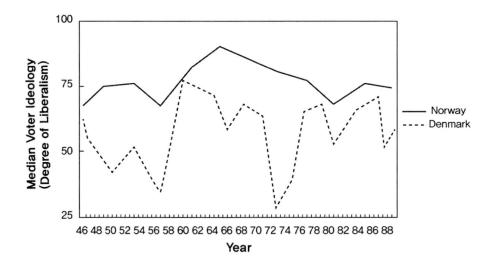

Figure 2. Examples of ideological stability and volatility: Norway and Denmark

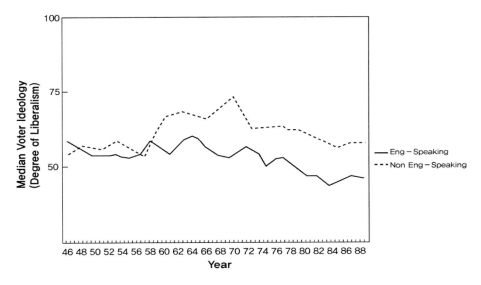

Figure 3. Voter ideology by language spoken

Theory

Based on the trends shown in the previous section, we believe a model of voter ideology ought to include two general types of variables. On the one hand, ideology can be thought of as being influenced by forces within a country.

Alternatively, we can conceptualize ideology as being influenced by forces originating from outside a country's borders. We discuss both types of factors below.

Internal Factors

The trends in voter ideology reported in the previous section suggest several hypotheses concerning the sources of ideology in these countries. In particular, the trends in Figure 3 appear to be rather consistent with general economic conditions in these countries. In his analysis of public opinion in the United States, Durr (1993) finds that the relationship between the economy and left-right ideology is straight forward W. hen the economy is expected to be "bad," Durr finds, voters are likely to be more conservative, and hence less supportive of expansionist leftist policies, since, as Durr argues, voters are more likely to be concerned about their personal financial well-being. When the economy is expected to be "good," however, voters are more liberal due to the relative availability of resources and the generosity that prosperity inspires.

Based on Durr's findings and a visual inspection of Figure 3, we can speculate that to a large extent, the period of liberalism experienced throughout the West during the 1960s and early 1970s may have been due to a combination of favorable economic conditions. Likewise, the shift to the right beginning in the 1970s may have been a consequence of a reversal of these economic conditions.

Based on this speculation, we examine the relationship between voter ideology and three indicators of the performance of the national economy that are commonly used to evaluate the national government: the gross domestic product as a measure of overall living standard, and unemployment rates and inflation rates as measures of economic hardship (see Lewis-Beck, 1988).

Although we expect that voters will shift ideologically in response to the state of the economy, since the incumbent government tends to get the credit (or the blame) for a good (or poor) economy we believe that the magnitude of this shift may depend on the ideological makeup of the incumbent government. These theoretical expectations lead to the following hypotheses:

Hypothesis 1: Economic growth causes leftward movement in voter ideology.

Hypothesis 2: Increases in unemployment cause rightward movement in voter ideology.

Hypothesis 3: Increases in inflation cause rightward movement in voter ideology.[8]

Hypothesis 4: The magnitude of the effect of the economy on ideological change is dependent upon the ideology of the government in power.

External Factors

We suspect that a process of ideological diffusion across countries may explain some of the common trends in ideology cited by political commentators over the years and evidenced by Figure 3. Perhaps the most obvious hypothesis about ideological diffusion between countries is that ideological change within a country will influence the ideology of countries with which it most frequently has contact. One likely source of ideological diffusion is geographic proximity.

Hypothesis 5: Voter ideology in a given country is related to voter ideology in neighboring countries.

Finally, an additional external influence on ideology may be the international environment. Eichenberg and Dalton, in their 1993 study of public support for European integration, find an inverse relationship between East-West tension (measured by the Soviet "net conflict" actions toward the U.S.) and the support for European integration among Europeans. The authors offer an explanation that "[w]hen European dependence on the United States is crystallized by security threats, there is increased public support for the Atlantic alliance [NATO] compared with purely European effort" (p. 515). In a similar vein, one may expect a "protect the capitalist democracies" or "rally around the U.S." mood among the Western democracies at the time of heightened East-West tension. To the extent that this is the case, we expect that voter ideology moves to the right when East-West tension is relatively high

Hypothesis 6: High levels of East-West tension cause rightward movement in voter ideology.

Empirical Measures, Methods, and Analysis

In our effort to explain ideological change, we examine voter ideology in 13 Western democracies, throughout a period that spans the years 1952-1989[9]. Our dependent variable is measured as the level of voter ideology in each election year, resulting in an N of 146.

Independent Variables

Internal Factors

Based on hypotheses 1-3 presented above, we include three economic indicators as independent variables. Economic Growth and Inflation are respectively measured as the annual percentage change in the gross domestic product and consumer price index within each country. Unemployment is measured as the annual percentage of unemployed workers in each country. These measures are consistent with other aggregate comparative studies of the effects of the economy on voting behavior, as is the time lag of one year for each variable (see Paldam, 1991, and Powell and Whitten, 1993)[10].

In hypothesis 4, we speculate that the effect of economic variables may depend on the ideology of the incumbent government. To test this hypothesis, we construct a measure of government ideology as follows. We begin with the party ideology measure used by Kim and Fording (1998) in constructing the measure of voter ideology. We then collect data for the number of cabinet portfolios for each party in each country in our sample, for the entire postwar period though 1989.[11] For each year, we combine this information with the party ideology scores by taking a weighted average of party ideology scores, where the weights are the proportion of total cabinet portfolios held by each party. Thus, for some countries where unified control of government occurs on a regular basis, the government ideology score reduces to the party ideology score for the party in power. For multiparty governments, however, the measure takes advantage of the information we have about the varying ideologies of the parties and their relative shares of power. Since the Kim-Fording measure of party ideology is an interval level measure of liberalism, taking on a possible range of 0 to 100, our measure of government ideology also becomes a measure of relative liberalism and takes on a possible range of 0 to 100. To test for interaction between economic variables and government ideology, we include a series of multiplicative terms in the model as follows: Economic Growth * Government Ideology, Inflation * Government Ideology, and Unemployment * Government Ideology.

External Factors

Our hypothesized external influences on voter ideology include the impact of ideological diffusion and the influence of the international political environment. Although one can imagine a variety of possibilities by which changes in ideology in one country may affect the ideology of other countries, we attempt to model a rather straightforwardd iffusion process. We hypothesize that voter ideology in a country is influenced by the ideology of its "neighbors," defined here as countries sharing a physical border.[12] For each country this variable, which we label Neighbor Ideology, is computed by first identifying that country's neighbors and then computing a weighted average of the neighbors' ideology scores, where country populations (as a percentage of the total neighbor population) are used as weights.

We are obviously hindered in our efforts to model this process due to a lack of data for some countries (i.e., we don't have data for each and every neighbor for some countries).[13] An additional problem concerns population differences between a country and its neighbors. Obviously, we should not expect a country as large as the United States to be influenced as strongly by what goes on in Canada as we would expect Canada to be influenced by what goes on in the United States. To capture this anticipated weaker effect for countries that are relatively large in size compared with their neighbors, we create an additional variable, Neighbor Ideology * Population Ratio, where Population Ratio is defined as the ratio of a country's population to the total population of its neighbors. While we expect voter ideology in a country to be positively influenced by the ideology of neighboring countries (Neighbor Ideology), we expect that this effect will decrease as the ratio of a country's population to that of its neighbors (Population Ratio) increases.

Finally, we hypothesize that ideology may be influenced by the international political environment. Specifically, we hypothesize that a high level of East- West tension causes a rightward shift in voter ideology and thus a decrease in our voter ideology measure. The specific variable we use is a yearly measure that taps the degree to which relations between the United States and the Soviet Union were either "warm" or "cold" during any given year. International relations scholars have developed several International Climate measures. We use the one developed by Bae (1992) based on a combination of COPDAB (Conflict and Peace Data Bank) and WEIS (World Events Interaction Survey) events data. As employed in our analysis, the measure ranges from -1 to +1, with higher values representing "colder" or relatively hostile relations between the two nations.

To determine the effects of these variables on voter ideology, we "pool" the 13 individual series and apply regression analysis, or more specifically in this case, pooled time-series analysis. Following Beck and Katz (1995), we estimate the coefficients for the model using Ordinary Least Squares. We address serial correlation by including a lagged dependent variable and calculate panel corrected standard errors, which are consistent in the presence of heteroskedasticity and spatial autocorrelation. The final model to be estimated is given below:

$$
\begin{aligned}
\text{Voter Ideology}_{i,t} =\ & \alpha + \beta_1 \text{Voter Ideology}_{i,t-1} + \beta_2 \text{Economic Growth}_{i,t-1} \\
& + \beta_3 \text{Inflation}_{i,t-1} + \beta_4 \text{Unemploymen t}_{i,t-1} + \beta_5(\text{Economic Growth}_{i,t-1} * \\
& \text{Government Ideology}_{i,t-1}) + \beta_6(\text{Inflation}_{i,t-1} * \text{Government Ideology}_{i,t-1}) + \\
& \beta_7(\text{Unemployment}_{i,t-1} * \text{Goverment Ideology}_{i,t-1}) + \beta_8 \text{Goverment} \\
& \text{Ideology}_{i,t-1} + \beta_9 \text{Neighbor Ideology}_{i,t-1} + \beta_{10}(\text{Neighbor Ideology}_{i,t-1} \\
& * \text{Population Ratio}_{i,t-1}) + \beta_{11} \text{Population Ratio}_{i,t-1} + \beta_{12} \text{International} \\
& \text{Climate}_{i,t-1} + \varepsilon_{i,t}.
\end{aligned}
$$

Results

The estimates of the coefficients in our model are given in column I of Table 1. As for the effects of internal factors, we do find some evidence that voter ideology is significantly influenced by economic conditions. In contrast to several studies of incumbent support, however, both unemployment and economic growth prove insignificant in our analysis, and only inflation is strongly related to voter ideology. This does not preclude the possibility that unemployment or economic growth do not matter within selected countries but simply suggests that it is inflation that is perhaps the most important, if not consistent determinant of voter ideology.

Although inflation is significantly related to voter ideology, the direction of the effect is influenced by the ideology of the incumbent government. This conditional relationship is reflected by the significance of the interaction term in Table 1 (16), and is represented graphically in Figure 4, which displays predicted slope values for inflation across the range of values of government ideology.

For the most conservative government (Government Ideology = 0), our results suggest that each 1 percent increase in inflation is expected to cause an increase in voter liberalism of approximately 1.2 points. This is reflected by the value of the slope coefficient for the additive inflation term (p3) in Table 1 and equivalently by the value of the intercept of the line in Figure 4. Substantively speaking, this suggests that when conservatives are in power, a disappointing economic performance is expected to move voters to the left. In contrast, when a left-wing government is in power, inflation is predicted to have the opposite effect. For the most leftist government (Government Ideology = 100), an increase of 1 percentage point in the inflation rate causes voter ideology to decrease by approximately 1.7 points (1.2 + 16 *100). Thus, it appears that voters look to inflation as an important measure of government performance and subsequently update their beliefs about what approach works.

Table 1. Regression Results for Voter Ideology

Independent Variables	Model I		Model II	
	β	PCSE	β	PCSE
Voter Ideology	0.16	0.12	0.20*	0.11
Government Ideology	0.33*	0.18	0.25	0.17
Inflation	0.17	0.87	0.83	0.79
Inflation * Government Ideology	−0.03*	0.01	−0.03*	0.01
Unemployment	−0.49	1.15	−0.78	1.10
Unemployment * Government Ideology	0.00	0.02	0.01	0.02
Economic Growth	−0.02	0.96	0.13	0.85
Economic Growth * Government Ideology	0.00	0.02	0.00	0.02
Neighbor Ideology	0.14	0.13	0.13	0.14
Neighbor Ideology Population Ratio	−0.03*	0.02	−0.03*	0.02
Population Ratio	−1.25	2.05	−1.01	2.41
International Climate	−0.28	3.03	−	−
International Climate * 1950s	−	−	−24.45*	7.79
International Climate * 1960s	−	−	6.98	6.43
International Climate * 1970s	−	−	13.11*	6.41
International Climate * 1980s	−	−	−0.64	7.06
1960s	−	−	−2.03	3.28
1970s	−	−	1.20	3.13
1980s	−	−	−1.52	3.50
R^2	.57		.63	
N	146		146	

Note: For the each model, column entries are unstandardized slope estimates, followed by panel corrected standard errors (PCSEs). All model were estimated in STATA (XTPCSE proceduce), with country dummy variables includes.

*p <.05, one−tailed

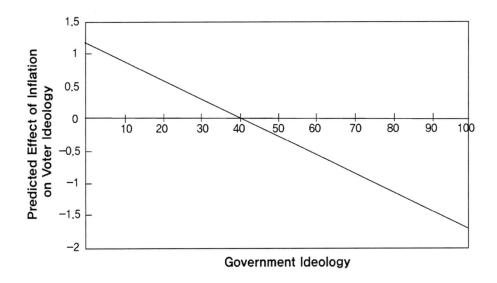

Figure 4. Predicted effect of inflation on voter ideology by ideology of incumbent government

Note: Government ideology is a measure of government liberalism, so that higher values corre-spont to more left-learning governments. Values for the vertical axis represent predicted slope values for the effect of inflation on voter ideology, holding other variables constant

Perhaps the most interesting finding in Figure 4 is the effect of inflation under moderate governments, or those near the middle range of the ideological scale. Under these governments, economic conditions are predicted to produce little change in voter ideology, at least in the aggregate. This may be due to uncertainty concerning which ideology-left or right-should be held responsible for the state of the economy.

Moving on to the effects of external variables, we find little initial support for the hypothesis that the international environment influences ideology. While the coefficient estimate does take on the hypothesized sign, the standard error is large and the t value does not approach conventional standards of significance. The effects of ideological diffusion, however, do prove significant. The coefficient values representing the effect of ideological diffusion suggest that as hypothesized, diffusion processes are strongest within countries that are small relative to their neighbors. Based on our estimates, for a country whose population is only 10% of that of its neighbors, an increase of 1 in neighbor ideology results in an increase of approximately .[14] in that country's ideology. This effect diminishes, however, as the population of a country increases relative to its neighbors. For a country whose population is twice as large as its neighbors, for example, the effect of neighbor ideology is predicted to decrease to .075 ($\beta9 + \beta10*2$)

Additional Analysis

Given the plausibility of our initial hypotheses, and in combination with the lack of support for some of them in Table 1, we explored several possible elaborations of our model above.[15] Among the most intriguing extensions of our initial model is the possibility that the effects of certain variables may vary across different historical periods. This is especially plausible for the economic variables, as the oil shocks experienced by most countries in the 1970s may have led to a different evaluation of economic performance among voters. We might also expect temporal variability in the effect of East-West tension as the threat of nuclear war might have given rise to different ideological reactions over time.

We explored each of these possibilities by examining the results of our model in the context of an interactive specification, allowing us in each case to examine how the effects of these variables changed across the historical periods of interest. For the economic variables, we examined the effects of the variables both before and after the first oil shock in 1973. These results generally do not differ from the results reported in column I of Table 1, so we do not report them here.

For our variable representing the state of the international climate, we examined temporal stability through an interactive specification that allowed us to compare the effect of this variable across decades. This analysis yielded some very interesting results, which are reported in column II of Table 1. The effect of the international climate by decade can be evaluated by examining the coefficients for a series of multiplicative terms that in each case consist of our measure of U.S.-Soviet relations and dummy variable for the decade of interest. Based on the specification of this model, each of the coefficients for the inter-action terms thus represents the effect of East-West tension on voter ideology during that decade.

Proceeding chronologically, we can see that for the decade of the 1950s, increases in East-West tension did have the predicted effect of causing a right-ward shift in voter ideology. By the 1970s, however, increasing tension appears to have the opposite (and significant) effect of moving voters to the left. This is a very interesting result and actually fits nicely with the general mood in these countries over time. In the 1950s, the United States was viewed by many European countries as their protector, especially after Europeans witnessed the Soviet aggression in their neighboring countries in Eastern Europe. Thus, when the tension mounted, they turned to more conservative positions. The late 1960s and 1970s, however, witnessed the rise of the radical student movements, the Greens, and general European dissent concerning the U.S. deployment of nuclear weapons on their continent. Out of this rose the fear that Europe would be a battleground should there be a conflict between the United States and the USSR. This explains the greater successes of the Greens as well as our finding of significant voter shifts to the left at the time of heightened East-West tension in the 1970s (see Bark and Gress, 1989, for a German example).

Discussion

In this article, we have investigated the origins of shifts in voter ideology in 13 Western democracies during the postwar era by utilizing the Kim and Fording (1998) measure of voter ideology. Their measure allows a meaningful comparison of voter ideology across different countries as well as across differ-ent time periods. Based on the results of our analysis, we find that shifts in voter ideology can be attributed to both domestic and international factors.

With respect to domestic influences, the state of the country's national economy, primarily inflation, seems to drive movement in voter ideology in a most significant way. As we saw above, the impact of economic factors is moderated by the ideological disposition of the incumbent government. This has a very important implication for parties and politicians, since the movement of voters on an ideological spectrum will depend not only on the state of national economy but on voters' perception of the location of the incumbent government on an ideological spectrum.

Our analysis reveals that there are international elements in the shifts in voter ideology, as we found significant ideological diffusion across neighboring countries of Western democracies. The effects of ideological diffusion are strongest within countries that are small relative to their neighbors. As a result, we suspect that a process of ideological diffusion across countries may explain some of the common trends in ideology cited by political commentators over the years, and evidenced by Figure 3.

We also found that ideology may be influenced by the international political environment, especially the level of East-West tension at the time of the Cold War. Our analysis suggests that the effect of East-West tension on voter ideology in Western democracies varies across decades. For the decade of the 1950s, increases in East-West tension caused a rightward shift in voter ideology. By the 1970s, however, increasing tension appears to have the opposite effect of moving voters to the left. We suspect that this is due to the changing European view of the U.S. role in Europe, the rise of the Greens, and general European dissent concerning the U.S. deployment of nuclear weapons, among other things.

Acknowledgments

An earlier draft of this article was presented at the annual meeting of the American Political Science Association, 2000 and at the World Congress of the International Political Science Association, 2000. We thank three anonymous reviewers of the Journal for their valuable comments. Juan Copa and Carl Dasse provided research assistance. We thank the Economic and Social Research Council at the University zu Koln for providing the ECPR party Manifesto Data to us. We also thank Bruce Western and Andre Blais for use of their data.

Notes

1. While the role of ideology has often been ignored in the American voting literature, both experimental (e.g., McKelvey and Ordeshook, 1990) and survey-based (e,g,. Levitin and Miller, 1979) find ideology th be an important determinant of choice in the United states.

2. Using party manifesto data, Laver and Budge(1993) convincingly show that the left-right dimension not only exists but is essential in the party programs in Western democracies.

3. Out of 20 countries in the manifesto data set, Kim and Fording include 15 in their study. The countries they include are Australia, Belgium, Canada, Denmark, Ireland, Italy, Luxembourg, Netherlands, New Zealand, Norway, Sweden, the United Kingdom, the United states, and the former West Germany.

4. The specific categories, as listed in the codebook, are as follows. Leftist categories are: Regulation of capitalism, Economic Planning, Protectionism: positive, Controlled economy, Nationalization, Decolonization, Military: negative, Peace, Internationalism: positive, Democracy, Social services expansion: positive, Education: positive, and Labor groups: positive. Rightist categories are: Free enterprise, Incentives, Protectionism: negative, Economic orthodoxy and efficiency, Social services expansion: negative, Constitutionalism: positive, Government effectiveness and authority, National way of life: positive, Traditional morality: positive, Law and order, National effort and social harmony, M ilitary: positive, and Freedom and domestic human rights. Detailed definitions of these categories are listed in the codebook, as well as in Laver and Budge (1993, 20-24). The salience of the left-right dimension is indicated by the frequency with which ideologically relevant statements appear in party manifestos. Overall, left-right statements comprise about half (47%; s.d. = 13.9%) of all statements in the entire sample of documents (N = 1,009). The salience of left-right statements is also consistent over time. Since 1966, the percentage of left-right statements averages 45% (N = 567), only slightly lower than the average for the entire period.

5. Kim and Fording offer evidence that suggests that this measure of party ideology is indeed a valid and reliable one. In particular, the manifesto-based measure of party

ideology correlates highly with alternative measures of party ideology constructed by political scientists in these countries (Castles and Mair, 1984) and a measure of party ideology relying on the perceptions of voters (based on Eurobarometer surveys). See Kim and Fording (1998) for details. The advantage of the manifesto-based measure over alternative measures is the fact that it is available for a number of countries for virtually the entire postwar period.

6. Although the validity of the median voter ideology measure is more difficult to ascertain due to a lack of comparable measures, Kim and Fording do present evidence that supports its validity. See Kim and Fording (1998). As most comparative scholars would anticipate, averaging over the entire postwar period, the most liberal countries turned out to be Sweden, Norway, and the Netherlands, while the most conservative countries were the United States, Ireland, and Australia. One may question if the Kim-Fording measure of voter ideology is telling us anything beyond changes in vote share for left and right parties (across time and countries). That is, one may argue that we can trace the nature of the ideological shift in the electorate simply by seeing whether the vote goes to, or away from the left or right parties. This would be accurate if the ideology of left and right parties is the same across countries, or even across time within a country. As many previous studies of the manifesto data have shown, both left-wing and right-wing parties differ greatly across countries, and perhaps more importantly for our analysis, party ideologies change over time (see Budge, 1994, and Budge and Robertson, 1987, for example). Based on our analysis of the manifesto data, we find that on average, party ideology scores (as described in this article) are correlated at .73 (N = 855) over time (i.e., from election at time t-1 to time t) within each country. This suggests that although party ideology is fairly stable, there is indeed a significant amount of change over time. Thus, the Kim-Fording measure provides significantly more information than a simple measure of vote shares for left vs. right parties.

7. For all the figures in this section, values for the manifesto-based series include observed ideological scores in election years and estimates based on linear interpolation in non-election years.

8. We can expect voter response to high (or low) levels of inflation based on the causes of inflation. First of all, "demand-pull" inflation is caused by excessive demand in an economy operating near full capacity and full employment. It can be fueled by the government's mismanagement of its fiscal policies. That is, excessively expansionary

fiscal policies in the sense of increasing expenditures and/or decreasing revenues, thereby increasing the deficit can overstimulate the economy by providing too much demand, leading sellers to raise prices and buyers to willingly pay those prices (one typical example would be the federal income tax cut under the Johnson administration at the time of the booming economy). Therefore, once inflation goes up, typical voter response would be a demand for decreasing expenditures (rather than raising taxes) along with a tight monetary policy. That is, voters demand a small government and move to the right. We can also think of "cost-push" inflation as well. The most important cost in an advanced capitalist economy is the compensation for the labor went to compensation of employees (Economic Report of the President, 1983). Therefore, to discuss cost-push inflation, one natural starting point is the impact of compensation patterns on inflation. If aggregate compensation in the economy increases more rapidly than productivity (output per hour), then the cost of labor for each unit of output should also increase. Sellers of the products then have choices between taking less profit and passing additional cost along to consumers in the form of higher prices. We can safely assume that in nearly every case the latter becomes reality. This being the case, inflation partly reflects successes of certain segments of labor in that their compensation surpassed the productivity level. (More radical interpretations of this process resulted in the class-conflict theory of the business cycle. See Mitchell, 1913, Kalecki, 1943, Boddy and Crotty, 1975, and Cameron, 1984a). Once inflation pushed by the labor cost rises, voters would demand the control of labor and move to the right. Obviously the rising labor cost is not the only cause of the cost-push inflation. As we saw in the 1970s, the rising oil price can also cause inflation, as oil is such an important input in production in the industrialized economies.

9. The time period analyzed is restricted by the availability of manifesto data and economic data. Although Kim and Fording (1998) constructed voter ideology estimates for a total of 15 countries during this period, we exclude Luxembourg in the present analysis due to a lack of economic data. We also exclude Belgium due to problems we encountered with matching political parties to both cabinet portfolio data and manifesto data, which is necessary to build our government ideology variable. Given the large number of short-lived parties, their tendency to form frequent short-lived alliances (and issue joint manifestos), as well as frequent name changes, the computation of government ideology scores was for the most part impossible in Belgium.

10. Sources for these data are as follows. GDP: Penn World Tables (http://cansim.epas.utoronto.ca:5680/pwt/pwt.html); Inflation and Unemployment: OECD data made available by Bruce Western (thru 1985), and Andre Blais (post-1985).

11. We use cabinet composition data contained in Woldenborp, Keman, and Budge (1993, 1998).

12. We consider New Zealand and Australia to be "neighbors" although they do not share a physical border.

13. The specific "neighbors" used in this measure are, for each country: Sweden: Norway and Denmark; Norway: Sweden; Denmark: Germany and Sweden; Netherlands: Germany; Italy: Austria; West Germany: Denmark, Netherlands, and Austria; Austria: Germany and Italy; United Kingdom: Ireland; Ireland: United Kingdom; United States: Canada; Canada: United States; New Zealand: Australia; Australia: New Zealand.

14. In addition to the elaboration we report below, we also experimented with alternative lag structures and different measures of the dependent and independent variables (levels vs. firstdifferences). None of these modifications led to results that were significantly different or more theoretically pleasing than the results reported in Table 1. We also considered the possibility that our results may be affected by multicollinearity. Indeed, an inspection of diagnostic statistics does find multicollinearity to be quite high for the variables involved in the interactions. This may pose a problem for estimation of the effects of unemployment and economic growth, neither of which were found to significantly affect voter ideology. Upon estimating an additive specification for these two variables, although the coefficients do take on the hypothesized sign, the t values are still quite small and do not approach conventional levels of statistical significance.

15. The results of this interactive model still find non-significant effects for unemployment and growth, but find that the effect of inflation was stronger prior to the oil shock. These results are available on request.

03.

Does Tactical Voting Matter?
The Political Impact of Tactical Voting in
Recent British Elections

Heemin Kim[*] & Richard C. Fording[**]

* Florida State University

** University of Kentucky

Abstract. Although much has been written about tactical voting, few studies have attempted to show its impact on the seat distribution within Parliament and subsequent government makeup in countries with single-member plurality systems. The authors attempt to assess the magnitude and impact of tactical voting in recent British general elections. They build a model of tactical voting by identifying factors known to affect the level of tactical voting measurable using available data. Based on this model, they generate predicted levels of tactical voting for all parties within each district. Based on these predicted values, they adjust actual election data to produce a new set of data containing a would-be election outcome in the

1) AUTHORS' NOTE: Earlier versions of this article were presented at the annual meetings of the Public Choice Society, 1998, and the American Political Science Association, 1997. We thank William Berry, Ian Budge, William Claggett, Han Dorussen, Tatiana Kostadinova, and Nancy Zingale for their helpful comments. Juan Copa provided valuable research assistance. Data from the 1983, 1987, and 1992 British Election Studies (BES) were supplied by the Inter-University Consortium for Political and Social Research Data Archive. Data from the 1997 BES were supplied by the European Consortium for Political Research Data Archive.
COMPARATIVE POLITICAL STUDIES, Vol. 34 No. 3, April 2001 294-311

absence of tactical voting. By comparing actual election data, adjusted election data, and the seat share of political parties in the parliaments after these elections, they discuss the political impact of tactical voting in the United Kingdom.

Sincere voting assumes that voters always choose their most preferred candidates and/or parties. It has been argued in both the formal and empirical literature, however, that voters may not always vote for their most preferred candidates. This is known as tactical (or strategic, sophisticated) voting and refers to voting contrary to one's nominal preferences. Tactical voting, as usually described in the literature, primarily takes place under single- member district plurality electoral systems and takes the form of third-party supporters voting for one of the major parties. The logic of tactical voting, of course, is that of Duverger's (1963) law, which states that the supporters of a small party would not "waste" their votes by voting for their most preferred party (candidate) because it does not have a chance to win under a plurality system with single-member districts. Instead, they vote for the major party that is most acceptable to them and that has a chance of winning (Duverger, 1963). Since Duverger, ample theoretical literature has shown incentives to vote tactically under different electoral institutions (Bowler & Farrell, 1991; Jesse, 1995; Riker, 1976, 1982; Tsebelis, 1986).[1]

Until now, empirical studies of tactical voting have taken two different paths: The first evaluates whether indeed some voters vote tactically under single-member district plurality electoral institutions (primarily Britain and Canada) and, if so, how many of them do so. These studies investigate the level of tactical voting for a single election using existing survey data and have shown that tactical voting does occur, usually at a rate of somewhere between 5% and 10% of the electorate (Alvarez & Nagler, in press; Blais & Nadeau, 1996; Curtice & Steed, 1988; Evans & Heath, 1993; Fisher, 1973; for different estimates of the level of tactical voting, see Niemi, Whitten, & Franklin, 1992, 1993).

The second direction taken by empirical studies of tactical voting is the investigation of the causes of tactical voting for a given election. These studies have shown that several individual factors as well as contextual factors within districts affect the level of tactical voting in a given election (Black, 1978; Bowler & Lanoue, 1992; Cain, 1978; Gailbraith & Rae, 1989; Johnston & Pattie,

1991; Lanoue & Bowler, 1992).

We take yet another approach. In this article, we investigate the political impact of tactical voting over a period of time. That is, we assess whether tactical voting has had an impact on the actual distribution of seats within the Parliament and eventually the partisan composition (and thus subsequent policies) of the government. If indeed the magnitude of tactical voting in single-member plurality systems is large enough to affect the power distribution within the Parliament and subsequent policy outcomes, this will provide additional empirical evidence that theoretical arguments based on voter rationality are valid in the real world and that voters are quite successful in not wasting their votes and preventing their least preferred parties from coming to power.[2]

In this article, we study four recent general elections in the United Kingdom, whose electoral system is characterized by single-member district plurality rule. We estimate levels of tactical voting for all major parties within each constituency for these elections. Based on these estimates, we adjust the actual election data to produce a revised set of results that represents would-be election outcomes in the absence of tactical voting (i.e., had everybody voted sincerely). In the last section of this article, we discuss the impact of tactical voting in the United Kingdom by comparing these new results to the actual election data.

Estimating the Political Impact of Tactical Voting: An Operationalization

Ideally, to accurately gauge the political impact of tactical voting, we would like to compare observed election results (which reflect tactical voting) to the election results that would have been observed if all voters had voted sincerely. This would be easy to do if district-level public opinion polls measuring voters' sincere preferences were ailable prior to each election. Unfortunately, they are not. In the absence of such data, we are left with two (albeit rather crude) choices.

First, we might simply calculate the national rate of tactical voting, along with the direction of tactical vote flows, based on national level surveys. We might then apply these national-level estimates to elections at the district level, using this information to estimate the distribution of sincere preferences within each district. The most obvious weakness of this strategy, however, is that it assumes that the rate of tactical voting, which would be estimated from national-level data, is the same across all districts. This is not likely to be the case, as a large literature suggests that the rate of tactical voting in a given election is in part a function of various aspects of the electoral context within each district, and as we would suspect, the electoral context across districts is likely to vary to a significant degree.

A second approach to measuring the impact of tactical voting does not make such an implausible assumption and therefore is adopted for this research. Our approach proceeds in three general stages. First, we estimate an individual-level model of tactical voting in which it is assumed that the probability that an individual votes strategically is a function of key characteristics of the electoral environment in his or her district. Having obtained the coefficients from this model, we then shift the level of analysis to the district level and, based on equivalent contextual variables, predict the rate of tactical voting for each party within each district. Along with estimates of vote flows obtained using national-level data, we then proceed to calculate the percentage of "sincere" supporters of each party within each district. This information is then compared to actual election results to determine how frequently tactical voting affects the outcome of an election.

A contextual model of tactical voting

To estimate the impact of contextual variables on tactical voting at the individual level, we rely on the British Election Study for the elections of 1983, 1987, 1992, and 1997.[3] To identify tactical voters, we use the operationalization advocated by Evans and Heath (1993). This indicator of tactical voting is based on a single item that asks respondents why they voted as they did and identifies tactical voters as those who responded by saying that their preferred party had no chance of winning (for a controversy over which survey items represent "tactical voting," see Evans&Heath, 1993; Niemi et al., 1992, 1993). In estimating our individual-level model, we estimate a separate model for each election, thus allowing the propensity for tactical voting among different parties as well as the effects of the variables in the model to vary over time.[4]

A large literature in political science has addressed the impact of electoral context on tactical voting. This literature has identified two important aspects of an election as being critical to determining the rate of tactical voting. The first one is the probability that one"s party can win the election. That is, voters are expected to be more likely to abandon their preferred party when their party is not competitive in the election (Blais & Nadeau, 1996; Niemi et al., 1992). This contextual dimension is captured by including the variable COMPETITIVENESS, measured as the percentage of the vote obtained by one's preferred party in the election .A second dimension of electoral context suggested by the literature is the closeness of the election (Black, 1978; Blais & Nadeau, 1996; Cain, 1978; Gailbraith & Rae, 1989; Niemi et al., 1992; Tsebelis, 1986). Consequently, we include the variable CLOSENESS, defined as the distance (in votes) between an individual"s second and third most preferred parties in the election.[5] All else equal, it is assumed that voters are more likely to abandon their most preferred party and vote strategically when their party is not competitive and when the distance between the other parties is small. In other words, we expect COMPETITIVENESS as well as CLOSENESS to be negatively related to tactical voting.

In addition, we expect COMPETITIVENESS and CLOSENESS to interact in their effect on tactical voting. For example, when a voter's preferred party is the frontrunner in a particular district (and thus COMPETITIVENESS is high), the value of CLOSENESS should not matter in that voter"s decision to vote tactically. More generally, we should thus expect the effect of closeness to diminish in magnitude as COMPETITIVENESS increases. To allow for this possibility, we include a multiplicative term (COMPETITIVE- NESS * CLOSENESS) to the model, where the coefficient for this interactive term is expected to be positive.

Finally, we adddummyvariables for the party of the respondent to capture election-specific forces that might be expected to affect the propensity for tactical voting among members of each of the major parties. As the dependent variable is dichotomous, we use logit analysis to estimate the model, the results of which are presented below in Table 1.

As expected, both contextual variables are negatively related to tactical voting and are generally statistically significant ($< .05$). The interaction term is positive, as expected, in three of the four models but does not quite reach conventional levels of statistical significance. However, given our theoretical preference for the interactive specification as well as the multicollinearity inherent in such models, we chose to keep the interactive terms in the models for our final results.

Table 1. Logit Results for Tactical Voting in British Elections, 1983–1997

Variables	1983 Election Coefficient		1987 Election Coefficient		1992 Election Coefficient		1997 Election Coefficient	
Competitiveness	−.075*	(.016)	−.067*	(0.18)	−.112*	(.017)	−.135*	(.021)
Closeness	−.023	(.020)	.025	(.020)	−.032*	(.012)	−.043*	(.018)
Competitiveness *Closeness	.001	(.001)	−.001	(.001)	.001	(.001)	.001	(.001)
Conservative supporter	−1.050*	(.312)	−.318	(.372)	.646*	(.315)	−.511	(.433)
Labour supporter	−.128	(.196)	−.172	(.251)	.258	(.263)	.392	(.327)
Intercept	−.079	(.437)	−.571*	(.514)	.841*	(.309)	1.481*	(.439)
Chi−square(df=5)	127.79		96.17		200.10		182.30	
Pseudo R^2	.14		.18		.24		.31	
n	3,133		1,544		2,191		1,549	

Note: Cell entries are logit coefficients, with robust standard errors in parentheses. Estimates were generated by STATA 6.0
* $p < .05$

The coefficients for the dummy variables indicating party support indicate that even after controlling for CLOSENESS and COMPETITIVENESS, supporters of the Labour Party and especially the Alliance/Liberal Democrat Party (LDP) were more likely to vote tactically than were Conservatives. The one exception here is the 1992 election in which, controlling for the electoral environment, Conservatives were more likely to vote tactically. Overall, the results support the literature that suggests tactical voting is sensitive to electoral context. As a result, although national rates of tactical voting have consistently averaged 5% to 7% in these elections, there is reason to believe that rates of tactical voting may actually be significantly higher in certain constituencies due to variation in electoral context at the constituency level.

Estimating tactical voting at the constituency

Having estimated our individual-level model of tactical voting for each election, we now shift the analysis to the constituency level, where our units of analysis now become political parties rather than individuals. Our ultimate goal at this stage is to estimate the extent and source of tactical voting within each district. We accomplish this task in a series of steps. First, we estimate the rate of tactical voting for each party within each district, defined as TACTPARTY$_i$, by using observed contextual data for the constituency and the coefficient estimates from the appropriate equation in Table 1. In other words, for each election, we calculate:

$$TACTPARTY_i = 1/(1+e-(\alpha+\beta CLOSENESS+\beta COMPETITIVENESS$$
$$+\beta COMPETITIVENESS^*CLOSENESS+\beta LABOUR+\beta$$
$$CONSERVATIVE)), \quad (1)$$

for each party within each district, where the form of the equation is dictated by the fact that the coefficient estimates were generated using the logit model.

Next, using our estimate of TACTPARTYi along with the observed vote share for each party (%VOTEi), we calculate the percentage of voters (across the entire district) who consider party i their most preferred party but instead voted tactically. More formally, we define TACTDISTi as:

$$TACTDIST_i =(\textit{Number of tactical voters preferring party i}$$

$$/ \textit{Number of all voters in the district})*100, \qquad (2)$$

which can be calculated as follows:

$$TACTDIST_i = [\% VOTE_i/(1 - TACTPARTY_i)] - \% VOTE_i. \qquad (3)$$

Note that the first component of this equation [%VOTEi / (1 − TACTRATEi)] is equal to the sum of two groups of voters: those who prefer party i and those who prefer another party but voted strategically for party I. By subtracting the proportion of the district voting for party i (%VOTEi), we are thus left with the percentage of voters who prefer but do not vote for party i (TACTDISTi).

Calculating sincere supporters at the constituency level

The final step in the analysis is to estimate election results that would have been observed if tactical voting had not occurred. First, we estimate vote flows (i.e., how tactical voters distributed their tactical votes across parties) using national-level data.[6] Let FLOWRATEji be the proportion of tactical voters from party j that give their votes to party i. Then, the percentage of vot-ers who prefer party j but vote tactically for party i, to be denoted VOTEFLOWji, can be estimated as follows:

$$VOTEFLOW_{ji} = TACTDIST_j^* FLOWRATE_{ji}, j = 1, 2, \qquad (4)$$

where FLOWRATEji is the proportion of tactical voters from party j that give their votes to party I.

Our ultimate goal in this stage of the analysis is to estimate the distribution of sincere preferences within each constituency. This requires that we estimate for each party in each constituency the proportion of voters who regard that party as their most preferred. To accomplish this task, we rely on the following formula that decomposes sincere vote shares for each party into several constituent parts. The percentage of voters who consider party i their most preferred party, to be denoted SINCEREi, can then be estimated as:

$$SINCERE_i = \%VOTE_i + \sum_{j=1}^{2} VOTEFLOW_{ij} - \sum_{j=1}^{2} VOTEFLOW_{ji}, \quad (5)$$

where VOTEFLOWij is the proportion of voters who consider party i their most preferred party but vote for some other party j. In other words, this final equation states that the percentage of the district electorate who (sincerely) prefer party i (SINCEREi) is equal to the percentage of voters who voted for party i (%VOTEi) plus (a) the percentage of voters who prefer party i but voted for party j minus (b) the percentage of voters who preferred party j but voted for party i.

Results

The impact of tactical voting in british elections, 1983-1997

Using this logic along with the coefficient estimates from the logit model above and observed electoral data from the elections of 1983, 1987, 1992, and 1997, we estimated the percentage of sincere voters for the Conservative Party, the Labour Party, and the Liberal/Social Democrat Party Alliance (or LDP) within each constituency. Based on our estimates of tactical voting for each of the parties in these elections, it appears that there is considerable variation in the rate of tactical voting across constituencies. This is evident from examining Figures 1 through 3, which display frequency distributions of estimated constituency-level tactical voting rates for the parties in these elections. In Figure 1, we can see that very little tactical voting has occurred among Conservative Party supporters. This is expected, as Conservative Party supporters have had little reason to expect their party to lose in recent elections. Alternatively, as Figures 2 and 3 indicate, tactical voting has been considerably higher among supporters of the other major parties. This is especially the case among Alliance/LDP supporters, whose rates of tactical voting in the range of 40% to 50% are estimated in a sizable number of districts in the 1990s.

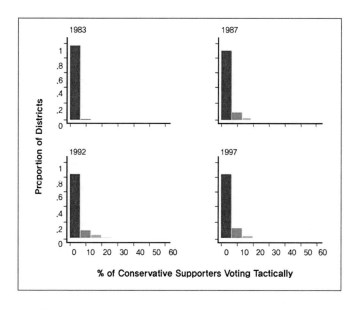

Figure 1. Predicted levels of tactical voting among Conservative Party supporters, 1983–1997.

Given this variation and thus the many constituencies where rates of tactical voting are predicted to have been extremely high, the next question to be answered is whether tactical voting has had a significant effect on election outcomes. We address this question by comparing observed election outcomes to estimated election outcomes assuming sincere voting. For each of the elections, this comparison is presented in the form of a cross-tabulation in Table 2.

An examination of the results yields two important findings. First, generally speaking, the predicted effect of tactical voting on actual election outcomes has been modest at best. This is easily seen by an examination of the off-diagonal entries of the table, where nonzero entries represent election outcomes that would have differed if tactical voting had not occurred. Of the 2,342 constituency outcomes examined across the four elections, in only 39 cases did

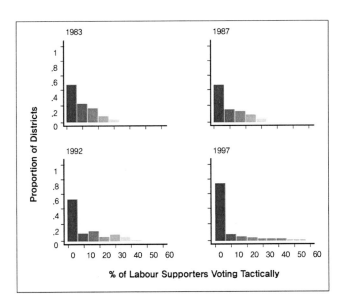

Figure 2. Predicted levels of tactical voting among Labour Party supporters,
1983–1997

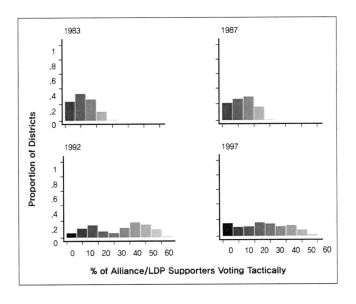

Figure 3. Predicted levels of tactical voting among Alliance/Liberal
Democratic Party supporters, 1983–1997

the actual winner differ from the winner predicted assuming sincere voting.

Table 2. Predicted Winners Based on Sincere Voting by Actual Winners, 1983–1997

Predicted Winner Based on Sincere voting	Actual Winner (reflecting tactical voting)			
	Conservative	Labour	Alliance/LDP	Total
1983 elction				
Conservation	391	0	0	391
Labour	6	209	0	214
Alliance	0	0	24	24
Total	396	209	24	629
1987 election				
Conservation	367	0	1	368
Labour	4	210	0	216
Alliance	0	0	20	20
Total	373	210	21	604
1992 election				
Conservation	323	3	4	317
Labour	0	213	1	222
Alliance	0	0	09	12
Total	325	214	12	551
1997 election				
Conservation	164	4	14	182
Labour	0	352	2	354
Alliance	0	0	22	22
Total	164	356	38	558

Note: LDP = Liberal Democrat Party

Assessing the sensitivity of our projections

For many reasons, it is possible that our results underestimate the impact of tactical voting. First, the omission of relevant explanatory variables and the possibility of measurement error in our individual-level model may serve to attenuate coefficient estimates used to predict rates of tactical voting. The ability of the model to predict such high rates of tactical voting in many constituencies (as evidenced in Figures 1 through 3) leads us to believe that this may not be a serious problem. A more likely source of bias, however, may exist due to the use of national-level tactical vote flows to generate our pre-dicted set of sincere election results. To the extent that these vote flows vary across districts (as we expect they do), it is quite likely that we underestimate the true impact of tactical voting.

Although survey limitations do not allow us to assess the variability in vote flows across constituencies, we assessed the sensitivity of our estimates to variation in vote flows by generating a series of alternative (sincere) election results using hypothetical (assumed) sets of vote flows between parties. In this experiment, we generated election outcomes assuming that tactical vote flows were either 100% or 0% for each combination of parties. For example, for one set of election outcomes, we assume that Conservatives gave 100% of their tactical votes to the LDP/Alliance, that Labour supporters gave 100% of their tactical votes to Conservatives, and that the LDP/Alliance gave 100% of their tactical votes to Labour. Exhausting all possible combinations, this results in eight unique sets of vote flows generated from the assumption that party supporters gave 100% of their tactical votes to a single party.

Based on these hypothetical sets of vote flows, we generated eight sets of sincere election outcomes. For each election (year), we then calculated the percentage of district outcomes that were the same under every one of the eight combinations of vote flows. Assuming the adequacy of the individual-level model presented in Table 1, these percentages thus reflect the number of districts where it is mathematically impossible for tactical voting to have affected the outcome. Thus, to the extent that these estimates are reasonably large, we can conclude that the true impact of tactical voting has been modest at best.

For 1983 and 1987, our estimates indicate that for approximately 84% of the constituencies, the result could not possibly have been affected. This figure decreases somewhat for 1992 and 1997, however, where it is estimated that for each of these years, approximately 67% of constituency outcomes could not possibly have been affected by tactical voting. Put somewhat differently, by the 1990s, it was mathematically possible that about 33% of the constituency outcomes could have been affected. Although this figure is not insignificant, we must stress that this value was generated based on a change in the outcome observed under any of eight possible vote flows within each district and thus represents the universe of districts where it is only mathematically possible that tactical voting could have mattered. Obviously, many of these vote flows are highly implausible. For example, national surveys repeatedly show that Labour Party supporters rarely gave their tactical votes to Conservative candidates, yet our experiment allows for such a possibility (at a rate of 100%). Consequently, the true impact of tactical voting must be significantly less than these estimates and is most likely (we feel) closer to our point estimates presented in Table 2. Nevertheless, this exercise does lead us to believe that variability in vote flows, which we believe may exist to some extent, probably leads us to underestimate the true impact of tactical voting to some degree. As a result, we conclude that the true impact of tactical voting has likely been politically significant in recent years, although relatively modest in magnitude.

Explaining the modest effect of tactical voting

Although our projections indicate that tactical voting has had only a modest impact on election outcomes, it is not immediately obvious why this might be the case. One possible reason might be that there are relatively few constituencies where the election is close. This appears not to be the case. Across the four election years, approximately 12% of all elections were decided by 5 or fewer percentage points. Rather, the reasons for such a small impact may lie elsewhere. Three possibilities seem likely.

The first reason is inherent in the nature of the relationship between electoral context and tactical voting. The individual-level analysis suggests that the level of support of one"s party is the most important factor in determining the probability of tactical voting. As a result, although there are many instances of predicted tactical voting rates of 30% or more, this would necessarily mean that these high rates of tactical voting are coming from parties that enjoy relatively little support and thus have relatively few tactical votes to give.

A second reason lies in the fact that the two most important electoral variables influencing tactical voting – COMPETITIVENESS and CLOSENESS – tend to be negatively correlated across districts. Although the magnitude of the correlation is modest by our estimates ($-.42$, $p < .05$), this does suggest that these important influences on tactical voting tend to cancel each other out to some degree in the empirical world.

Finally, a third reason lies in the fact that tactical voters from a given party often do not seem to agree on their second-choice parties. Based on the national-level (survey) data, it is clear that tactical voters from the same party are far from unanimous in their selection of the party to receive their vote. This is clear by examining Table 3, which displays the distribution of vote flows from party to party based on pooled samples of tactical voters over the four elections. As can be seen, only for the Labour Party do tactical voters seem to be in strong agreement as to who should receive their vote, as approximately 80% gave their votes to the Alliance/LDP across the four elections. For both the Alliance/LDP and Conservatives, tactical voters were significantly less unanimous in their choice, with the distribution of vote flows ranging between 40% and 60% in the four-election sample. Even granting the likelihood that these vote flows vary across districts, it is still likely that we would find considerable disagreement among party supporters could we observe district-level data, suggesting that even if there were significant numbers of tactical votes to be had, these votes tend to flow in opposing directions, attenuating the cumulative impact of tactical voting.[7]

Table 3. Distribution of Tactical Votes across Parties, 1983–1997

Vote of Respondent	Sincere Preference of Respondent							
	Conservative		Labour		Alliance/LDP		Total	
Conservative			2	(4.9%)	23	(41.8%)	25	(24.0%)
Labour	2	(25.0%)			32	(58.2%)	34	(32.7%)
Alliance/LDP	6	(75.0%)	39	(95.1%)			45	(43.3%)
Total	8	(100.0%)	41	(100.0%)	55	(100.0%)	104	(100.0%)

Source: Heath, Jowell, & Curtice (1989); Heath, Jowell, Curtice, Brand & Mitchell (1992); Heath, Jowell, Curtice, & Field (1983); Heath, Jowell, Curtice, & Norris (1997)

The increasing impact of tactical voting over time

Although we estimate that the impact of tactical voting has been relatively modest in the past, it has been growing. Of the 39 constituencies in which tactical voting was estimated to have made a difference, 20 occurred in the 1997 election alone. This finding confirms the conventional wisdom that tactical voting played a more important role in the 1997 election (Budge, Crewe, McKay, & Newton, 1998; Curtice & Steed, 1997). Furthermore, our results show that in 18 of these 20 cases, Conservative Party candidates lost the election due to tactical voting by Labour Party or LDP supporters. This is in sharp contrast to previous elections (1983 and 1987) in which Conservatives were predicted to be the primary beneficiaries of tactical voting.

Why might the tide have turned in 1997? The answer may lie in the recent ideological movement of the Labour Party. Based on recent evidence, it is clear that the Labour Party moved to the right in 1997, sending a clear mes-sage to both Labour and LDP supporters about what their second-choice party should be in case they voted tactically. The parties" ideological movement over time (based on a content analysis of party manifestos) is presented in Figure 4.

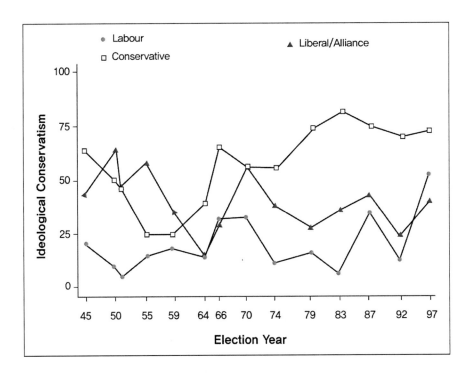

Figure 4. British parties' left–right movement, 1945–1997.

Source: Based on work from Budge (1992) on the ECPR Party Manifestos Project.

As can be seen, by 1997, the Labour Party had moved considerably to the right, thus strengthening the relationship between Labour and the LDP. This fact is also supported by the pattern of vote flows during the four elections. In the three elections prior to 1997, Alliance tactical voters had given a majority of their votes (55%) to Conservatives. By 1997, however, the data suggest that the Labour Party had replaced the Conservatives as the second choice of LDP supporters as 58% of the 1997 sample of LDP tactical voters gave their votes to Labour Party candidates. Whereas Labour Party tactical voters have overwhelmingly favored the Alliance/LDP as their second choice throughout the four elections, the 1997 level of support significantly exceeded levels seen in earlier elections as 95% of the 1997 sample of Labour tactical voters gave their votes to LDP candidates.

Conclusion

Previous empirical studies using existing survey data have shown that some voters do vote tactically under single-member district plurality electoral institutions (Alvarez & Nagler, in press; Blais & Nadeau, 1996; Curtice & Steed, 1988; Evans & Heath, 1993; Fisher, 1973; Niemi et al., 1992, 1993).

These studies provide empirical evidence that some voters try to avoid "wasting" their votes by not voting for their most preferred party (candidate) under the Duvergerian reasoning. Our study, over a period of time, further affirms the fact that in some cases, tactical voting does indeed lead to election outcomes that are different from those in the absence of tactical behavior. This means that voters can be successful in not wasting their votes and preventing their least preferred party candidates from being elected, thus providing additional evidence that theoretical arguments based on voter rationality are to some degree valid in the real world.

At the same time, however, our results convincingly demonstrate that until recently, tactical voting has had a modest impact on election outcomes in the United Kingdom. Tactical voting had a modest impact on the actual distribution of seats within the Parliament and no impact on the partisan composition of the government.[8] Even in 1997, when tactical voting had a much greater impact due to the ideological convergence of the Labour Party and the LDP, it did not affect the partisanship of the government given the margin of the Labour majority. At the micro level, individual voters may try not to waste their votes by voting tactically. Our results suggest, however, that this individual act may not always lead to its intended outcome, which is to prevent voters" least preferred party from winning. This may be due to a variety of reasons, including the electoral contexts within districts, the small pool of tactical voters, a lack of information about party positions, and different preferences among tactical voters themselves about their second-choice parties. There may exist individual-level incentives to vote tactically and thus rationally, in the Duvergerian sense, but the collective choice may not result in the intended effect. As social choice theorists would suggest then, individual rationality does not necessarily lead to group rationality.

As we suggested in the first section of this article, the study of tactical voting in single-member district plurality systems has been a growth industry in comparative politics. Our study is an attempt to go beyond simply measuring the level of tactical voting after each election or evaluating the factors determining this level. Given our results, more studies about voter perception of party positions and the determinants of voters" ordinal preferences of political parties are warranted.

Notes

1. Although the notion of tactical voting has been primarily applied to plurality electoral systems, incentives to vote tactically may exist in countries with different electoral systems as well. Some recent studies indicate that such incentives exist in electoral systems with an ordinal ballot structure (voters order preferences among the candidates) where vote transfer is possible (e.g., Ireland and the Australian Senate; see Bowler & Farrell, 1991; Jesse, 1995). An incentive to act tactically on the part of small-party supporters arises in these countries as their party fails to meet the quota, and they subsequently transfer their votes to big parties (which may not be their second most preferred party). Also see Tsebelis (1986) for potential incentives for tactical voting in proportional representation systems.

2. There have been a few studies in the past that tried to estimate the number of constituencies in Britain whose election outcomes were altered by tactical voting. These estimates were based on somewhat crude assumptions and methodology. See Curtice and Steed (1988, 1992, 1997) and Evans (1994). See Catt (1990) for a critique of the approach taken by these studies.

3. We chose to begin with the 1983 general election because it was in the mid-1980s when tactical voting became a major subject of public and media interest (Butler & Kavanagh, 1988; Fieldhouse, Pattie,&Johnston, 1996). Furthermore, surveys for prior elections do not allow one to reliably distinguish "pure" tactical voters from "insincere" voters who stray from their preferred party for other, nonstrategic reasons.

4. We only consider cases of tactical voting in which both the preferred party and the party actually supported were among the Labour, Conservative, and Alliance/Liberal

Democratic Parties (LDP). This is due primarily to the fact that there are only a handful of tactical voters in these samples who either truly supported or voted for another party, preventing us from estimating tactical vote flows to and from these other parties. Estimates of these vote flows are necessary to make the final election adjustments in the sections ahead.

5. For the contextual variables, we use actual election outcomes to determine pre-election support. Ideally, one should use individual preelection expectations or poll results. In the absence of such data for all constituencies in Britain for all four elections, we use actual election results, following the tradition of Black (1978), Cain (1978), and Niemi et al. (1992).

6. For vote flows between Labour and Alliance/LDP, these vote flows are calculated using national-level data for each of the four elections. For vote flows involving the Conservative Party, however, the sample sizes for each group of tactical voters are reduced to unacceptably low levels when using yearly figures (i.e., n < 20). We therefore use the average distribution of votes across the four elections for these cases.

7. Although the vote flow estimates presented in Table 3 are based on pooled data, yearly estimates of vote flows (which were used in the estimation of tactical voting rates) of Alliance/ LDP supporters reveal similar levels of disagreement. Yearly estimates of vote flows originating from Conservative Party supporters were not calculated due to extremely small sample sizes (see Note 6).

8. A caveat applies here: Our study assesses the impact of the act of tactical voting on the day of election. However, the expectation of tactical voting can shape parties" pre-election electoral strategies, such as the choice of candidates for individual constituencies, the amount of party support in each constituency, the cooperation with other parties (thus the birth of Alliance), and so forth. Therefore, this aspect of tactical voting, although unobservable and thus unmeasurable, can still have great impact on election outcomes.

04.

Government Partisanship in Western Democracies, 1945-1998

Heemin Kim[*] & Richard C. Fording[**]

* *Department of Political Science, Florida State University, USA*

** *Department of Political Science, University of Kentucky, USA*

Abstract. In this article, we put forward a continuous measure of government partisanship, which allows meaningful comparisons across countries and across time, for 17 Western democracies for the period of 1945 through 1998. Our measure is predicated upon a manifesto-based measure of party ideology recently developed by Kim and Fording (1998), along with yearly cabinet post data. After discussing the validity of our measure, we replicate one of the most cited works in comparative political economy over the last ten years - Alvarez, Garrett and Lange's (1991) analysis of economic performance — by utilizing our own measure of government partisanship. We conclude that comparativists need to exercise greater caution in interpreting and evaluating the past findings of a large number of multi-variate studies in comparative politics.

Introduction

Government partisanship has become an increasingly important explanatory variable in comparative politics, as comparativists have tried to assess the impact of the parties in power on various policy outputs and outcomes. In the case of Western democracies, government partisanship has mostly been measured on a left-right ideological dimension. This is the case because ideology has been the most important and common cleavage in these countries throughout the postwar period (Blais et al. 1993; Budge & Robertson 1987; Kim & Fording 1998; Knutsen 1988; Lijphart 1984; Warwick 1992), and political parties are assumed to reflect the dominant cleavage in society (Budge 1994; Laver & Budge 1993).

To assess the impact of government partisanship, we must first measure the ideological positions of political parties since government partisanship reflects party positions and the power distribution among the parties in power. Too often, however, we have been forced to assess party ideological positions in a rather limited fashion. Most research has either focused on comparing parties and party movement within countries (e.g., Budge et al. 1987), or comparing parties across countries at one relatively short period in time (e.g., Castles & Mair 1984; Janda 1980).[1] While these studies have undoubtedly contributed to our understanding of the dynamics of party competition and ideological change, their restricted scope leaves many questions unanswered. Most importantly, perhaps, until recently most of the classification schemes used to measure party ideology have been based on subjective assessments, thus introducing significant measurement error into analyses of party behaviour.

Despite the weaknesses of existing measures of party ideology, many scholars have relied on relatively crude measures of party ideology to construct measures of government partisanship for use in quantitative (often pooled) analyses. Others have bypassed this strategy and have constructed measures of government partisanship that do not rely on measures of party ideology, but instead are based on subjective (ordinal) assessments of the entire set of parties in power. As we argue below, these measures are flawed in fundamental ways, thus introducing significant measurement error into multivariate analyses that rely on government partisanship as an explanatory variable. Our goal in this article is to develop a measure that allows meaningful comparisons of government partisanship across different countries as well as across different time periods. We believe that this measure will improve the methodological quality of the debates in comparative politics concerning the impact of government partisanship on public policy outcomes.

In the first section of the article, we review existing methods of measuring government ideology and their weaknesses. In the following section, we describe how we operationalize the concept of government ideology. In the third section, we provide support for the validity of our measure by presenting a brief comparison of patterns of government ideology across space and time, thus establishing face validity. In the final section, we investigate the potential consequences of relying on inferior methods of measuring government ideology by replicating one of the most cited works in comparative political economy over the last ten years – Alvarez, Garrett and Lange's (1991) analysis of economic performance. We conclude that comparativists need to exercise greater caution in interpreting and evaluating the findings of a large number of multivariate studies in comparative politics.

Alternative Measures of Government Ideology

Conceptually speaking, most analysts would agree that a valid measure of government ideology should tap two distinct characteristics of the parties (or party) in power. First, the measure should incorporate information concerning the relative share of power held by each of the governing parties. Second, the measure should take into account the preferences, or the ideology of the governing parties as measured on a left-right scale. More specifically, for any given government we define government ideology as:

$$\sum \{Ideology_i * (\#Posts_i/Total\ Posts)\}$$

where:

$\#Posts_i$ = the totalnumber of cabinet posts controlled by partyi,
$Ideology_i$ = the ideology of partyi, and
Total Posts = the total number of posts

Over the years, scholars have used various approaches to incorporate both dimensions in their measures of government partisanship. In some studies, government partisanship has been considered either left or right (Alt 1985; Hibbs 1977; Rose 1980; Williams 1990). Such an approach implicitly codes each dimension of government ideology as dichotomous, where the ideology of governing parties is either "left" or "right", and the degree of power held by each party is determined by whether or not parties of the same ideology form a majority of posts.

A second and more common approach improves upon this simple measure of government ideology by measuring the degree of power using some type of continuous variable. For example, some studies have used the weighted mean of the leftist and rightist parties in the government, weighted by the number of votes that leftist and rightist parties received (e.g., Cameron 1978). Probably the most popular measure of government partisanship has been the percentage of cabinet portfolios held by left or right parties (e.g., Alvarez et al. 1991; Cameron 1984a; Hicks 1988; Jackman 1987; Korpi 1989; Lange & Garrett 1987). Still others have used the proportion of cabinet seats held by parties of the left minus the proportion of cabinet seats held by parties of the right (e.g., Blais et al. 1993, 1996). Despite what appear to be differences in these measures of government ideology, all of these measures share one common characteristic: party ideology is still dichotomous, that is, either right or left, and is constant over time. Clearly, both conventional wisdom and the findings of Budge, Robertson, and Hearl (1987) demonstrate that such a conceptualization of party ideology is quite a distortion of reality, both in longitudinal and cross-sectional terms. As a result, these measures of government ideology based on dichotomous measures of party ideology are likely subject to significant measurement error.

Recently, some ordinal measures of government partisanship have been developed (e.g., Budge & Keman 1990; Crepaz 1992; Hicks & Swank 1992; Schmidt 1982; Woldendorp et al. 1993, 1998). Most of them rely on ordinal classifications of parties in power. They employ three to five categories of political parties and, like the dichotomous measure of party ideology, they assume ideology is constant across time.

Government Ideology: An operationalization

Measuring government ideology requires the completion of two major estimation tasks. First, it is necessary to develop a reliable, continuous measure of party ideology that is comparable across countries and time. We can then combine this measure with cabinet post data to compute a measure of government ideology as proposed above. In a recent paper, Kim and Fording (1998) developed a measure of party ideology for 17 Western democracies. Their measure of party ideology is based on manifesto data collected by Budge, Robertson, Hearl, Klingeman and Volkens (contained in Budge 1992; and updated by Volkens 1995) and on manifestos (platforms) issued by parties at the time of each election. The manifesto data set, which includes 20 major democracies and spans most of the postwar period, is based on an exhaustive content analysis of manifestos issued by all significant parties competing in each postwar election. The data set employs a total of 56 common issue categories. For each document (and thus for each party) the data represent the percentage of all statements comprised by each category. In effect, this standardizes the data with respect to document length, yielding a measure of party emphasis that is comparable across documents.

Kim and Fording (1998) develop a measure of ideology for each party in each election for a total of 17 countries.[3] The first task in measuring party ideology is to choose an appropriate set of categories that capture the left-right dimension. In so doing, they rely on Laver and Budge (1993), who analyzed all 20 countries over the entire period in the data set to build a left-right scale. Using a series of exploratory factor analyses, Laver and Budge identified 13 categories as comprising left ideology and another 13 as comprising right ideology. These ideological categories consistently loaded together in a series of factor analyses (Laver & Budge 1993: 24-27) and formed the basis for their measure of party ideology. Based on the analyses of the entire data set by Laver and Budge, Kim and Fording use the same 26 categories in their attempt to build a measure of party ideology in 17 industrialized democracies during the postwar period.[4]

The manifesto data are collected such that statements in each of these 26 categories represent either pro-left or pro-right tendencies. Based on these 26 categories, Kim and Fording (1998) develop separate measures of left and right ideology for each party in each election for these countries in the following manner:

$$IDLeft = \sum Pro-LeftStatements$$
$$IDRight = \sum Pro-RightStatements$$

In other words, IDLeft represents the percentage of all party statements that advocate left-wing positions, and IDRight represents the corresponding percentage of all party statements that represent right-wing positions. They then compute their measure of party ideology (IDParty) as follows:

$$IDParty = (IDLeft - IDRight)/(IDLeft + IDRight)$$

In sum, they evaluate parties on their net ideological position (scores) with respect to the left-right dimension. The measure is thus computed by subtracting the rightist score from the leftist score (per cent leftist statements minus per cent rightist statements), dividing by the total percentage of leftist and rightist statements. This procedure yields a measure of party ideology that ranges from -1 to +1 where the larger score indicates greater support for leftist policies. For ease of presentation and interpretation, they transform this measure so that it takes on a possible range of 0 to 100.[5]

Having created a measure of party ideology for each country for each election year, Kim and Fording then compute a yearly series of party ideology scores within each country. They estimate missing (non-election) years using linear interpolation, which assumes steady change in ideology between elections. While ideology is not likely to change this steadily in every case, in general this approach is reasonable since it is likely that ideology is relatively stable in the short run. More importantly, estimation of missing years facilitates comparisons across countries, which would otherwise be biased due to the irregularity of the timing of elections across countries.

In this paper, we use the Kim-Fording measure of party ideology to build a continuous measure of government partisanship for Western democracies as follows.[6] We first collect yearly data for the number of cabinet portfolios for each party in each country in our sample for the entire postwar period through the late 1990s.[7] For each year, we then combine this information with the party ideology scores by taking a weighted average of party ideology scores, where the weights are the proportion of total cabinet portfolios held by each party (as in the equation above). Thus for some countries where unified control of government occurs on a regular basis, the government partisanship score reduces to the party ideology score for the party in power. For multi-party governments, however, the measure takes advantage of the information we have about the varying ideologies of the parties and their relative shares of power. Using the Kim-Fording measure of party ideology, this new measure of government partisanship was built for 17 countries for the entire postwar period.[8] Since the Kim-Fording measure of party ideology is a continuous measure of left-leaning tendencies taking on a possible range of 0 to 100, our measure of government partisanship also becomes a measure of relative left-leaning tendencies and takes on a possible range of 0 to 100.

Establishing validity

Validity of Party Ideology Across Time and Space

While it is not necessarily obvious that the manifesto data can be used to create valid and reliable measures of party ideology, recent analyses suggest that this is indeed the case. This evidence of validity comes from a variety of sources. First, it has been shown by "country experts" that manifesto-based measures of party ideology "fit convincingly with general historical impressions of where the parties were in various periods, which is important for their validation as realistic policy representations" (Budge 1994: 458; also see Budge & Hofferbert 1990, 1992; Hofferbert & Klingemann 1990; and Klingemann et al. 1994). Second, Kim and Fording (1998) find that their measure of party ideology is highly correlated with equivalently scaled party scores constructed by aggregating ideological self-placement data (from the Eurobarometers) by party identification. Third, Kim and Fording also find that their party ideology measure is highly correlated with one of the most respected cross-sectional measures of party ideology, that of Castles and Mair (1984).[10] Fourth, McDonald and Mendes (2001) extensively evaluate the validity and reliability of the manifesto-based left-right scales by asking how well they square with the existing expert surveys. They conclude, 'with respect to validity and reliability, ...the evidence here tells us that, to the extent one has confidence in the party positioning from expert surveys, there is every reason to have just as much confidence in party positioning based on the manifesto data' (McDonald & Mendes 2001: 15). Finally, the utility of the manifesto data in constructing party ideology scores is firmly established in a series of extensive analyses reported by Huber and Gabel (2000). After constructing several different versions of party ideology based on alternative factor analysis methods, they find that manifesto-based measures of party ideology correlate highly with party ideology estimates constructed by Huber and Inglehart (1995), and scores obtained by aggregating data from the World Values Survey.[11]

Validity of Government Partisanship across Time and Space

The many analyses cited above provide strong support for the validity of manifesto-based measures of party ideology, thus indirectly establishing some measure of support for our measure of government partisanship. It is worthwhile, however, to examine the validity of our measure of government partisanship directly to insure that our method of aggregating party scores does indeed provide a valid and reliable representation of government partisanship. There are a number of different strategies that one might use to establish the validity of any indicator. However, in this specific case, our range of options is rather limited. One possible strategy might be to examine the correspondence between our measure and the policies pursued by the respective governments of the countries in our data set. This would help in establishing the predictive validity of our measure. Unfortunately, this proves to be an extremely difficult, if not impossible, task. This is due to the extreme level of disagreement among political scientists concerning the impact of government partisanship on the economic/social policies pursued by, or economic outcomes attainable under, governments of different ideological complexion.[12] As there is no commonly accepted set of expectations about the causal relationships between government partisanship and economic policies or outcomes, it is impossible to establish the predictive validity of any measure of government partisanship by performing empirical analyses of these presumed relationships.

A second possible strategy would be to examine the relationship between our manifesto-based measure of government partisanship and existing measures of government partisanship, thus establishing convergent validity. This strategy is not available to us for two reasons. First, there are very few measures of government partisanship that have been constructed. Second, and most importantly, we specifically argue that existing measures lack a great deal of validity. This is especially the case for one of the most commonly used measures of government partisanship, the percentage of cabinet portfolios held by leftist parties (hereafter 'PLCP'). This general approach to measuring government partisanship has been used in a number of quantitative studies, including Alvarez et al. (1991), Blais et al. (1993, 1996), Cameron (1984a), Hicks (1988), Jackman (1987) and Korpi (1989) among others. The PLCP measure and our measure are conceptually similar in the sense that they both weight a measure of party ideology by the proportion of cabinet portfolios held by different political parties. However, there are two major differences between the two measures: (i) the PLCP measure assumes that there are only two types of parties, leftist and non-leftist parties, while our measure does not impose such restrictions by adopting a continuous measure of party ideology ranging between the scores of 0 and 100;[13] and (ii) the PLCP measure assumes that party ideology is constant across time, while our measure allows change in party ideology by computing the party ideology scores each time elections are held.[14] As the simple time series correlations between the two government partisanship in western democracies, 1945–1998 measures attest, the PLCP measure is not strongly related to our manifesto-based measure of ideology ($r = 0.46$).[15] And based on the theoretical argument above, we believe that our measure must be more valid than the PLCP measure.[16]

Given an absence of alternative strategies, we rely on face validity to examine the adequacy of our measure of government partisanship. A brief examination of the computed government partisanship scores offers some support for the measure, as the patterns across countries and across time are consistent with our general understanding of the ideological tendencies of the governments in these countries. In Figure 1, we present average government partisanship scores for each of the countries, averaged over the period 1970-95. As we would expect, Norway, Luxembourg, Finland and Sweden have been among the most left-leaning countries during this period, while Great Britain, the United States and Iceland have been the most right-leaning.

Trends over time are consistent with expectations as well. In Figure 2, we present government partisanship scores across time for the entire 1945-95 period, where the score for each year is the average across all countries in our data set.[17] As the figure shows, generally speaking, the 1960s and 1970s was a relatively left-leaning period, while the 1980s witnessed an increasing shift to the right.

In sum, many analyses establishing the validity of manifesto-based measures of party ideology, along with the face validity of our measure of government partisanship established in Figures 1 and 2, suggest that our manifesto-based measure of government partisanship is indeed valid. Further, there are strong theoretical reasons to believe that our measure is superior to existing measures that necessarily rely on dichotomous and ordinal measures of party ideology, and which implicitly assume that party ideology, however measured, is constant over time. While any measure of government partisanship that relies on such implausible assumptions is likely to suffer a loss of validity, this problem is most severe, we believe, for the PLCP measure described above.This is important since this has been the most commonly used measure of government partisanship, especially among the growing number of studies employing pooled analyses. It is for this reason that we replicate one of the most cited pieces in comparative political economy that relies on the PLCP measure: Alvarez, Garrett, and Lange (1991).

Do parties *really* matter?
A replication of Alvarez, Garrett and Lange

One of the areas of comparative politics where the concept of government partisanship plays a critical role is the 'Do Parties Matter?' debate. This debate initially centered around the question of whether leftist parties, once they are in power, can pursue economic policies (such as the level of government spending and monetary policy) that are sufficiently different from those of rightist parties (e.g., Cameron 1978; Castles & McKinlay 1979; Keman 1984, 1997; Schmidt 1989, 1996, 1997;Williams 1990; Blais et al. 1993, 1996; Castles 1994, 1998). Lange and Garrett (and later Alvarez) among others extended this debate to the question of economic performance (such as level of inflation, unemployment and economic growth) (Lange & Garrett 1987; Garrett & Lange 1989; Alvarez et al. 1991). They argue that 'there are two different paths to desirable macroeconomic performance. In countries with densely and centrally organized labor movements, leftist governments can promote economic growth and reduce inflation and unemployment. Conversely, in countries with weak labor movements, rightist governments can pursue their partisan-preferred macroeconomic strategies and achieve similarly beneficial macroeconomic outcomes. Performance will be poorer in other cases' (Alvarez et al. 1991: 539). In other words,Alvarez, Garrett and Lange propose an interactive model, where government ideology and labour organizational strength interact to affect economic performance. Based on pooled analyses of data for 16 Western democracies spanning the years 1968–84, Alvarez, Garrett and Lange report results that are highly supportive of this interactive relationship.

Over the years, the Alvarez, Garrett and Lange model has been hallenged on different methodological grounds including the influence of outliers (Jackman 1987, 1989) and the estimation method used (Beck et al. 1993; Western 1998). While Beck et al. (1993) find that the interactive model is not supported for unemployment and inflation, Alvarez, Garrett and Lange's 'major finding' (i.e., their results for economic growth which support the presence of an interactive relationship) has survived empirical scrutiny (Beck et al. 1993:

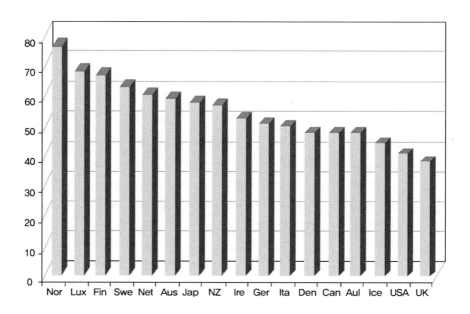

Figure 1. Average government ideology in 17 Western democracies, 1970–1995

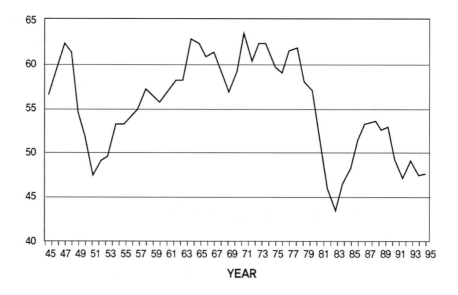

YEAR

Figure 2. Government ideology (average of 16 countries) over time

945). In order to determine if their results are sensitive to measurement choices, we replicate their economic growth model below. To rule out the possibility that our findings might be affected by differences in the estimation sample (we do not have a manifesto-based measure of government ideology for France), we first replicate their model using their measure of government ideology for a sample that includes the common set of countries for which we have data for both our measure and theirs.[18] The specific model is given below:

$$\text{Growth}_{i,t} = \alpha + \beta_1 \text{Growth}_{i,t-1} + \beta_2 \text{OECD Demand}_{i,t} + \beta_3 \text{OECD Export}_{i,t} + \beta_4 \text{OECD Import}_{i,t} + \beta_5 \text{Labour Organization Index}_i + \beta_6 \text{Government Partisanship}_{i,t} + \beta_7 \text{Labour Organization Index}_i * \text{Government Partisanship}_{i,t} + \varepsilon_{i,t}.$$

$\text{Growth}_{i,t-1}$ = Lagged dependent variable.
$\text{OECD Demand}_{i,t}$ = Annual OECD economic growth rates weighted by the 'openness' (export/GDP) of the countries in the sample.
$\text{OECD Export}_{i,t}$ = Annual growth in OECD export prices weighted by openness.
$\text{OECD Import}_{i,t}$ = Annual growth in OECD import prices weighted by openness.
Labor Organization Index$_i$ = The sum of standardized scores for the density and centralization of labour movements (Lange & Garrett 1985: 805).
Government Partisanship$_{i,t}$ = Annual percentage of cabinet portfolios held by leftist parties.
Labour Organization Index$_i$ * Government Partisanship$_{i,t}$ = A multiplicative term capturing the conditional relationship between labour organization and government partisanship.

To estimate the model, we employ the strategy of Beck et al. (1993). As they report, serial correlation is adequately handled by the inclusion of the lagged dependent variable, while heteroskedasticity and contemporaneous error correlation are dealt with by the estimation of panel corrected standard errors (PCSEs). The results of our replication using their measure of government ideology for our sample of countries are given in column 2 of Table 1. By comparing these to the results in column 1, which represent the results reported by Beck et al. (1993) for the original sample of countries used by Alvarez, Garrett and Lange, we can see that the two sets of results are nearly identical. As a result, we can be confident that any differences we find by substituting our measure of government ideology are due solely to the substitution of our government partisanship variable for theirs.

The results reflecting this substitution are contained in column 3 of Table 1. As can be seen, when the manifesto-based measure of government partisanship is used instead of their measure, the results change significantly. While the results in columns 1 and 2 strongly support the existence of a conditional relationship between labour organization and government partisanship, the results in column 3 provide little if any support for the existence of an interaction.[19]

At the very least, it thus appears that the manner in which government partisanship is measured can potentially play a significant role in affecting the conclusions drawn from the analysis. We acknowledge that the difference in results could logically be traced to deficiencies in either measure, and therefore it is possible (hypothetically speaking) that the original results (using the PLCP measure) are indeed the 'true' results. However, this would necessarily require that a measure relying on a dichotomous and temporally invariant measure of party ideology is superior to a measure that relies on a continuous and temporally variable measure of party ideology. At this point, we know of no such argument that would lead us to believe this is the case, and therefore are led to conclude that the original results are due to bias in coefficient estimates known to be caused by measurement error.

Conclusion

In this article, we have developed a continuous measure of government ideology which allows for meaningful comparisons across countries and across time for 17 Western democracies for the entire postwar period. It is based on the manifesto-based measure of party ideology recently developed by Kim and Fording (1998), along with the cabinet post data collected by Woldendorp et al. (1993, 1998).

To the extent that our measure is an improvement over existing measures, we believe that comparativists need to exercise caution in interpreting and evaluating the findings of past empirical studies of the role of government

Table 1. Pooled regressions of economic growth on alternative measures of government ideology and relevant control variables

Independent variables	Original results		Replication I		Replication II	
	β	PCSE		PCSE	β	PCSE
Lagged growth	.077	.094	.147	.0755	.1769*	.0756
Vulnerability to OECD demand conditions	−.0025	.0019	−.0023	.0020	−.0026	.0019
Vulnerability to OECD demand conditions (import prices)	−.0009	.0017	−.0024	.0020	−.0029	.0020
Vulnerability to OECD demand conditions (export prices)	.002*	.0012	.0033*	.0013	.0035*	.0014
Labour organization index (LORG)	−.700**	.216	−.7020**	.2474	−1.0045	.6137
% left cabinet posts (LFCAB)	−.023**	.007	−.0285**	.0080	−	−
LORG * LFCAB	.012**	.003	.0134**	.0032	−	−
Government ideology (manifesto)	−	−	−	−	−.0011	.0258
Government ideology * LORG	−	−	−	−	.0104	.0098
Constant	4.65**	.65	6.511**	.5942	6.021**	1.581
R^2	Not reported		−.54		.53	
N	224[b]		238[c]		238[c]	

* $p < 0.05$, two–tailed

** $p < 0.01$, two–tailed

Note: For each model, column entries are unstandardized slope estimates followed by panel corrected standard errors (PCSEs). All models estimated in STATA 6.0, using the XTPCSE procedure

[a] These results are from Beek et al. (1993) and correct for problems inherent in the estimation procedure originally used by Alvarez, Garrett & Lange (1991)

[b] This regression utilizes data for 16 countries over a period spanning the years 1971–84

[c] Our replication utilize data for 14 countries over a period spanning the years 1968–84, the time period originally used by Alvarez, Garrett & Lange (1991)

partisanship. Our replication of Alvarez, Garrett and Lange's model of economic performance provides just one example of how measurement may matter, but we urge comparativists to revisit the role of government partisanship by replicating other studies as well.

Appendix: Manifesto categories capturing ideological tendencies

The Right–Wing Categories	The Left–Wing Categories
Free Enterprise	Regulation of Capitalism
Incentives	Economic Planning
Protectionism: Negative	Protectionism: Positive
Economic Orthodoxy and Efficiency	Controlled Economy
Social Services Expansion: Negative	Nationalisation
Constitutionalism: Positive	Decolonisation
Government Effectiveness and Authority	Military: Negative
Nation Way of life: Positive	Peace
Traditional Morality: Positive	Internationalism: Positive
Law and Order	Democracy
National Effort, Social Harmony	Social Services Expansion: Positive
Freedom and Domestic Human Rights	Education: Positive
Military: Positive	Labour Group: Positive

Acknowledgements

We thank William Berry and Ian Budge for their valuable comments. Jun Y.Choi and Carl Dasse provided research assistance. The Economic and SocialResearch Council at the University of Essex and Zentralarchiv für EmpirischeSozialforschung an der Universität zu Köln provided the ECPR Party Manifesto Data to us. We thank Duane Swank for providing his data on government partisanship.

Notes

1. Budge and Robertson (1987) do compare parties across countries for a prolonged period of time, but they do so for a limited number of parties. More recently, Laver and Budge (1993) and Kim and Fording (1998) have developed a more comprehensive measure of party ideology that incorporates most postwar European parties.

2. We build a measure of government ideology as a proxy for government partisanship in Western democracies for the reasons stated above. Obviously party (and thus, government) differences can include non-ideological factors. See Castles (1994) and Schmidt (1996), for example.

3. All political parties included in the data set for these countries are listed in the codebook accompanying the manifesto data.

4. We list these 26 categories in the Appendix to this article. For details about the specific categories, see the codebook and Laver and Budge (1993: 20–24). The salience of the left-right dimension is indicated by the frequency with which ideologically relevant statements appear in party manifestos. Overall, left-right statements comprise about half (47 per cent; SD = 13.9 per cent) of all statements in the entire sample of documents (N = 1,009). The salience of left-right statements is also consistent over time. Since 1966, the percentage of left-right statements averages 45 per cent (N = 567), only slightly lower that the average for the entire period.

5. Although Kim and Fording use the same manifesto categories as Laver and Budge (1993), they construct their measure of party ideology somewhat differently. The Laver-Budge measure is equivalent to the numerator of the Kim-Fording measure or, in other words, the difference of IDLeft and IDRight as a percentage of all statements in the document. McDonald and Mendes (2001) call the Laver-Budge measure a 'subtractive measure' and the Kim-Fording measure (as well as the Laver-Garry (2000) measure, which employs the same formula as Kim and Fording) a 'ratio measure' (pp. 4–5). There are some philosophical differences between these two measures, and as McDonald and Mendes correctly point out, 'validity depends on what the researcher intends to measure. If one's intention is to locate a party in a space defined by its emphasis on Left versus Right values relative to all values (thereby stressing the overall

saliency of Left and Right values), then the subtractive measure is preferred. If, on the contrary, one's intention is to locate the party along the Left-Right dimension as such, then the ration is preferred' (2001: 5). Regardless of this difference in the two measures, the two are nearly identical in empirical terms as they are correlated at 0.95.

6. We actually rely on an updated version of the Kim-Fording measure, which is based on updated manifesto data (Budge et al. 2001). The updated version not only expands the number of countries for which we are able to computer government ideology scores, it also extends all party ideology series into the late 1990s.

7. We use cabinet composition data contained in Woldendorp et al. (1993, 1998).

8. The number of countries for which we are able to computer government ideology scores is limited by the availability of both manifesto data and government composition data The specific countries included are: Australia, Austria, Canada, Denmark, Finland, Germany, Great Britain, Iceland, Ireland, Italy, Japan, Luxembourg, Netherlands, Norway, New Zealand, Sweden and the United States. Although we have party ideology data for France and Belgium, we were unable to create a government partisanship for France and are only able to do so for a limited number of years in Belgium due to differences in the coding of parties across data sets.

9. We have posted our data on government ideology on our website for public inspection/consumption. They are available at http://garnet.acns.fsu.edu/~hkim/dataset.htm.

10. The correlation between the Eurobarometer-based measure of party ideology and the manifesto-based measure is 0.74, while the correlation between Castles and Mair's measure and Kim and Fording's measure is 0.85. See Kim and Fording (1998) for details.

11. Although Huber and Gabel do find that each of the manifesto-based measures of party ideology performs satisfactorily, they express a preference for their version of the measure which is based on a somewhat different (and more parsimonious) group of manifesto categories than those used by Laver and Budge (1993) and subsequently employed by Kim and Fording (1998) and by Laver and Garry (2000) in constructing their versions of party ideology from the manifesto data). Our preference for using the Kim-Fording version, and thus the manifesto categories identified by Laver and Budge, lies merely in the fact that these categories have been used in a number of

published studies examining party systems and party competition in recent years. Our measure of government partisanship could easily be replicated using the Huber-Gabel selection of manifesto categories – however, we leave this task to future research. Our purpose in this article is merely to demonstrate the utility of the manifesto data in creating a measure of government partisanship.

12. For disagreements about the impact of government partisanship on economic policies such as the size of the government revenues, public domestic spending, social welfare expenditure, monetary policy, fiscal policy and capital control, see Cameron (1978); Frey (1978); Castles & McKinlay (1979); Golden & Poterba (1980); Solano (1983); Hicks & Swank (1984); Keman (1984, 1997); Lewis-Beck & Rice (1985); Rice (1986); Berry & Lowery (1987); Pampel & Williamson (1988); Swank (1988); Hicks et al. (1989); Schmidt (1989, 1996, 1997); Williams (1990); Hicks & Swank (1992); Castles (1994, 1998); Beck & Katz (1995); Blais et al. (1993, 1996); and Oatley (1999) among many others. For disagreements about the impact of government partisanship on economic outcomes such as inflation, unemployment and economic growth, see Hibbs (1977); Cameron (1984a, 1984b); Alt (1985); Williams (1990); Lange & Garrett (1985, 1987); Garrett & Lange (1986, 1989); Jackman (1986, 1987, 1989); Hicks (1988); Hicks & Patterson (1989); Alvarez et al. (1991); Crepaz (1992); Beck et al. 1993; and Castles (1998) among others.

13. Since the PLCP looks only at the percentage of cabinet portfolios held by leftist parties, it in effect assigns the party ideology score of 1 to all the parties classified as leftist and the score of 0 to all non-leftist parties.

14. The following example illustrates the limitations of the PLCP measure rather well. At no time between 1968 and 1984 did leftist parties have power in Japan, Canada or the United States. In addition, due to the single-party control of the governments in these countries during this period, non-leftist parties held 100 per cent of the cabinet portfolios. Thus, the government partisanship scores for all three of these countries were 0 for all years. Thus, according to this measure, we are able to believe that Japanese, Canadian and US governments occupied exactly the same ideological positions and that, over nearly two decades, their ideological positions remained constant!

15. This correlation is based on PLCP data from Alvarez et al. (1991) for the time period of their analysis (1967–84). The correlation reported above is based on pooled data.

The country-specific correlations are as follows: Australia (0.29), Austria (0.45), Belgium (-0.34), Canada (no variation in PLCP), Denmark (0.44), Finland (-0.01), Germany (0.80), Ireland (0.79), Italy (0.57), Japan (no variation in PLCP), Netherlands (0.51), Norway (0.83), Sweden (0.58) and the United Kingdom (0.88).

16. In the absence of such a theoretical argument, we are not willing to make a definitive judgment about another family of commonly used measures of government partisanship, the ordinal measures of government ideology (e.g., Budge & Keman 1990; Crepaz 1992; Hicks & Swank 1992; Schmidt 1982; Woldendorp et al. 1993, 1998). Laver and Budge (1993), along with their collaborators, developed a measure of government policy intentions based on a content analysis of government policy declarations in several multi-party systems. While their measure might seem to be a reasonable candidate to compare to ours to help establish the validity of our measure, their measure is conceptually distinct from our measure and thus it is not obvious that the two should be highly correlated. Our measure is a weighted average of the ideology of the parties in the government and is mainly intended to test whether the partisanship (or ideological makeup) of the government does/does not affect policy outcomes as is typical in the so-called 'Do Parties Matter?' debate we discuss below. The Laver-Budge measure (based on policy declarations), on the other hand, reflects the outcome of coalition bargaining among political parties since it measures government policy intentions during/after coalition formation. One obvious future research path would be the study of the institutional impact of the process of coalition bargaining by comparing our measure (which represents how governmental policies should look without coalition bargaining) and the Laver-Budge measure (which reflects the compromise struck during the bargaining process).

17. We drop Japan from this analysis due to a lack of manifesto data prior to 1955.

18. The specific countries are: Australia, Austria, Belgium, Canada, Denmark, Finland, Germany, Ireland, Italy, Japan, Netherlands, Norway, Sweden, United Kingdom and United States.

19. Although we do not report results for models with unemployment or inflation as dependent variables, we did replicate these models as well. Consistent with the findings of Beck et al. (1993), we find no evidence of an interaction between labour organization and government partisanship when our manifesto-based measure is substituted.

05.

Voter Ideology in Western Democracies: An Update

Heemin Kim[*] & Richard C. Fording[**]

* Florida State University, USA

** University of Kentucky, USA

Abstract. In this article, we update and expand the measure of voter ideology we originally proposed in this journal in 1998. Our new measure combines party manifesto data most recently updated by Budge et al. (2001) with election return data. Assuming the comparability and relevance of left-right ideology, we estimate the median voter position in 25 Western democracies throughout most of the postwar period.With this measure, we are able to make cross-national comparisons of voter ideology among these countries, as well as cross-time comparisons within individual countries.

Introduction

In our earlier article published in this journal, we developed measures that allow meaningful comparisons of party and voter ideology across different countries as well as across different time periods (Kim & Fording 1998). Although we developed measures of party and voter ideology, our emphasis was primarily on voter ideology. Since it was not feasible to describe the exact shape of the voter distribution on an ideological dimension in all Western democracies, we estimated the median voter position in these countries as our indicator of voter ideology. To do so, we first developed a measure of party positions using party manifesto data compiled by Budge, Robertson, Hearl, Klingemann and Volkens (Budge et al. 1992) and updated by Volkens (1995). We then estimated the median voter position by combining our party ideology measure with election return data for each country.

Since then the party manifesto data have been expanded to include 25 Western democracies and updated up to 1998. In this article, we expand and update our measures of party and voter ideology utilizing the newest manifesto data. In the first section, we describe how we operationalize the concept of 'ideology'. In the following section, we present cross-national and cross-time comparisons of voter ideology in 25 Western democracies (listed in the Note to Figure 2).

Measurement of voter ideology: an operationalization

Our measure of ideology rests on three basic assumptions about how voters think and behave when making voting decisions: (1) we assume that a leftright ideological dimension can be found in most industrialized democracies, (2) that it is an important and often primary determinant of vote choice in Western democracies and that it has been so for the entire postwar period, and (3) we assume that the left-right dimension is comparable across countries (see Kim & Fording 1998: 76–77).

Assuming the comparability, continuity and relevance of the left-right dimension, it is then possible to develop a measure of the ideological position of a particular electorate that is comparable across countries and across time. To do so, one must first begin to conceive of elections as large-scale opinion polls. In this sense, one might think of ballots as questionnaires that instruct the 'respondent' to choose the party that is closest to them on a left-right ideological scale. Assuming we have accurate, comparable interval-scale measures of party ideology for each party in an election, we can then treat election results, along with the corresponding measures of party ideology, as a grouped frequency distribution and calculate fairly reliable estimates of measures of central tendency such as the median and the mean. In other words, we infer ideological tendencies based on the rational choices of ideological voters.

Measuring party ideology

Such a strategy requires the completion of two major estimation tasks. First, it is necessary to develop a reliable, interval-level measure of party ideology that is comparable across countries and time. We construct such a measure based on manifestos (platforms) issued by parties at the time of each election. Our measure of party ideology is based on manifesto data originally collected by Budge, Robertson, Hearl, Klingeman and Volkens (Budge et al. 1992) and most recently updated by Budge et al. (2001). The newest manifesto data set, which includes 25 major democracies and spans most of the postwar period, is based on an exhaustive content analysis of manifestos (platforms) issued by all significant parties competing in each postwar election.The data set employs a total of 56 common categories, including external relations categories (e.g., anti-imperialism), freedom and democracy categories (e.g., human rights), political system categories (e.g., governmental and administrative efficiency), economic categories (e.g., nationalization), welfare and quality of life categories (e.g., environmental protection), fabric of society categories (e.g., multiculturalism) and social group categories (e.g., underprivileged minority groups). For each document, the data represent the percentage of all statements comprised by each category. In effect, this standardizes the data with respect to document length, yielding a measure of party emphasis that is comparable.

We develop a measure of ideology for each party in each election in each of the 25 countries. The first task in measuring party ideology is to define 'left-right ideology' and to choose an appropriate set of categories that capture the left-right dimension. 'Ideology' is a set of ideas that relate to the social/ political world and that provide a general guideline for some action (Mahler 1995: 36–37). As such, "ideology provides politicians with a broad conceptual map of politics into which political events, current problems, electors' preferences and other parties' policies can be fitted" (Budge 1994: 446) and thus incorporates a broad range of political, economic and social issues.

There have been a few recent attempts to identify a left-right dimension utilizing party manifesto data. Each of these studies uses a correlation-based statistical technique, such as factor analysis or principal components analysis, to identify a common left-right dimension from an analysis of manifesto data (Bowler 1990; Budge & Robertson 1987; Laver & Budge 1993; Warwick 1992). The most comprehensive measure is that of Laver and Budge (1993) in that they analyze all countries and the entire period in the data set. They use a series of exploratory factor analyses to identify potential combinations of categories to build a left-right scale. From these analyses, they identify 13 categories as comprising left ideology and another 13 as comprising right ideology. These 26 ideological categories consistently loaded together in their factor analyses (Ibid.: 24–27). Based on their analyses of the entire data set, we use the same 26 categories in our attempt to build a measure of party ideology in 25 industrialized democracies during the postwar period.

The data in the manifesto set are collected such that statements in each of these 26 categories demonstrate either pro-left or pro-right tendencies. Based on these 26 categories, we first develop separate measures of left and right ideology for each party in each election for these countries in the following manner:

$$IDLeft = \sum Pro - Left\,Categories$$
$$IDRight = \sum Pro - Right\,Categories$$

In other words, IDLeft represents the percentage of all party statements that advocate left-wing positions and IDRight represents the corresponding percentage of all party statements that represent right-wing positions. We then compute our measure of party ideology (IDParty) as follows:

$$IDParty = (IDLeft - IDRight)/(IDLeft + IDRight)$$

We assume that voters evaluate parties on their net ideological position (scores) with respect to the left-right dimension. The measure is thus computed by subtracting the rightist score from the leftist score (%leftist statements − %rightist statements), then dividing by the total percentage of leftist and rightist statements. This procedure yields a measure of party ideology that ranges from -1 to 1, where the larger score indicates greater support for leftist policies. For ease of presentation and interpretation, we transform this measure so that it takes on a possible range of 0 to 100.[1]

Measuring voter ideology

Having developed a measure of party ideology, our second major estimation task is to estimate the median ideological position within the electorate of each country, at each election.We proceed in a series of three steps. First, for each election, we obtain ideology scores for each party in that election and place the parties on an ideological dimension by their score. Second, for each party, we find an interval on this dimension where its supporters are located. This was done in the following manner: for each party we calculate the midpoint between this party and the one immediately left of it and another midpoint between this party and the one immediately right of it. We assume that those who vote for this party fall into this interval between these two midpoints on the left-right ideological dimension. This is a simple application of Euclidean preference relations: voters choose the candidates/parties that are closest to them. Voters on the left side of this interval will vote for the party on the left of this party, and the ones on the right side of this interval will vote for the party on the right of it (see Kim & Fording 1998: 92–93).

Third, for each election, we find the percentage of the vote received by each party (from Mackie & Rose 1990, supplemented by the Annual Data Yearbook of the European Journal of Political Research). At this point, we have the percentage of the electorate that falls into each interval that we have created. Having now transformed the data to a grouped frequency distribution, we estimate the median position by using a formula outlined in almost any introductory statistics text (we use Bohrnstedt & Knoke 1982: 52). The particular variant of this formula that we use is as follows:

$$M = L + \{(50 - C)/F\} * W \qquad (1)$$

where:

M = Median voter position (ideological score).

L = The lower end (ideological score) of the interval containing the median.

C = The cumulative frequency (vote share) up to but not including the interval containing the median.

F = The frequency (vote share) in the interval containing the median.

W = The width of the interval containing the median.

Having created a measure of voter ideology for 25 countries for 364 election years, we then compute a yearly series of voter ideology scores within each country. We estimate missing (nonelection) years by using linear interpolation, which assumes a steady change in ideology between elections. While we realize that ideology is not likely to change this steadily in every case, we feel that in general this approach is reasonable since it is likely that ideology is relatively stable in the short term. More importantly, estimation of missing years facilitates comparisons across countries which would otherwise be biased due to the irregularity of the timing of elections across countries (see Kim & Fording 1998: 80-84; Kim & Fording 2002).

Voter Ideology: cross-national and cross-time comparisons

In Figure 1 we present a cross-national comparison of the average ideological scores of 21 Western democracies during the entire period 1945–1998. In sum, Figure 1 presents a snapshot describing the entire period of analysis. During this period, it is clear that Norway, Luxembourg and Sweden have been the most left-leaning states, while Iceland, the United States and Turkey have been at the opposite end of the ideological spectrum of Western democracies.

There are four countries in the manifesto data set for which the data are available for shorter time periods (Greece, Japan, Portugal and Spain). To take advantage of all of the information in the data set, we present a cross-national comparison of the average ideological scores of 25 Western democracies during

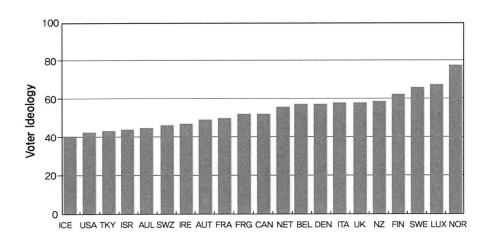

Figure 1. Voter ideology in Western democracies, 1945–1998 (average median voter position)

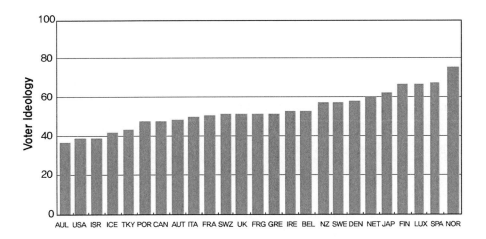

Figure 2. Voter ideology in Western democracies, 1974–1998 (average median voter position)

Note: The 25 countries included in the data set are: Australia, Austria, Belgium, Canada, Denmark, France, Finland, Germany, Greece, Iceland, Ireland, Israel, Italy, Japan, Luxembourg, Netherlands, New Zealand, Norway, Portugal, Spain, Sweden, Switzerland, Turkey, the United Kingdom and the United States. All political parties inclued in the data set for these countries are listed in the codebook accompanying the manifesto data the period 1974–1998 in Figure 2. During this period, we see roughly the same set of most left-leaning and right-leaning states, with the exception of Spain replacing Sweden as one of the most left-leaning countries.

Next, we examine aggregate movement in ideology among our panel of countries between the years 1950 and 1994, the years for which ideological scores are available for all 21 countries in Figure 1. The results of this analysis can be found in Figure 3, which displays ideology scores averaged across these countries. Consistent with conventional wisdom, Figure 3 indicates that the period of the 1960s and early 1970s was indeed a relatively left-leaning period followed by shifts to the right in the late 1970s and 1980s.

Although Figure 3 displays ideological movement among most countries in our sample, there is no reason to believe that all of these countries have followed this identical pattern during this period. Indeed, although the majority show some type of movement toward the left during the 1960s, in general there are significant differences across countries in the magnitude of such ideological shifts, not only during the 1960s, but throughout the entire period of analysis. Although a presentation of all 25 countries is beyond the scope of this article, we present two examples of different patterns of ideological movement in Figure 4. This Figure displays ideological movement in both the United States and Iceland, and we can see that although there have been some shifts, voter ideology in the United States has been relatively stable as it has stayed between the ideological scores of 35 and 50 for most of the period of analysis. Voter ideology in Iceland, however, displays a different pattern with greater short-term fluctuations.

Although space does not permit a presentation of each individual country, we can get some idea of the relative ideological volatility across countries during this time period by computing the standard deviation for each country series. Since our measure of voter ideology is comparable across countries, such a measure of ideological volatility is comparable as well. Figure 5 presents such a comparison. During this period, the United States, Israel and Germany have maintained relatively stable ideological trends, while voter ideology in Sweden, Iceland and the United Kingdom has exhibited significant variation over the years 1945 to 1998. It needs to be noted that here the standard

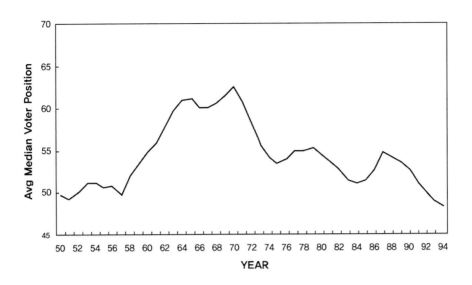

Figure 3. Voter ideology in Western democracies, 1950–1994

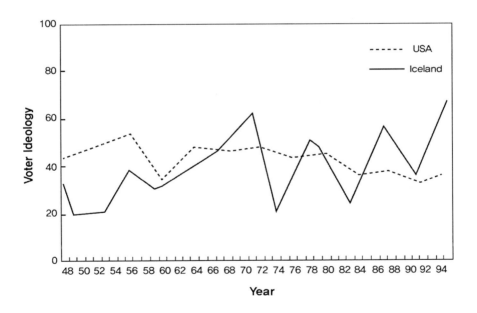

Figure 4. Examples of ideological stability and volatility.

deviation analysis captures different types of ideological volatility – for example, some countries exhibit an ideological pattern with continued short-term fluctuations (e.g., Iceland and Ireland). Other countries have experienced just a few periods of marked ideological shifts (e.g., Sweden in the 1990s and Austria in the 1970s and the 1990s). Still others have shown gradual, but significant, change (e.g., the United Kingdom). Countries with all of these types of ideological change scored high on the volatility analysis in Figure 5.

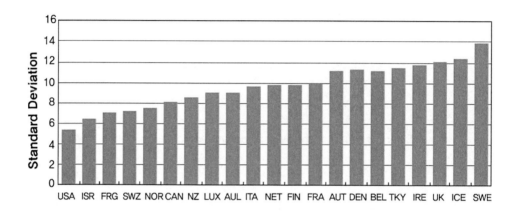

Figure 5. Ideological volatility, 1945–1998

In our earlier piece, we also examined ideological trends among the English-speaking countries (Australia, Canada, Ireland, New Zealand, the United Kingdom and the United States) separately from the other Western democracies in order to investigate the claim that the rightward movement which begins in the 1970s and extends into the 1980s in Figure 3 is not common to all the countries in our sample and that it is either most pronounced, or even entirely driven, by a movement toward the right among the English-speaking democracies. Such a possibility is suggested by Francis Castles (1990), who argues that, in recent years, a movement toward the right has been strongest in these countries, as evidenced by the economic policies of these countries.

Our investigation with the new data set in Figure 6 largely confirms our earlier findings. First, though a divergence in ideology can be seen among the two sets of countries, the real departure between the ideologies of the

English-speaking and other Western countries occurred in the late 1950s rather than the 1980s. Since then, these two groups of countries have maintained a fairly substantial distance in ideology, with non-English-speaking countries substantially more left-leaning than English-speaking countries. Second, and more importantly for the question at hand, these two groups of countries have displayed similar trends in voter ideology. Generally speaking, both groups experienced a general shift to the left during the 1960s, as we might expect given the fact that this was a period of relative economic prosperity throughout the West. We also find that both groups began to shift back to the right during the early 1970s, which also coincided with the first oil shock and the subsequent downturn in most Western economies.

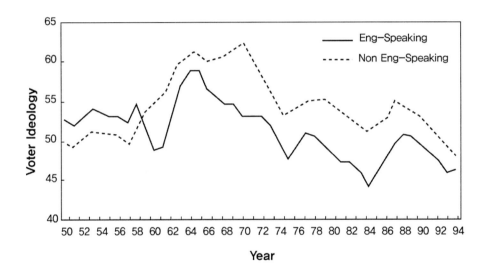

Figure 6. Voter ideology in Western democracies.

The fact that these trends were, at least to some extent, a common experience among Western democracies contradicts evidence presented by Host and Paldam (1990) that suggests that 'international opinion swings' do not exist among Western nations.With regard to Castles' argument that the shift toward the right in the 1980s has been stronger in English-speaking countries, we need to note that he is talking about a policy shift to the right in these countries.

Since the magnitudes of shifts to the right in voter ideology in the 1980s are quite similar in these two groups of countries, this suggests a non-ideological explanation for the differences Castles finds between the two sets of countries.

Discussion

In this article, we have updated and expanded the Kim-Fording measure of voter ideology that originally appeared in this journal. Our updated measure largely confirms many interesting insights concerning voter ideology in Western democracies provided by our original measure. The trends in ideology in these countries themselves are important findings, but there are many other ways to use our measures of party and voter ideology either to study political phenomena in ways that were not previously feasible or to improve existing research in comparative politics (see Kim & Fording 1998: 88-91). The research presented in this article should therefore be considered as the beginning point of a larger body of research concerning the origin of voter ideology, its impact on government and public policy, and the development of theories of democracy.

Notes

1. Although we use the same manifesto categories as Laver and Budge (1993), we construct our measure of party ideology somewhat differently. Their measure is equivalent to the numerator of our measure or, in other words, the difference of IDLeft and IDRight as a percentage of all statements in the document.We believe that the denominator of our measure should be restricted to the total number of left-right statements only since we necessarily assume that voters evaluate parties strictly with respect to the left-right dimension. Regardless of this difference in the two measures, the two are nearly identical in empirical terms as they are correlated at 0.96.

06.

Electoral Systems, Party Systems, and Ideological Representation
An Analysis of Distortion in Western Democracies

Heemin Kim, G. Bingham Powell Jr. & Richard C. Fording

Abstract. The effects of party system features and election rules on ideological representation can be seen in parliamentary elections in Western democracies over a fifty-year period. "Distortion" is short-term representation failure—the distance between the median voter and the legislature or government immediately after the election. Electoral choice and left-right positions of parties (from the manifesto data) can be used to estimate median voter positions. The number of parties, party polarization, and the election rules all independently affect ideological distances. But party system polarization seems to be the predominate factor shaping distortion of governments" relationship with the median voter. Examining the effects of party systems under different election rules helps clarify the causal connections between legislative and government levels.

Democracy means government by the people. In modern nation-states policies are predominately made by elected representatives of the people, rather than by the people themselves. Political scientists have invested a great deal of effort in exploring the connections between the people and these representatives. One element that looms large in both theoretical and empirical studies is systematically generated correspondence between the preferences of the people and the commitments of their chosen representatives. Such correspondence is sometimes identified as the definition of democracy,[1] as its best justification,[2] or as essential to its overarching goal.[3] We need not debate alternative definitions or explore the complexities of interests and preferences to accept that agreement between citizens and representatives is "one of the most important notions within the broad family of theories of representative democracy." [4] If elections systematically fail to generate close correspondence between the preferences of citizens and the stated positions of those they elect, what is here called "distortion," the quality of the democratic process may be diminished.

In comparative studies of representation, two general empirical approaches can be discerned. One of these assumes that what voters want is best summarized by their partisan vote; representation is measured by comparing the distribution of party votes with partisan distributions of legislative or executive officeholders. Following Douglas Rae's work in 1967, a large literature has developed this approach.[5] The other approach, pioneered by Warren Miller and Donald Stokes in 1963 and reflected in several studies of industrialized democracies and the European Union, begins with direct measures of voter preferences and compares these to the preferences or public commitments of those they elect.[6]

A limitation of vote-based studies, despite their valuable descriptions and explanations of vote-seat distortions, is that they can say little by themselves about the substantive content of election outcomes. Vote-seat distortions are only one possible element in shaping whether vote winners' commitments correspond more closely to citizens' desires in one system than another. Preference-based studies rest primarily on surveys of citizen preferences in one or a handful of specific political systems, making it difficult to see how these are shaped by institutional settings. Moreover, the empirical tradition of these studies, following Miller and Stokes, has emphasized the constituency or party voters and their representative(s) as a dyadic unit of analysis, rather than comparing voters and legislators (or governments) as a whole. Concentrating on dyadic connections illuminates the process in valuable ways but obscures the collective outcomes.

This article adds to the empirical comparative literature on representative distortion by showing the effects of two widely studied institutions in the national political setting: election rules and the party system. Both of these institutions, especially the polarization of the party system, have an important impact on the distortion of preference correspondence in democracies and shape the collective outcome—correspondence between the electorate as a whole and the representatives as a whole rather than the voter-party dyads.[7] In normatively successful ideological representation, the representative commitments should correspond to the position of the median citizen. The position of the median is normatively privileged because it is the only policy position that cannot be defeated by another position in a head-on vote. In any system, the further from the median voter the legislative median, or government, is located, the larger the electoral majority that would prefer an alternative.

Dependent Variable: Distortion

Distortion in representation is defined as the absolute distance (on a 0-100 point, left-right scale) between the median voter and the representative. The position of the median voter is estimated on a left-right scale, derived from treating elections as preference polls and locating the positions of parties according to the coding of their election manifestos, as originally developed by HeeMin Kim and Richard Fording.[8] For the positions of representatives, the manifesto data are used to compute the position on the left-right scale of the party at the parliamentary median and the position of the government,[9] weighting the parties' positions by the proportions of their cabinet portfolios.[10]

Perfect ideological representation in a one-dimensional space expects the median voter and the representative to be at the same position on the left-right scale. Therefore, the greater the distance between the median voter and the representative, the greater is the distortion in representation.[11] The variation in both legislative and government distortion is analyzed for twenty western democracies across a period that begins in the early 1950s for most countries through the 1990s.

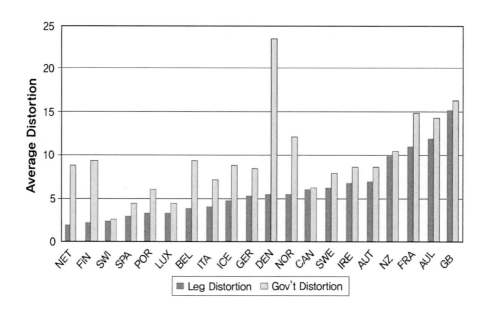

Figure 1. Average Levels of Legislative and Government Distortion in Western Democracies across the Entire Period of Analysis

Figure 1 presents average legislative and government distortion values for each of the twenty countries in the sample across the entire period analyzed, yielding several important conclusions concerning levels of distortion across countries. First, there is significant variation across countries in the level of distortion. This is especially true for government distortion, where the country with the highest level of distortion (Denmark) displays an average distortion value approximately ten times that of the country with the lowest distortion value (Switzerland). Second, although the average level of government distortion exceeds legislative distortion in every country, government and legislative distortion appear to be moderately related to one another (r5.57). Third, with the exception of Canada, countries with single-member-district (SMD) electoral systems generally display higher levels of distortion than countries with proportional representation systems

Independent Variables: Election Rules and Party Systems

There are good reasons to expect that election rules affect representation. There is, of course, a large literature about election rules and vote-seat disproportionality,[12] and a growing one on election rules and ideological distortion.[13] As sketched below, there should be both direct effects of and interactions with the party system. The many complexities of election rules are treated very simply, reducing them to the minimal (but very powerful) distinction between PR election rules and SMD election rules. The mixed systems (Germany, post-1992 Italy, and post-1993 New Zealand) involve compensation for disproportionality and are treated simply as PR. The SMD majority and Alternative Vote systems of Fifth Republic France (except 1986) and Australia, respectively, are treated as SMD, along with the plurality rule systems of Canada, Britain, and pre-1996 New Zealand.

Party systems are the institutions designed to link citizens and leaders, aggregating and bringing to bear the electoral resources of citizens. The literature on party systems shows their many facets, including the "parties in people's minds," the sets of organizations linking activists, members and leaders, the configurations of citizen voting support, and the groupings of legislators. Of course, these are connected in many complex ways. The treatment of party systems here focuses on the configurations that emerge from the party strategies and citizen choices in the election. These configurations open some possibilities for representation and constrain others. They tend to have great continuity across elections because of the weight of voter images and organizational structure,[14] yet they are also capable of sharp changes as new issues emerge or new electoral strategies are chosen (or eschewed).[15]

The two classic features of party systems in this sense are the number of competing political parties and the polarization of those parties. A critical conceptual and empirical issue is whether to conceive of these properties in terms of the pure offerings by the parties or also to incorporate information about voter choices. The former conception focuses solely on the number of parties offering candidates and the way the offerings of those parties are distributed in the issue space. It has the advantage of simplicity and is free of post-election influence from voters" responses to those choices. But it has the disadvantage of not discriminating between massive parties and trivial ones, between contenders taken seriously by all voters and annoying gadflies. We tend to consider a party system with two very large parties and two very tiny ones as basically a two-party system, not a four-party system. For that reason, the literature on party systems has come to rely almost entirely on the "effective number of parties," a measure originally developed by Marku Laakso and Rein Taagepera and mathematically equivalent to Douglas Rae and Michael Taylor's "fractionalization" measure.[16] The effective number of parties takes account of the voting support received by the parties, rather than simply counting the number of parties offering candidates. The formula is $1 / (\sum_{i=1}^{n} P_i^2)$ where P is the percentage of vote won by party i. We follow this conceptualization and the practice in the literature in our primary analysis of this property of party systems. In these countries the smallest effective number of parties, found in Britain and New Zealand in the early 1950s, for example, is about 2.1, while the largest number is about 9.9 (Belgium in 1991). The average effective number of parties in the twenty countries over the fifty-year time span is about 4.0. A dividing median line that roughly separates a small number of competing parties from a larger number is under or over three and one-half parties.

Polarization is conceptually the ideological "stretch" of the party system in terms of the positions and strength of the parties. The same logic concerning the pure party offerings or a range or distribution weighted by voter support applies here also. The party manifesto positions, converted into a cross-nationally comparative, right-left scale by the percentages of statements devoted to various themes, are used to locate each party in the party system.[17] The pure polarization of party offerings could be captured either by the distance between the right-most and left-most parties,[18] or by the standard deviation of the party distribution, with the latter providing more information about the full party system. But as in the case of the number of parties, the usual conception of a very centrist party system is one in which most voters are supporting parties fairly close to the mean or median, even if a small party offers a choice at one of the extremes. In a very polarized party system, most voters are supporting parties far from the center, even if there is a small party at the center.

In this analysis, therefore, polarization is estimated by taking the standard deviation of the distribution of party votes across the left-right scale, assuming each voter is at the manifesto position of the party supported.[19] The standard deviation is a useful measure because in a normal distribution 68 percent of the cases will fall within one standard deviation of the mean. In the case of a 100-point, left-right scale with a mean around 50, this implies that a standard deviation of 15 reflects two-thirds of the votes given to parties between 35 and 65. A standard deviation of 25 reflects two-thirds of the votes given to parties between 25 and 75. By this measure the average polarization across our countries over the fifty-year time span is about 18 (roughly two-thirds of the cases fall between polarization scores of 11 and 25).[20]

Both the number of parties and their polarization vary fairly sharply across countries and are fairly stable from election to election. However, Figure 2 shows that party system features can vary across elections within a single country and that the two features can and do vary independently of each other. In Figure 2 we see the effective number of parties (dashed line) and polarization (solid line) in Britain over time.

The effective number of British parties increases only slightly from the 1950s to the mid–1970s and afterwards, but polarization changes sharply over time. The immediate post-war period saw quite a polarized two-party system, which converged sharply to a very centrist one in the mid–1950s to mid–1960s (as Anthony Downs, in voter).[21]

The effective number of parties increased somewhat in the mid–1970s, although the large parties still dominated, followed by sharp party divergence into the polarization of the early Thatcher period. The 1983 election showed a high polarization (SD) of 29 (between the Conservatives at 19 and the Labour Party at 88, despite substantial voter support for the centrist Liberals). The 1997 British election showed a new convergence towards the median with a polarization score of only 9 (shaped by the Conservatives at 30 and New Labour at 43) although the effective number of parties does not diminish. The British party system measures fit our general intuition about the British party system, and show that occasionally the country averages can conceal important changes

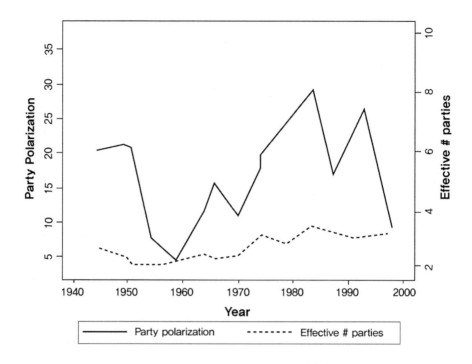

Figure 2. The Changing Party System in Britain:
Polarization and Number of Parties

over time, while the two party system features can vary independently of each other.

Theoretical Expectations about Party System Properties, Election Rules, and Ideological Representation

There is not a highly advanced body of theory concerning party systems, election rules, and ideological representation comparable to that on vote-seat distortion. But building on studies of party competition and election rules, initial hypotheses can be suggested.

Legislative Distortion   For election rules we follow the suggestion of Gary Cox, G. Bingham Powell, and Georg Vanberg that, in general, the stringency of conditions necessary for good congruence under SMD gives an expected advantage to PR, which is consistent with the empirical findings by Michael McDonald, Ian Budge, and others.[22]

H1: SMD election rule increases legislative distortion.

However, this has become a matter of some dispute, as André Blais and Marc André Bodet suggest that competing factors, such as number of parties, convergence to the median (depolarization), and vote-seat distortion, may cancel each other, leaving no net effects.[23] Our multivariate analysis disentangles these contrasting factors. Indeed, we might expect the effect of election rules to be contingent on the party system features whose vote distributions they convert into legislative representation. If, as expected from Duverger's Law, SMD election rules tend to create two-party systems and, as expected from Downs's theory of convergence to the median voter,[24] this depolarizes the party system, then SMD election rules could result in the major parties taking positions very close to the median voter—and thus eliminating legislative ideological distortion, even if there is substantial vote-seat distortion.

H1a: If polarization is low, SMD election rules do not increase legislative distortion.

The effect of the number of parties on ideological legislative congruence depends on two features: the availability of a party proximate to the median voter and the representation of the parties in the legislature.[25] Consider, first, multiple parties competing in national PR elections. While theoretical expectations are not completely clear, if there were equilibrium in one-dimensional competition, it should result in the parties dispersing themselves evenly across the spectrum, in the sense that an equal number of voters should fall between each party.[26] The more parties competing, the closer to the median the center parties should be (the niches between them are smaller). Moreover, as long as we have national PR elections with a low threshold, or the number of parties is not so great as to run into threshold problems, as is the case in most of these mature democracies, then under PR there should be fairly accurate reflection of the centrist parties into the legislature, where one of them should become the median legislative party. Thus, more parties should result in less distance between median voter and the party containing the median legislator.

> H2a: Under PR election rules, the greater effective number of parties reduces legislative distortion.

Although the great majority of our elections are fought under some version of PR, about thirty percent were held under SMD election rules. In these circumstances our expectations are not so clear. It is expected that under SMD there will be fewer competing parties.[27] If there is pure two-party competition, these parties may converge towards the political median, rather than dispersing across the spectrum.[28] More parties will inhibit this process and thus potentially create greater distances between median voter and the closest party.[29]

Moreover, more parties competing under SMD rules should create a higher potential for vote-seat disproportionality, as the "carrying capacity" of the election rules are exceeded. (Depending on how the support for these parties is distributed, various geographic sources of distortion may also emerge).[30] Vote-seat disproportionality does not itself necessarily create greater ideological distortion, but it has the possibility of doing so when, for example, a small centrist party is underrepresented in the legislature, as in the case of the British Social Democrats or the Australian Democrats, or when the plurality loser wins the election. Much depends on where the competing parties are located.

These competitive and vote-seat disproportionality considerations lead us to expect the reverse of our PR expectations: under SMD more parties should lead to greater legislative distortion. On the other hand, more competing parties may imply availability of parties closer to the center, especially if we are already taking account directly of the dispersion of parties across the spectrum in our polarization measure. Thus, the distance implications of more parties under SMD election rules are indeterminate and depend on conflicting factors.

H2b: Under SMD, the effect of the number of parties on legislative distortion is indeterminate.

Party system polarization implies that the weight of the competing parties is away from the center. The parties are more dispersed in the left-right ideological space. Here we take the level of polarization, like the number of parties, as exogenous with respect to representation. The distribution of party strategies and citizen support may be shaped by historic domestic and international cleavages;[31] contemporary social, political, and organizational conditions;[32] the way multiple issues are reduced into the unidimensional discourse space;[33] and so forth. Under either PR or SMD, potential gaps in the center associated with greater polarization should lead to greater distances between the median voter and median legislator. Because SMD tends especially to reward the larger parties and penalize smaller ones,[34] the effect of party polarization on legislative representation should be exaggerated under SMD.

H3: Party polarization increases legislative distortion.
H3a: Party polarization increases legislative distortion by greater amounts under SMD.

Government Distortion In parliamentary systems governments are responsible to the legislature and thus dependent on the configuration of parties in the legislature.[35] Under PR election rules, a single party only rarely wins a legislative majority. So elections are usually followed (and occasionally preceded) by bargaining between parties to form a government that can be sustained by their legislative support. Under SMD, on the other hand, the vote-seat distortion usually results in a direct legislative majority for a single party or pre-election coalition. Thus, legislative distortion should play a role in government formation under both PR and SMD. However, under PR the role is through the median legislative party, which is included in about 80 percent of government coalitions,[36] drawing them towards the center in a coalition also including other parties. Under SMD, the median legislative party usually has a controlling majority, so its distance from the median will completely determine the government distortion.

> H4: Legislative distortion increases government distortion
> H4a: The effect of legislative distortion on government distortion is greater under SMD.

The effects of party system characteristics on government distortion depend on the election rules because these rules largely determine whether or not there will be negotiation between parties. Under SMD, the effects of party system characteristics are completely mediated through legislative distortion and should have no additional effect once legislative distortion is taken into account.

> H5: Under SMD, greater number of parties and less party polarization are associated with less government distortion, but both effects are entirely mediated through legislative distortion (thus vanishing when legislative distortion is controlled).

Under PR we also expect that the effect of the number of parties is mediated through legislative distortion. Government negotiation is not systematically distorted by the presence of more parties, once we take account of the position of the median legislative party.

> H6a: Under PR, greater number of parties is associated with less government distortion, but the effect is mediated entirely by legislative distortion (thus vanishing when we control for legislative distortion).

But polarization affects the distances of the large parties from the median voter and these large parties are also necessary for government formation. For example, we know that the plurality party is also almost always included in the government.[37] Because of its size, its position has a strong impact on the government's position; its distance from the median voter will affect the government's distance. Polarization reflects that large party distance. Moreover, it seems reasonable to expect that where the system is more polarized, it will be harder to build coalitions across the median, rather than on one side of it.[38] For that reason, it is expected that party polarization will directly affect the distance between the government and the median voter, even taking account of the distance of the median legislator (which may also be affected by polarization).

H6b: Under PR, greater party polarization has both direct and indirect effects on government distortion (thus remaining significant even when we control for legislative distortion).

Party System Features and Ideological Representation: Additive Multivariate Analyses

The representative performance of a typology of party systems based on the average effective number of parties and polarization scores is shown in Table 1. The party systems are divided into "two-three party" and "multiparty" at the dividing point of three and one-half effective parties; and into centrist, moderate, and polarized party systems according to the polarization index. Taking the country averages, Germany and New Zealand emerge as centrist two-three party systems, while Spain, Portugal, and Luxembourg emerge as centrist multiparty systems. Austria, Australia, Canada, Ireland, and UK are two-three party systems that are moderately polarized; while Belgium, Iceland, Italy, Netherlands, Norway, and Switzerland are multiparty systems that are generally moderately polarized. No two-three party systems are highly polarized, while Denmark, Finland, France, and Sweden on average are multiparty systems with high polarization. (The polarization cutting points are 15.0 and 20.9.)

Table 1. Representation Failure

Party System Type	Legislative Distortion	Government Distortion
Centrist – 2/3 pty (72)	5.10	5.26
Centrist – Multipty (50)	2.62	4.30
Moderate – 2/3 pty (38)	9.22	12.12
Moderate – Multipty (51)	3.09	9.69
Polarized – 2/3 pty (40)	13.42	15.96
Polarized – Multipty (51)	6.28	16.99

This typology of individual elections in Table 1 shows the average ideological representation failures of distortion for the median legislator and for the government, indicating that the polarization dimension has a large effect on distortion. Reading down the columns, distortion increases. The effective number of parties also seems to have a strong effect on legislative representation, which is better (the distortion scores are smaller) in the multiparty systems. But the number of parties, unlike their polarization, apparently has rather little effect on the average failure of government representation. As expected, there is a general relationship, although only a weak one, between effective number of parties and polarization–the four very polarized systems are all multiparty systems, but simple correlation is only .16. Moreover, we have not yet taken account of the election rules, which are expected to be related to both party system variables. The British example (Figure 2) shows that party system properties can vary sharply across elections. Therefore, inferences should be checked with a multivariate analysis. This can be done by regressing the representation measure on the effective number of parties and their polarization. Initially we can also control for election rules in two ways: by adding a dummy variable for the election rules (Model I) and by a fixed effects model with dummy variables for each country (Model II). As the election rules rarely change from one election to the next (twice in France and once in New Zealand), putting in the country dummies wipes out the effects of election rules. Both approaches are interesting, because the former allows us to check our expectations about election rules (SMD yielding poorer ideological representation) while the latter gives us more confidence in the causal impact of the party system characteristics. Table 2 shows the regression results with simple additive models. Panel corrected standard errors are shown in parentheses, as these are pooled time series data.

The first two columns in Table 2 show the effects on legislative distortion (distance after each election).[39] Looking at the effects of election rules as a simple additive variable, the SMD systems produce median legislators significantly further, about six points on the 100-point scale, from the median voter than PR systems.[40] These results support Hypothesis 1.

Table 2. Party System and Representation

Independent Variables	Legislative Distortion		Government Distortion	
	I	II	I	II
Effective # Parties	−1,02*	−.64**	−.28	−.13
	(.19)	(.25)	(.31)	(.56)
Polarization	.39**	.50**	.78**	.74**
	(.04)	(.05)	(.07)	(.07)
SMD	6.20**	−	4.15**	−
	(.86)		(.81)	
Constant	1.63	−.56	−3.70	−3.97
	(1.16)	(1.48)	(1.73)	(3.10)
R^2	.41	.48	.34	.45
	(N= 302)	(N=302)	(N=300)	(N=300)

Note: Panel−corrected standard errors in parentheses. Model II is estimated with country−specific dummy variables (results not shown)
  * $p < .05$, ** $p < .01$

The effects of party system features on legislative representation also work very consistently for both models. As expected, a larger effective number of parties is significantly helpful in reducing distortion, taking account of election rules or country-level effects. (However, as the standard deviation of the effective number of parties is only 1.4, an increase of one standard deviation only reduces distortion by less than two points.) Further, the causal reasoning about the number of parties is supported by entering a variable for the distance of the political party closest to the median voter into these equations. In the PR systems, this variable is correlated at -.36 with the effective number of parties and very strongly correlated (.82) with legislative distance.[41] Most important, it completely mediates the significance of effective number of parties in all these equations, as expected theoretically.

Polarization, as expected, significantly increases representation failures in a robust way. (each increase in the polarization gap creates about a half point greater distortion; as the standard deviation of polarization is about 7, then an increase of one standard deviation in polarization leads to about three points greater legislative distortion.) These results support Hypothesis 3.

As shown in the last two columns of Table 2, the effects on government distortion in this simple additive model are somewhat different. The direct effects of election rules are smaller, albeit significant and in the expected direction. SMD election rules produce governments more distant from the median voter. Surprisingly, given the effect on legislative distortion, the effects of the number of parties on government distance are tiny and statistically insignificant. This difference presumably has to do with the indirectness of government formation in multiparty contexts. Although coalition studies show that the median legislative party participates in 80 percent of government coalitions, the larger plurality party is equally likely to be included,[42] and has more effect on government positions.[43]

On the other hand, polarization would have a doubled impact on government distances. Because of the indirect effect through legislative distortion and the direct effects through distance of the largest party, and in making centrist coalition formation more difficult, the polarization coefficients for government distortion are much larger than for legislative distortion (especially in the Model I specifications, where they are more than doubled). An increase of a standard deviation in polarization increases government distortion by nearly six points. Centrist party systems, and all systems when they are more centrist, are more likely to have close correspondence of voters and representatives; polarized ones generate more frequent failures.

Party System Features, Election Rules, and Distortion: Interactive Analyses

The analysis in Table 2 treats election rules simply as a variable that may affect ideological representation directly. However, as shown in the discussion of theoretical expectations, there is good reason to anticipate interactions between the election rules and the features of the party system. In shaping legislative representation, our expectations about the number of parties were in conflict under SMD (Hypothesis 2b) with arguments that greater fractionalization of the party system could be either helpful or harmful, whereas under PR (in this range of thresholds and numbers of parties), more parties were expected to be associated with less distortion (Hypothesis 2a). Party system polarization was expected to be less, on average, under SMD, but the effects of polarization on distortion might be even stronger because of the exaggeration of larger party representation (Hypothesis 3a).

Table 3 introduces interaction terms to compare legislative and government distortion under PR and SMD. In this specification, the simple party system coefficients show the effect of the party system under PR. The interaction shows the difference in that effect under SMD rules; to get the party system effect under SMD, we sum the two coefficients. The first two columns show legislative distortion; the second two columns show government distortion.

First, the effects of the party system on legislative distortion are considered. The conflicting expectations about the number of parties under SMD are resolved in the direction of more parties being helpful to legislative representation, under both PR and SMD. Under PR the coefficients are negative and highly significant, supporting Hypothesis 2a. The interaction terms are not statistically significant, as they have large standard errors, but the direction of the effect suggest that the helpful effect of parties is at least as great under SMD rules as it is under PR (thus resolving the underdetermined direction of Hypothesis 2b). Party polarization significantly increases distortion under both PR and SMD, thus supporting Hypothesis 3. As expected from Downsian theory of party competition, the number of parties is associated with polarization, although the relationship is not very strong (r5.36.). But taking account of the number of parties, there is an even stronger effect of polarization on distortion—the interaction terms are significant and the effect is more than doubled under SMD. This finding supports Hypothesis 3a.

Table 3. Conditional Effects of Party System Characteristics on Legislative and Government Distortion.

Independent Variables	Legislative Distortion		Government Distortion	
	I	II	I	II
Effective # Parties	−1,08**	−.62**	−.34	−.15
	(.19)	(.23)	(.37)	(.58)
Effective # Parties * SMD	−.82	−1.16	−.13	−.10
	(.63)	(.66)	(1.00)	(.80)
Polarization	.23**	.30**	.70**	.65**
	(.04)	(.05)	(.08)	(.09)
Polarization * SMD	.90**	.76**	.40**	.33*
	(.11)	(.10)	(.13)	(.13)
SMD	−6.05*	−	−2.15	−
	(2.33)		(3.79)	
Constant	4.86**	.23	−2.09	−2.82
	(1.16)	(3.00)	(2.22)	(4.60)
R2	.54	.59	.36	.46
	(N=302)	(N=302)	(N=300)	(N=300)

Note: Panel—corrected standard errors in parentheses. Model II is estimated with country—specific dummy variables (results not shown)
* p < .05, ** p < .01

The second two columns in Table 3 show government distortion. Interestingly, the effective number of parties has no effect on government distortion under PR, despite its helpful reduction of legislative distortion. The effective number of parties is associated with decreased government distortion under SMD, but the coefficients are very small and not significant.

However, as expected, the party system polarization under PR has a sharper effect on government polarization than it did on legislative polarization. In the SMD systems, polarization had a significantly stronger effect on government polarization than under PR, but the total effect (adding the PR and SMD coefficients) is very similar to the impact of polarization on legislative distortion. This is consistent with Hypothesis 5.[44]

The effect of the election rules themselves cannot be read directly from Table 3 because of the interactions. Rather, just as the effects of the party system varied across different electoral rules, the effects of electoral rules vary as a function of different party system characteristics. These conditional effects are displayed in Table 4 for different combinations of party system variables.

Table 4 displays predicted effects of SMD's on legislative distortion, conditional on two characteristics of the party system: the effective number of parties and the level of party polarization. There is relatively little variation in the predicted effects within columns, reflecting the fact that the conditional effect of the number of parties is trivial (as shown in Table 3). However, there is significant variation across rows, as the predicted effect of SMDs on legislative distortion increases significantly with the level of party polarization. Thus, with the exception of the least polarized systems—where SMD and PR systems perform similarly (which supports Hypothesis 1a)—-SMD systems appear to result in moderate to significant increases in distortion.

Table 4. Predicted Difference in Legislative Distortion across SMD and PR Systems at Different Combinations of Party System Characteristics.

#Effective Parties	Party Polarization		
	Low (10)	Medium (17.5)	High (25)
Low (2.5)	.91	7.67**	14.42**
Medium (3.5)	.09	6.85**	13.61**
High (4.5)	−.73	6.03**	12.79**

Note: Cell entries represent predicted effects of SMD systems (SMD distortion − PR distortion) and are based on the model presented in Table 3, Model I

Table 5 further clarifies the causal process through which the party system shapes government distortion by taking legislative distortion directly into account. It is expected that under PR, most elections are followed by interparty bargaining to build a government coalition or a sustainable minority government. Legislative distortion should affect government distortion because of the greater distance of

Table 5. The Conditional Effects of Party System Characteristic and Legislative Distortion on Government Distortion.

Independent Variables	Government Distortion	
	I	II
Effective #Parties	−.13	.04
	(.40)	(.59)
Effective #Parties * SMD	1.25	1.11
	(.84)	(.67)
Polarization	.66**	.59**
	(.09)	(.10)
Polarization * SMD	−.49**	−.41**
	(.15)	(.15)
Legislative Distortion	.20	.21
	(.14)	(.14)
Legislative Distortion * SMD	.62**	.54**
	(.17)	(.17)
SMD	−.06	–
	(3.30)	
Constant	−3.06	−2.70
	(2.25)	(4.22)
R^2	.41	.50
	(N=300)	(N=300)

Note: Panel−corrected standard errors in parentheses. Model II is estimated with country−spe−
cific dummy variables (results not shown)
* $p < .05$, ** $p < .01$

the median party, usually in the government, from the median voter (Hypothesis 4). But the impact of the plurality party will be larger and polarization should affect both the distance of the plurality party and the improbability of forming coalitions across the median. Thus, under PR it is expected that both legislative distortion (distance of the median party from the median voter) and polarization directly affect government distortion. This can be seen in Table 5, which adds legislative distortion to the specification in Table 3. However, the coefficient for legislative distortion under PR is just below the margin of conventional statistical significance, while the polarization coefficient is very large and significant.[45] This result supports Hypothesis 6b. The impact of polarization in PR systems, then, seems to come primarily from the difficulties it creates in forming centrist governments, less from the path through the median legislator.[46]

Under SMD, most elections are followed by a single party or pre-election coalition winning an absolute majority, which by definition both contains the median legislator and forms a majority government. In fact, the simple correlation between legislative distortion and government distortion is only .27 under PR, emphasizing the distinct, two-stage nature of the government formation process, whereas it is .87 under SMD, emphasizing the dominance of legislative outcomes. In the regression analysis in Table 5, the effect of polarization is significantly less than in PR, and the total effect (subtracting the interaction term) is statistically indistinguishable from 0 in this specification. However, there is a very strong path through legislative distortion, which is itself (as shown in Table 3) powerfully shaped by party system polarization (Hypothesis 6).

Thus, the party system effects on government distortion are fairly similar in PR and SMD systems (the effective number of parties is insignificant, while polarization is strong and significant), but the causal path is quite different.

Conclusion

Party systems, which organize and reflect the preferences of voters, are a primary connector between citizens and elected policymakers. Therefore, properties of party systems should shape the representation connection. Yet, despite the large literature on party systems discussing causes and consequences of such features as the number and polarization of parties, few studies have developed the ideological representation linkage in theory or empirical analysis. No doubt, the fact that most studies of the correspondence of citizen preferences and the positions of representatives are limited to one or two elections in a single country or a handful of political systems has greatly constrained such analysis. Moreover, the tradition in comparative research on issue correspondence has focused on voter-representative dyads, rather than collective correspondence. In this article, the sources of distortion in the relationship between the median voter, the median legislator, and the government are analyzed. A few exceptional studies have emphasized the election laws. Because election laws and party systems are closely related in theory and practice, it is essential to consider them and their interactions explicitly. Here, the impact of election rules and party systems, additively and interactively, on collective left-right representation are considered by utilizing measures of voter, parliament, and government ideology that permit cross-national comparisons over an extended period of time.

In general, the theoretical expectations in this analysis, based on theories of multiparty competition and on earlier studies of election rules, are reasonably well met. Distortion of the voter-representative relationship was generally greater under SMD election rules, even taking account of the party system. However, the interactive specification (Tables 3 and 4) suggested that under conditions of low party system polarization, the election rules made little difference for collective citizen-representative correspondence. Although it makes a great deal of sense intuitively, this important feature of the effect of election laws has not previously been observed.

Although beyond the bounds of most of this analysis, taking advantage of the new cases recently added to the manifesto data,[47] currently low polarization seems directly responsible for less distortion in SMD systems in the last decade.[48] The depolarization of the British system since the convergence towards the center of New Labour in 1997 exemplifies this trend but is not unique. A regression analysis of government distortion in eighty-four SMD systems with dummy variables for decades indicates that the most recent decade

(1996-2004) has significantly less distortion than the other decades (with the decade 1956–65 a close second). Entering the polarization measure completely eliminates the significance of all the decade dummy variables. SMD systems in this period of their low polarization show no more distortion than PR systems.

The two general features of the party system configurations, effective number of parties and party system polarization, generally affected representation in the expected ways. Having more parties was somewhat helpful to legislative representation. Consistent with Downsian expectations of two-party convergence, having more parties under SMD was associated with greater polarization. After polarization was taken into account, the greater number of parties was associated with legislative medians closer to the citizen median, even under SMD. (Under PR, at least, this was associated with having available a party close to the citizen median.) Greater party system polarization, however, made good legislative representation more difficult, especially under SMD. These findings were relatively robust to alternative measures of party system properties, even those based purely on the party choices (range) offered without taking account of voter support.

Government distortion was affected by the party system features somewhat differently. The number of parties had little, if any, effect, once polarization was taken into account. The key feature for government distortion is polarization of the party system, not the number of parties.[49] Polarization made government distortion more likely under both PR and SMD, but apparently though somewhat different causal pathways. Under PR, polarization seemed to make centrist governments more difficult to form, with leg-islative distortion playing a small additional role. (The magnitude of this role depended somewhat on the conceptualization and measurement of party system.) Under SMD, the legislative distortion was the main direct cause of government distortion. Although it seems clear that features of the party system must play an important role in the electoral connections between citizen preferences and policymaker positions, the precise nature of the effects of different party system features, and especially the causal mechanism under different election rules, has not previously been explicated. This analysis clarifies the role of these critical institutions in the process of democratic representation.

Acknowledgments

This research was partially funded by a National Science Foundation Political Science Grant (SES-0237820) to the first author. The authors would like to thank Spencer Powell, Emilia Powell, and Sunhee Park for their able research assistance. We also thank Mark Kayser, Michael McDonald, Bonnie Meguid, Richard Matland, and participants in seminar series at the University of Michigan and the University of Rochester for helpful comments.

Notes

1. Michael Saward, The Terms of Democracy (Oxford: Blackwell Publishers, 1998), p. 51.

2. Robert A. Dahl, Democracy and Its Critics (New Haven, CT: Yale University Press, 1989), p. 95.

3. J. Westerstahl and F. Johansson, "Medborgarna och kommunen," Report 5, Kommunaldemokrtisk forskningsgruppen, Ds Kn Stockholm, 12 (1981), 20, cited by Soren Holmberg, "Issue Agreement" in Beyond Westminster and Congress, ed. Peter Esaiasson and Knut Keidar (Columbus: Ohio State University Press, 2000), pp. 155–80.

4. Ibid., p. 155.

5. Douglas Rae, The Political Consequences of Electoral Laws (New Haven, CT: Yale University Press, 1967). See especially, Rein Taagepera and Matthew S. Shugart, Seats and Votes (New Haven, CT: Yale University Press, 1989); and Arend Lijphart et al., Electoral Systems and Party Systems: A Study of Twenty-Seven Democracies 1945-1990 (New York: Oxford University Press, 1994).

6. Warren E. Miller and Donald Stokes, "Constituency Influence in Congress," American Political Science Review, 57 (1963): 165–-77; Russell Dalton, "Political Parties and Political Representation," Comparative Political Studies, 18 (1985): 276–-99; and Warren E. Miller et al., Policy Representation in Western Democracies (Oxford: Oxford University Press, 1999). For a more detailed review, see G. Bingham Powell, "Political Representation in Comparative Politics," Annual Review of Political Science, 7 (2004): 273–96.

7. For the latter, Bernhard Wessels, "System Characteristics Matter: Empirical Evidence from Ten Representation Studies," in Miller et al., pp. 1137-61, examines election rule majoritarianism and party polarization across ten elections in five nations.

8. HeeMin Kim and Richard C. Fording, "Voter Ideology in Western Democracies," European Journal of Political Research, 33 (1998): 73–97; and HeeMin Kim and Richard C. Fording, "Voter Ideology in Western Democracies: An Update," European Journal of Political Research, 42 (2003): 95–105.

9. Ian Budge et al., Mapping Policy Preferences (New York: Oxford University Press, 2001).

10. HeeMin Kim and Richard C. Fording, "Government Partisanship in Western Democracies, 1945–1998," European Journal of Political Research, 41 (2002): 187–206.

11. Some scholars have suggested that, given the slow pace of policy change in democracies, democratic representation should be analyzed as a long-term phenomenon, and distortion should be looked at with a longer time horizon. See Michael McDonald and Ian Budge, Elections, Parties, Democracy: Conferring the Median Mandate (New York: Oxford University Press, 2005). However, we have yet to determine a non-arbitrary way to choose an ideal time horizon to evaluate democratic representation of different party systems and election rules. Moreover, we believe that voters in specific elections expect immediate correspondence between their preferences and positions of the new legislatures and governments. In this article we offer a good starting point for studying what is also part of a long-term process, and we leave the task of introducing a longer time horizon for future endeavor.

12. For example, Rae, Electoral Laws Taagepera and Shugart, Seats and Votes and Lijphart et al., Electoral Systems.

13. G. Bingham Powell and Georg Vanberg, "Election Laws, Disproportionality and the Left-Right Dimension," British Journal of Political Science, 30 (2000): 383–411; and Michael D. McDonald et al., "What Are Elections For? Conferring the Median Mandate," British Journal of Political Science, 34 (2004): 1–26.

14. Seymour Martin Lipset and Stein Rokkan, Party Systems and Voter Alignments (New York: Free Press, 1967).

15. See Herbert Kitschelt, The Transformation of European Social Democracy (New York: Cambridge University Press, 1994).

16. Markku Laakso and Rein Taagepera, "'Effective' Number of Parties: A Measure with Application to Western Europe,"' Comparative Political Studies, 12 (1979): 3--27; Douglas W. Rae and Michael Taylor, The Analysis of Political Cleavages (New Haven, CT: Yale University Press, 1970.)

17. On this methodology, see M. J. Laver and Ian Budge, eds., Party Policy and Government Coalitions (London: Macmillan, 1992); and Budge et al., Mapping Policy Preferences.

18. As is done by Giacomo Sani and Giovanni Sartori, "Polarization, Fragmentation and Competition in Western Democracies," in Western European Party Systems, ed. Hans Daalder and Peter Mair (Beverly Hill, CA: Sage Publications, 1983), pp. 307-40, counting only "relevant" parties.

19. See Paul V. Warwick, Government Survival in Parliamentary Democracies (New York: Cambridge University Press, 1994), pp. 50 ff.; and Russell J. Dalton, "The Quantity and Quality of Party Systems: Party System Polarization, Its Measurement and Its Consequences," Comparative Political Studies, 41 (2008): 899–920, for similar approaches.

20. We appreciate that some readers may be interested in the pure offerings of the parties before the voters make their choices. For that reason we have also calculated a measure of polarization based on pure range (distance between most extreme parties) parties and a measure of the distribution (standard deviation) counting each party as one unit. We have conducted a parallel analysis with these measures. We do not present them in our tables and figures, both for simplicity and because we think the voter-weighted measures more closely correspond both to the usual conceptualization of party system configurations and to common practices in party system analysis. But we shall compare the findings with these measures with our standard ones (notes 40, 45, and 46 below), noting the few cases of noncorrespondence. Analysts focusing on the dynamics of party-voter interaction may wish to explore these in more detail in the future. It is worth noting that the simple range is correlated at .87 with our weighted polarization measure, which is correlated at .91 with an unweighted measure of party distribution. Insofar as the regression results are similar, as they are, they also provide reassurance to anyone who may feel that the voter-weighted measures are too close to the measurement of the median voter position, creating findings that are methodo-

logical artifacts.

21. Anthony Downs, An Economic Theory of Democracy (New York: Harper and Row, 1957).

22. Gary W. Cox, Making Votes Count: Strategic Coordination in the World"s Electoral Systems (Cambridge: Cambridge University Press, 1997); Powell and Vanberg, "Election Laws" G. Bingham Powell, "Election Laws and Representative Government," British Journal of Political Science, 36 (2006): 291-315. Empirical studies include McDonald et al., "What Are Elections For" and McDonald and Budge, Elections, Parties, Democracy.

23. André Blais and Marc André Bodet, "Does Proportional Representation Foster Closer Congruence between Citizens and Policymakers?" Comparative Political Studies, 39 (2006): 1243–63.

24. Maurice Duverger, Political Parties: Their Organization and Activity in the Modern State (New York: John Wiley, 1954); and Downs, Economic Theory but see Bernard Grofman, "Downs and Two-Party Convergence," Annual Review of Political Science, 7 (2004): 25-46.

25. Also see McDonald and Budge, Elections, Parties, Democracy, pp. 124–30.

26. Gary W. Cox, "Centripetal and Centrifugal Incentives under Alternative Voting Institutions," American Journal of Political Science, 34 (1990): 903–35; and Cox, Making Votes Count. But some scholars expect polarizing effects of multiparty competition, at least past some threshold of parties. See, for example, Giovanni Sartori, Parties and Party Systems (New York: Cambridge University Press, 1976).

27. Duverger, Political Parties and Cox, Making Votes Count.

28. Downs, Economic Theory and Cox, Making Votes Count but see Grofman.

29. See Thomas R. Palfrey, "Spatial Equilibrium with Entry," The Review of Economic Studies, 51 (1984): 139-56. Note that if we put polarization directly into the multivariate model, we would control for this hypothesized effect.

30. See Powell and Vanberg, "Election Laws" and Burt L. Monroe and Amanda G. Rose, "Electoral Systems and Unimagined Consequences: Partisan Effects of Districted Proportional Representation," American Journal of Political Science, 46 (2002): 67–89.

31. Lipset and Rokkan, Party Systems.

32. Kitschelt, European Social Democracy.

33. Ronald Inglehart, "The Changing Structure of Political Cleavages in Western Society," in Electoral Change in Advanced Industrial Societies, ed. Russell J. Dalton, Scott C. Flanagan, and Paul Allen Beck (Princeton, NJ: Princeton University Press, 1984), pp. 25–69.

34. Rae, Electoral Laws.

35. See, for example, Lanny Martin and Randy Stevenson, "Government Formation in Parliamentary Democracies," American Journal of Political Science, 45 (2001): 33–-50; and Powell, "Election Laws and Representative Government."

36. Michael Laver and Norman Schofield, Multiparty Government: The Politics of Coalition in Europe (Oxford: Oxford University Press, 1990); and Powell, "Election Laws and Representative Government."

37. Laver and Schofield, Multiparty Government, p. 113; and Martin and Stevenson, "Government Formation."

38. Powell, "Election Laws and Representative Government."

39. Replicating the analysis in Table 2 with alternative measures of polarization (both simple range between the most distant parties and left-right distribution of parties unweighted by voter support) yields results completely consistent with the following discussion, except that percentage of variance explained is much smaller.

40. This was also found by Powell and Vanberg, "Election Laws," with very different measures; and by McDonald et al., "What Are Elections For?," using a similar distortion measure.

41. This was also found by McDonald and Budge, Elections, Parties, Democracy and Hans-Dieter Klingemann et al., Mapping Policy Preferences II (New York: Oxford University Press, 2006), ch. 7.

42. Laver and Schofield, Multiparty Government, p. 113.

43. Martin and Stevenson, "Government Formation" and Powell, "Election Laws and Representative Government."

44. Replicating the analyses in Table 3 with an alternative measure of polarization, the left-right distribution of parties unweighted by voter support yields results completely consistent with the following discussion. A measure of polarization based simply on the range between far left and far right yields identical results with two exceptions:

for the model of legislative distortion, the coefficient for electoral system (SMDs) is still negative but is no longer statistically significant (the model without fixed effects). However, we see this as trivial because this coefficient represents a conditional effect that is defined for the case where the effective number of parties and polarization are both fixed at 0. We also find the interaction between the effective number of parties and SMDs to be negative and significant in the model of legislative distortion when using fixed effects. We believe that this finding simply strengthens our conclusions about the effects of party system characteristics on democratic performance.

45. We also replicated the analysis in Table 5 with alternative measures of polarization. Perhaps the most important difference is that the effect of legislative distortion is significant in the PR case for three of four alternative specifications (two alternative measures X fixed/no fixed effects models). In Table 5, based on our primary measure, it is not quite significant. But it is important to note that all of the alternative specifications continue to support the conclusion that the effect of legislative distortion is much greater in the SMD case. This supports our primary conclusion based on our primary measure of polarization. In addition, for each of the two fixed effects models, we do not find polarization to significantly interact with electoral system (SMDs) to affect government distortion. However, this interaction continues to be supported in models that do not rely on fixed effects. In addition, in one of the fixed effects models that does not find a significant interaction, the p-value for the interaction term is very close to significance at .07. For the other insignificant interaction, even though the p-value is not close to significance, the direction of the coefficient is still consistent with the results we find using the primary measure of polarization.

46. McDonald and Budge, Elections, Parties, Democracy, observe that most of the government distortion in PR systems emerges "principally in the step between the parliamentary median and the government" (125), but have no explanation for the variance in negotiating congruent governments.

47. Klingemann et al., Mapping Policy Preferences II.

48. This was also observed, using very different measures, by Blais and Bodet.

49. We have also replicated the (nonfixed effects) equations from Tables 2, 3, and 5 using the new Comparative Study of Electoral Systems data (thirty-six elections in their "old" democracies 1996–2004.) The median citizen position is based on right-left

self-placements; citizen placement of parties is used to estimate legislative median and government positions, as well as party polarization. (Thus polarization is calculated completely independently of estimation of the median citizen position.) The polarization coefficients, both direct and interactive, from these estimates are extremely similar to those in our tables; in the government equations they are all statistically significant at the .05 level.

07.

Does Tactical Voting Matter?
The Political Impact of Tactical Voting in
Canadian Elections

Heemin Kim[*] & Tatiana Kostadinova[**]

Florida State University and Seoul National University

**Florida International University*

Abstract. Tactical voting primarily takes place under single-member district plural-ity electoral institutions and takes the form of third-party supporters voting for one of the major parties. Although much has been written about tactical voting, few studies have attempted to show its impact on seat distribution within the parlia-ment or on the makeup of the subsequent government, in countries with sin-gle-member plurality systems. In this article, we assess the magnitude and impact of tactical voting in the Canadian general elections between 1988 and 2000. We build a model of tactical voting by identifying factors that are known to affect the level of tactical voting that we can measure using available data. Based on this model, we generate predicted levels of tactical voting for all parties within each district, and then use these predicted values to adjust the actual election data to produce a new set of data containing a would-be election outcome in the absence of tactical voting. By comparing actual election data, adjusted election data, and the seat share of political parties in the parliament after these elections, we discuss the political impact of tactical voting in Canada. The results of our study affirm that, in some cases, tactical voting does lead to election outcomes different from those in its absence and that arguments based on voter rationality are to some de-gree valid in the real world. At the same time, our results demonstrate that the impact of tactical voting on election outcomes, and thus on the actual distribution of seats within the parliament, has been minimal in Canada. It had no impact on the partisan composition of the government in any of the four elections studie

Introduction

Sincere voting assumes that voters always choose their most preferred candidates or parties. It has been argued in both the formal and empirical literature, however, that voters might not always vote for their most preferred candidates. This is known as tactical (or strategic, sophisticated) voting and refers to voting contrary to one's nominal preferences. Tactical voting, as usually described in the literature, primarily takes place under single-member district plurality electoral systems and takes the form of third-party supporters voting for one of the major parties. The logic of tactical voting, of course, is that of Duverger's law, which states that the supporters of a small party would not 'waste' their votes by voting for their most preferred party (candidate) since it does not have a chance to win under a plurality system with single-member districts. Instead, they vote for the major party that is most acceptable to them and that has a chance of winning (Duverger, 1963). Since Duverger, ample theoretical literature has shown incentives to vote tactically under different electoral institutions (Riker, 1976, 1982; Tsebelis, 1986; Bowler & Farrell, 1991; Jesse, 1995).[1]

Until now, empirical studies of tactical voting have taken two different paths: the first evaluates whether indeed some voters vote tactically under single-member district plurality electoral institutions (primarily Britain and Canada), and if so, how many of them do? These studies investigate the level of tactical voting for a single election using existing survey data; they have shown that tactical voting does occur, usually at a rate of somewhere between 5% and 10% of the electorate (Fisher, 1973; Curtice & Steed, 1988; Evans & Heath, 1993; Blais & Nadeau, 1996; Alvarez & Nagler, 2000. For different estimates of the level of tactical voting, see Niemi, Whitten & Franklin, 1992, 1993).

The second path taken by empirical studies of tactical voting is the investigation of the causes of tactical voting for a given election. These studies have shown that several individual factors as well as contextual factors within districts affect the level of tactical voting in a given election (Black, 1978; Cain,

1978; Gailbraith & Rae, 1989; Johnston & Pattie, 1991; Bowler & Lanoue, 1992; Lanoue & Bowler, 1992; Blais & Nadeau, 1996; Blais et al., 2001).

Kim and Fording (2001) take yet another approach. Using data from four recent general elections in Britain, they investigate the political impact of tactical voting over a period of time. That is, they assess whether tactical voting has had an impact on the actual distribution of seats within the parliament and eventually the partisan composition (and thus, subsequent policies) of the government in Britain. If indeed the magnitude of tactical voting in single-member plurality systems is large enough to affect the power distribution within the parliament and subsequent policy outcomes, they argue, this will provide additional empirical evidence that theoretical arguments based on voter rationality are valid in the real world and that voters are quite successful in not wasting their votes and preventing their least preferred parties from coming to power.

In this paper, we take the same approach as Kim and Fording: We study four recent general elections in Canada, whose electoral system is characterized by single-member district plurality rule. We estimate levels of tactical voting for all major parties within each riding for these elections. Based on these estimates, we adjust the actual election data to produce a revised set of results that represent would-be election outcomes in the absence of tactical voting (that is, had everybody voted sincerely). In the last sections of this paper, we discuss the impact of tactical voting in Canada by comparing these new results to the actual election data.

Estimating the Political Impact of Tactical Voting: An Operationalization

Ideally, to accurately gauge the political impact of tactical voting, we would like to compare observed election results (which reflect tactical voting) to the election results that would have been observed if all voters had voted sincerely. This would be easy to do if district-level public opinion polls that measured voters' sincere preferences were available prior to each election. Unfortunately they are not. In the absence of such data, we are left with two (albeit rather crude) choices.

We could simply calculate the national rate of tactical voting, along with the direction of tactical vote flows, based on national-level surveys. We could then apply these national-level estimates to elections at the district level, and use this information to estimate the distribution of sincere preferences within each district. The most obvious weakness of this strategy is that it assumes that the rate of tactical voting, which would be estimated from national-level data, is the same across all districts. This is not likely to be the case: As much literature suggests, the rate of tactical voting in a given election is in part a function of various aspects of the electoral context within each district, and as we would suspect, the electoral context across districts is likely to vary to a significant degree.

The other approach to measuring the impact of tactical voting does not make such an implausible assumption, so it is adopted for this research. Our approach proceeds in three general stages. First, we estimate an individual-level model of tactical voting in which it is assumed that the probability that an individual votes strategically is a function of key characteristics of the electoral environment in his or her district. Having obtained the coefficients from this model, we then shift the level of analysis to the district level and, based on equivalent contextual variables, predict the rate of tactical voting for each party within each district. Along with estimates of vote flows obtained using national-level data, we then proceed to calculate the percentage of sincere supporters of each party within each district. This information is compared to actual election results to determine how frequently tactical voting affects the outcome of an election.

A Contextual Model of Tactical Voting

To estimate the impact of contextual variables on tactical voting at the individual level, we rely on the Canadian Election Study (CES) for four elections: 1988, 1993, 1997, and 2000. We begin with the 1988 election, because the CES questionnaires changed significantly in that year making the comparison of elections before and after that election difficult.[2] The national-level outcomes of these elections are shown in Table I. The Progressive Conservative Party (PC), the Liberal Party, and the National Democratic Party (NDP) were the three major parties at the national level in Canada until 1993. In the 1993 general elections, both the PC and the NDP shrank to an insignificant size, and the Reform Party and the Bloc Quebecois (BQ) emerged as alternatives, although all the seats of the latter have been won in Quebec making it a dominant regional party in Canadian politics.[3]

Table 1. Federal election results in Canada, 1984–2000

Year	Progressive Conservative		Liberal		NDP		Reform		Bloc Quebecois		Others	
	Seats	Votes	Seats	Votes	Seats	Votes	Seats	Votes	Seats	Votes	Seats	Votes
1988	169	42.9	83	32.0	43	20.4					1	4.7
1993	2	16	177	41.3	9	6.9	52	18.7	54	13.5		
1997	20	18.8	155	38.5	21	11.0	60	19.4	44	10.7	1	1.6
2000	12	12.2	172	40.8	13	8.5	66*	25.5*	38	10.7	0	2.3

* Reform-Conservative Alliance in 2000

We analyze tactical voting not only across elections, but also for the province of Quebec and the rest of the country separately, because the major parties differ in these two regions of Canada starting with the 1993 election. In Quebec, the three traditional major parties, the PC, the Liberals, and the NDP, have competed along with the BQ, while in all the other provinces, the fourth major party has been the Reform Party.

Our first task is to identify tactical voters among all those who cast ballots. Unlike the British Elections Studies (BES), the recent CES do not contain a single survey item that asks respondents why they voted as they did.[4] Therefore, to identify tactical voters, we use the alternative operationalization advocated by Blais et al. (2001) for Canadian elections. It consists of three steps. First, we estimate a model for each of the parties (three in 1988, and four in 1993, 1997 and 2000), inside and outside Quebec, where each vote for them is explained by voters' preferences and the intensity of those preferences. The explanatory variables include party ratings, leader ratings, and strength of party identification. We also estimate a model that adds voters' expectations for the final outcome through a party performance variable.

Data come from CES items that reflect respondents' feelings toward federal parties and their leaders (ranked on a 0–100 thermometer scale), as well as the intensity of their attachment to particular parties (ranked as strength of identification). Relative expectations for party chances to win a seat in the respondent's constituency are indicated in percentages. All variables are further recoded, standardized, and transformed (for more detail on these procedures, see Appendix A in Blais et al., 2001).

Second, using the parameters obtained in step one, we estimate equations for each respondent's most preferred party (the party he or she would have voted for sincerely, based on preferences and party attachment), and the party he or she was most likely to vote for (when also considering expectations about the outcome of the local race). Finally, we compare the two sets of predicted voter choices. If the two predictions are consistent (that is, the respondent is predicted to support the same party regardless of his or her expectations about the outcome of the race), the case is considered one of sincere voting. If, however, there is a discrepancy in the two predictions, showing that the voter switched to a less preferred party while taking into account party chances to win the local race, we code such an instance as tactical voting.

Following the Blais et al. method, we identified groups of tactical voters in the four Canadian elections, whose relative size is quite modest. In the provinces except Quebec, tactical voting occurred at a rate of 3% to 4% (4.4% in 1988, 3.4% in 1993, 3.7% in 1997, and 2.8% in 2000). In Quebec, a decline in tactical voting can be observed over this time: It was at its highest point in 1988 (6.2%), decreased to 4% in 1993, 2.8% in 1997, and reached a low of 2.4% in 2000.[5]

Having identified the tactical voters, now we proceed with estimation of the impact of several contextual factors on the voters' choice to behave strategically. A large body of literature in political science has addressed this question. Previous studies have identified three important aspects of an election as being critical to determining the rate of tactical voting. The first one is the probability that one's party can win the election. That is, voters are expected to be more likely to abandon their preferred party when their party is not competitive in the election (Niemi, Whitten & Franklin, 1992; Blais & Nadeau, 1996). This contextual dimension is captured by including the variable

COMPETITIVENESS, measured as the proportion of the vote obtained in the district by one's preferred party. A second dimension of electoral context suggested by the literature is the closeness of the election (Black, 1978; Cain, 1978; Tsebelis, 1986; Gailbraith & Rae, 1989; Niemi, Whitten & Franklin, 1992; Blais & Nadeau, 1996). Consequently, we include the variable CLOSENESS, defined as the distance (in vote-share proportion) between the two largest parties in the district.[6] All else equal, it is assumed that voters are more likely to abandon their most preferred party and vote strategically when their party is not competitive and when the distance between the two large parties is small. In other words, we expect both COMPETITIVENESS and CLOSENESS to be negatively related to tactical voting.

We also expect COMPETITIVENESS and CLOSENESS to interact in their effect on tactical voting. For example, when a voter's preferred party is the frontrunner in a particular district (thus COMPETITIVENESS is high), the value of CLOSENESS should not matter in that voter's decision to vote tactically. More generally, we should thus expect the effect of CLOSENESS to diminish in magnitude as COMPETITIVENESS increases. To allow for this possibility, we include a multiplicative term (COMPETITIVENESS * CLOSENESS) to the model, where the coefficient for this interactive term is expected to be positive. Finally, we add dummy variables for the party of the respondent to capture electionspecific forces that might be expected to affect the propensity for tactical voting among members of each of the major parties.

The units of analysis are individual voters making their choices under the specific circumstances of their electoral districts. As the dependent variable is dichotomous, we use logit analysis to estimate the model. We estimate separate models for Quebec and the rest of the country for each of the elections since 1993, thus allowing the propensity for tactical voting among different parties (as well as the effects of the variables in the model) to vary over time. The results of our estimation are presented in Table II.

Table 2. Logit results for tactical voting in Canada elections, 1988–2000

(a) Coefficient Estimates for the 1988 Elections

Variables	1988 Election
Competitiveness	−8.204**** (1.178)
Closeness	.051 (.429)
Competitiveness * Closenness	1.118 (3.125)
PC supporters	.103 (.297)
Liberal supporter#	
NDP supporter	−.756** (.365)
Constant	−.888** (.359)
−2LL	436.270
N	1962

(b) Coefficient estimates for Quebec province, 1993–2000

Variables	1993 Election	1997 Election	2000 Election
Competitiveness	−12.124**** (1.931)	−10.733**** 2.734	−6.344** (2.691)
Closeness	.403 (.596)	.404 (.823)	.665 (1.039)
Competitiveness * Closeness	6.926** (3.257)	6.336* (3.959)	3.890 (2.987)
PC supporter	−.497 (.622)	.286 (.611)	−.745 (1.098)
Liberal supporter	−1.329** (.601)	−.623 (.840)	−.268 (.609)
NDP supporter#		−.463 (1.140)	
Reform/Alliance#			−18.305 (5950.930)
Bloc Quebecois#	−.893* (.504)		
Constant	−.228 (.441)	−1.406** (.627)	−2.098** (.948)
−2LL	177.343	106.668	126.313
N	889	624	657

(c) Coefficient estimates for provinces other than Quebec , 1993–2000

Variables	1993 Election	1997 Election	2000 Election
Competitiveness	−7.860**** (1.1900	−9.244**** (1.475)	−10.409****
			(2.086)
Closeness	−.511 (.600)	−.517 (.560)	−.069 (.635)
Competitiveness* Closeness	3.047 (3.605)	5.298* (2.947)	5.474 (3.531)
PC supporter#	.128 (.499)	1.035** (.447)	
Liberal supporter	.238 (.325)	.689 (.463)	1.022* (.577)
NDP supporter	.701* (.401)	.642 (.445)	.256 (.661)
Reform/Alliance#			.555 (.618)
Constant	−1.545**** (.307)	−1.859**** (−428)	−2.160**** (.585)
−2LL	457.597	349.347	199.366
N	1845	1559	1160

Cell entries are logit coefficients with robust standard errors in parentheses
* p < .1, ** p < .05; *** p < .01; **** p < .001
# The reference categories are: Liberal supporter for 1988, NDP supporter for Quebec 1993, Bloc Quebecois supporter for Quebec 1997 and 2000. Reform supporter for outside of Quebec 1993 and 1997, and PC supporter for outside of quebec 2000.

As expected, COMPETITIVENESS is negatively related to tactical voting and is statistically significant. CLOSENESS and the interaction term roughly correspond to the expected signs with varying degrees of statistical significance across elections.[7] The coefficients for the party support dummy variables indicate that even after controlling for CLOSENESS and COMPETITIVENESS, supporters of some parties were more likely to vote tactically in certain elections.

The substantive effects of an independent variable can best be evaluated by looking at how a switch from one value to another contributes to changes in the predicted probability of tactical voting. From the results for 1988, the model predicts an increase of 2.2% in the likelihood of a voter to cast a ballot strategically if he or she expected his or her favorite party to receive 30% rather than 40% of the vote. In a similar scenario in Quebec, changes in the probability of tactical voting produced by the impact of party competitiveness in the

1993, 1997, and 2000 elections amount to 3.6%, 1.4%, and 1.8% respectively. Further, the overall probabilities calculated for supporters of each party, while keeping all other variables constant, show that levels of likelihood for tactical voting vary across parties, elections, and regions. The highest overall probability outside Quebec is estimated for NDP, 2.9% in 1993, and for PC, 2.1% in 1997.

Overall, the results support the literature that suggests that tactical voting is sensitive to the electoral context. As a result, although national rates of tactical voting have consistently averaged 3% to 4% in these elections, there is reason to believe that rates of tactical voting may actually be significantly higher in certain constituencies due to variations in the electoral context at the constituency level.

Estimating Tactical Voting at the Constituency Level

Having estimated our individual-level model of tactical voting for each election, we now shift the analysis to the constituency level, where our units of analysis become political parties rather than individuals. Our ultimate goal at this stage is to estimate the extent and source of tactical voting within each district. We accomplish this task in a series of steps. First, we estimate the rate of tactical voting for each party within each district.[8] This rate, denoted as TACTPARTYi (where the subscript i indicates party i), is calculated by using observed contextual data for the constituency and the coefficient estimates from the appropriate equation in Table II. In other words, for each election we calculate:

$$TACTPARTY_i = 1/ (1+ e^{\alpha\ +\ \beta COMPETITIVENESS\ +\ \beta CLOSENESS\ +\ \beta COMPETITIVENESS^*\ CLOSENESS+ \sum \beta PARTYSUPPORTER)})$$

for each party within each district, where the coefficients are estimates generated by the logit model above, COMPETITIVENESS, CLOSENESS, and the interaction term are based on actual election results for the district, and PARTYSUPPORTER variables are party dummy variables.

For using our estimate of TACTPARTYi along with the observed vote share for each party, we calculate the percentage of voters (across the entire district) who consider party i their most preferred party but instead voted tactically. More formally, we define TACTDISTi as:

$$TACTDIST_i = (\#TacticalVotersPreferringParty_i/\#AllVotersintheDistrict)*100$$

which can be calculated as follows:

$$TACTDIST_i = [\%VOTE_i/(1 - TACTPARTY_i)] - \%VOTE_i$$

where $\%VOTE_i$ denotes the observed vote share of party I.

Note that the first component of this equation [$\%VOTE_i/(1-TACTPARTY_i)$] is equal to the sum of two groups of voters: those who prefer party i, and those who prefer another party but voted strategically for party i. By subtracting the proportion of the district voting for party i ($\%VOTE_i$), we are thus left with the percentage of voters who prefer, but do not vote for, party i ($TACTDIST_i$).

Calculating Sincere Supporters at the Constituency Level

The final step in the analysis is to estimate election results that would have been observed if tactical voting had not occurred. First, we estimate vote flows (that is, how tactical voters distributed their tactical votes across parties) using national-level data.[9] Let $FLOWRATE_{ji}$ be the proportion of tactical voters from party j that give their votes to party i. Then the percentage of voters who prefer party j but vote tactically for party i, to be denoted $VOTEFLOW_{ji}$, can be estimated as follows:

$$VOTEFLOW_{ji} = TACTDIST_j * FLOWRATE_{ji}, j = 1,2,3^{10}$$

where $FLOWRATE_{ji}$ is the proportion of tactical voters from party j that give their votes to party I.

Our ultimate goal at this stage of the analysis is to estimate the distribution of sincere preferences within each constituency. This requires us to estimate for each party in each riding the proportion of voters who regard that party as their most preferred. To accomplish this, we rely on the Equation (5), which decomposes sincere vote shares for each party into several constituent parts. The percentage of voters who consider party i their most preferred party, to be denoted SINCEREi can then be estimated as:

$$SINCERE_i = \%VOTE_i + \sum_{j=1}^{3} VOTEFLOW_{ij} - \sum_{j=1}^{3} VOTEFLOW_{ji} \quad [5]$$

where VOTEFLOWij is the proportion of voters who consider party i their most preferred party but vote for some other party j. In other words, this final equation states that the percentage of the district electorate that (sincerely) prefers party I (SINCEREi) is equal to the percentage of voters that voted for party i (%VOTEi), plus (i) the percentage of voters who prefer party i but voted for party j, minus (ii) the percentage of voters who preferred party j but voted for party i.

Results: The Impact of Tactical Voting in Canadian Elections, 1988–2000

Using this logic, along with the coefficient estimates from the logit model above and observed electoral data from the elections of 1988 through 2000, we estimated the percentage of sincere voters for all major parties within each riding. Based on our estimates of tactical voting for each of the parties in these elections, it appears that there is considerable variation in the rate of tactical voting across ridings, parties, and elections. This is evident from examining Figure 1, which displays frequency distributions of estimated constituency-level tactical voting rates for the parties in these elections. In Figure 1(a), we can see that very little tactical voting occurred among PC supporters in 1988. This is not surprising, as they had little reason to expect their party to lose in that year (see Table I). Apparently the situation changed in 1993 and 1997 when there were significantly more ridings than before where the rate of tactical voting was higher. On the other hand, the pattern of tactical voting is quite different among Liberal supporters, shown in Figure 1(b), as the Liberal Party maintained the majority of the parliamentary seats since 1993. In Figure 1(c), we see that tactical voting is widespread among the NDP supporters as their party remains a minor party throughout the period of analysis. Quite interestingly, the BQ supporters remained quite loyal to their party, as can be seen in Figure 1(d), showing the regional character of the party.

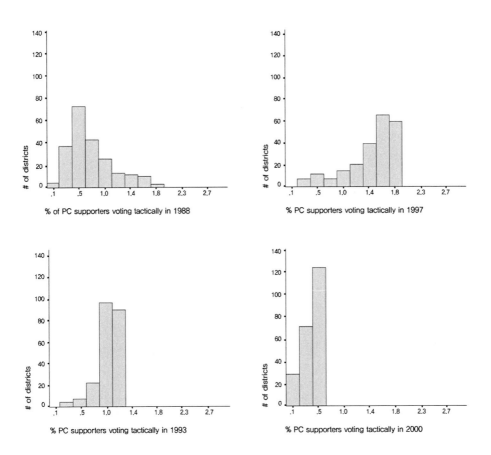

Figure 1. Predicted levels of tactical voting among various party supporters, 1988–2000

Given the variation in the rate of tactical voting across parties and the many idings where rates of tactical voting are predicted to have been high, the next question to be answered is whether or not tactical voting had a significant effect on election outcomes. We address this question by comparing observed election outcomes to estimated election outcomes assuming sincere voting. For each of the elections, this comparison is presented in the form of a cross-tabulation in Table III.

Table 3. Predicted winners based on sincere voting, by actual winners, 1988–2000

Predicted Winner Based on Sincere Voting	Actual Winner (Reflecting Tactical Voing			
1988 Election	PC	Liberal	NDP	Total
PC	169	0	0	169
Liberal	0	83	0	83
NDP	0	0	43	43
Total	169	83	43	395

1993 Election: **	PC	Liberal	NDP	Reform	Bloc	Total
PC	2	0	0	0	0	2
Liberal	0	172	0	0	3	175
NDP	0	0	9	1	0	10
Reform	0	3	0	51	0	54
Bloc	0	0	0	0	51	51
Total	2	175	9	52	54	292
1997 Election: **	PC	Liberal	NDP	Reform	Bloc	Total
PC	20	0	0	0	0	20
Liberal	0	154	0	0	0	154
NDP	0	0	21	2	0	23
Reform	0	0	0	58	0	58
Bloc	0	1	0	0	44	45
Total	20	155	21	60	44	300

2000 Election	PC	Liberal	NDP	Alliance	Bloc	Total
PC	12	0	0	0	0	12
Liberal	0	172	0	0	1	173
NDP	0	0	13	0	0	12
Reform	0	0	0	66	0	66
Bloc	0	0	0	0	37	37
Total	12	172	13	66	38	301

* An Independent won a seat in the 1997 election
** Two ridings were excludes from the analysis for the 1993 elections for lack data. The Liberals won in both of them, which makes their seat 177.

To see the impact of tactical voting on the seat distribution within the parliament, we simply need to examine the off-diagonal entries of the Table III, where non-zero entries (in italic) represent election outcomes that would have differed if tactical voting had not occurred. An examination of the results yields some interesting findings. First, the predicted effect of tactical voting on actual election outcomes was minimal across the four elections we study in this paper. Tactical voting did not change election outcomes in any ridings in 1988. Tactical voting altered the outcomes in 7, 3, and 1 ridings respectively in the 1993, 1997, and 2000 elections. We list those ridings in which the winners changed due to tactical voting in the Appendix. Our result is rather consistent with what Kim and Fording (2001) found in the four British elections they analyzed.[11] Tactical voting did not alter who would get into government in any of the four elections in Canada we study in this paper.

Our results show that in 1993, the Liberals came out even after tactical voting. That is, the party secured three extra seats due to the Reform Party supporters' tactical voting, but lost three seats in Quebec since its own supporters tactically voted for the BQ. In 1997, the Reform Party acquired two extra seats due to the NDP supporters" tactical voting, while the BQ lost a seat to the Liberals in Quebec. This situation was reversed in 2000 when the BQ gained a seat in Quebec due to the tactical voting of the Liberal supporters.

Table IV displays the distribution of vote flows from party to party, based on samples of tactical voters from the four elections. In 1993, the tactical voters from the Reform Party gave a majority of their votes (61.5%) to the Liberals, which may explain the seat swing from the former to the latter. Table IV, which contains the national aggregate figures, shows that 29.2% of the tactical voters from the Liberals gave their votes to the BQ in 1993. Looking at the province of Quebec only, however, 88.9% of the tactical voters from the Liberals supported the BQ.[12] This may explain the three-seat swing between the two parties in Quebec.

Table IV also indicates that, in 1997, outside Quebec, the Liberals were the most frequent second choice of PC, NDP, and Reform voters alike. In Quebec, BQ voters' second choices were primarily Conservatives. These findings about second-choice party challenge the view that the supporters of the PC and the Reform Party 'on the right' see themselves as part of a single ideo logical family, and so Reform voters' second choice might well be the Conservative party and vice versa. Rather, the Liberal Party was acceptable to a definite majority of Canadians in 1997. Our findings are consistent with Nevitte et al. (2000: 15–16).

Although our projections indicate that tactical voting has had only a modest impact on election outcomes, it is not immediately obvious why this might be the case. Two possibilities seem likely. The first reason is inherent in the nature of the relationship between electoral context and tactical voting. The individual-level analysis suggests that the level of support of one's party is the most important factor in determining the probability of tactical voting. As a result, even though there are many instances of predicted tactical voting rates of 6% or more, these high rates of tactical voting are coming from parties that enjoy relatively little district support and thus have relatively few tactical votes to give.

Table 4. Distribution of tactical votes across parties

1988 Election

		Sincere Preference of Respondent			Total
		PC	Liberal	NDP	
Vote of Respondent	PC		36 69.2%	8 66.7%	44 38.9%
	Liberal	38 77.6%		4 33.3%	42 37.2%
	NDP	11 22.4%	16 30.8%		27 23.9%
Total		49 100%	52 100%	12 100%	113 100%

1993 Election

		Sincere Preference of Respondent					Total
		PC	Liberal	NDP	Reform	Bloc	
Vote of Respondent	PC		5 14.3%	1 5.9%	4 30.8%	16 66.7%	26 25.2%
	Liberal	9 64.3%		13 76.4%	8 61.5%	7 29.2%	37 35.9%
	NDP	1 7.1%	9 25.7%		1 7.7%	1 4.1%	12 11.7%
	Reform	2 14.3%	13 37.1%	2 11.8%		0 0%	17 16.5%
	Bloc	2 14.3%	8 22.9%	1 5.9%	0 0%		11 10.7%
Total		14 100%	35 100%	17 100%	13 100%	24 100%	103 100%

1997 Election

		Sincere Preference of Respondent					Total
		PC	Liberal	NDP	Reform	Bloc	
Vote of Respon dent	PC		14	6	8	4	32
			53.8%	31.6%	32%	50%	32.9%
	Liberal	14		10	12	3	39
		73.7%		52.6%	48%	37.5%	40.2%
	NDP	1	1		5	1	8
		5.3%	3.9%		25%	12.5%	8.2%
	Reform	2	11	3		0	16
		10.5%	42.3%	15.8%		0%	16.5%
	Bloc	2	0	0	0		2
		10.5%	0%	0%	0%		2.2%
Total		19	26	19	25	8	97
		100%	100%	100%	100%	100%	100%

2000 Election

		Sincere Preference of Respondent					Total
		PC	Liberal	NDP	Reform	Bloc	
Vote of Respondent	PC		7	2	3	2	14
			36.8%	50%	18.75%	18.2%	23%
	Liberal	4		1	13	7	25
		36.3%		25%	81.25%	63.6%	41%
	NDP	2	5		0	0	7
		18.2%	26.3%		0%	0%	11.5%
	Reform	5	6	0		2	13
		45.5%	31.6%	0%		18.2%	21.3%
	Bloc	0	1	1	0		2
		0%	5.3%	15%	0%		3.2%
Total		11	19	4	16	11	61
		100%	100%	100%	100%	100%	100%

The second reason lies in the fact that tactical voters from a given party often do not seem to agree on their second-choice parties. Based on the national-level (survey) data in Table IV, it is clear that tactical voters from the same party are far from unanimous in their selection of the party to receive their vote. Even granting the likelihood that these vote flows vary across constituencies, it is still likely that we would find considerable disagreement among party supporters could we observe district-level data, suggesting that even if there were significant numbers of tactical votes cast, these votes tend to flow in opposing directions, attenuating the cumulative impact of tactical voting. The emergence of a politically salient issue, such as Canadian approval of the proposed free trade agreement with the United States in 1988, may have an impact on tactical voters' choices in favor of a party that stands closer to their position on that particular issue dimension (Bickerton, Gagnon & Smith, 1999: 11, 13-14, 213-214). [13] Speaking of the same elections in 1988, Johnston et al. (1992) point out the voters' potential inability to 'discern a difference between the parties or candidates in question; one alternative must yield greater utility than the other' (p.198), thus obscuring individual voter's second-choice parties.

One important question that deserves attention is how certain we can be in our final results. In generating the findings reported in this study, we moved from the individual to the constituency-level analysis. We first examined the effects of the constituency-level electoral context on individual voters' strategic behavior. The relationships were established using survey data collected from nationwide samples of respondents. These results are reliable because the samples are nationwide representative. At the next (constituency) level we apply information from the estimated impact of the district political environment on the occurrence of voting for a second-choice party. This transition becomes possible because the effects of constituency-level factors rather than personal characteristics of voters are used to model the rate of tactical voting at the aggregate level.

Conclusion

Previous empirical studies using existing survey data have shown that some voters do vote tactically under single-member district plurality electoral institutions (Fisher, 1973; Curtice & Steed, 1988; Niemi, Whitten & Franklin, 1992, 1993; Evans & Heath, 1993; Blais & Nadeau, 1996; Alvarez & Nagler, 2000; Blais et al., 2002). These studies provide empirical evidence that some voters try to avoid 'wasting' their vote by not voting for their most preferred party (candidate) (under the Duvergerian reasoning). Our study over a four-election cycle in Canada further affirms the fact that, in some cases, tactical voting does indeed lead to election outcomes that are different from those in the absence of tactical behavior. This means that voters can be successful in not wasting their votes and preventing their least preferred party candidates from being elected, thus providing additional evidence that theoretical arguments based on voter rationality are to some degree valid in the real world.

At the same time, our results demonstrate that the impact of tactical voting on election outcomes, and thus on the actual distribution of seats within the parliament, has been minimal in Canada. It had no impact on the partisan composition of the government in any of the four recent elections.[14] At the microlevel, individual voters may try not to waste their votes by voting tactically. Our results suggest, however, that this individual act may not always lead to its intended outcome, which is to prevent the voters' least preferred party from winning. This may be due to a variety of reasons, including the electoral contexts within districts, the small pool of tactical voters, a lack of information about party positions, and different preferences among tactical voters themselves about their second choice parties. There may exist individual-level incentives to vote tactically and thus rationally, in the Duvergerian sense, but the collective choice may not result in the intended effect. As social choice theorists would suggest, then, individual rationality does not necessarily lead to group rationality.

As we suggested in the first section of this paper, the study of tactical voting in single member district plurality systems has been a growth industry in comparative politics. Our study, like Kim and Fording (2001), is an attempt to go beyond simply measuring the level of tactical voting after each election or evaluating the factors determining this level. Given our results in this paper, more studies about voter perception of party positions and the determinants of voters' ordinal preferences of political parties are warranted.

Appendix

Ridings where winners changed due to tactical voting in four recent Canadian elections

Electoral District		Province	Change
1988		None	
	Moose Jaw Lake Centre	Saskatchewan	NDP → Reform Party
	Souris Moose Mountain	Saskatchewan	Reform Party → LP
	Edmonton East	Alberta	Reform Party → LP
1993	Edmonton North	Alberta	Reform Party → LP
	Anjou–Rivierre–des–Praires	Quebec	LP → Bloc Quebecois
	Bourassa	Quebec	LP → Bloc Quebecois
	La Prairie	Quebec	LP → Bloc Quebecois
	Selkirk– Interlake	Minitoba	NDP → Reform Party
1997	Saskatoon–Humboldt	Saskatchewan	NDP → Reform Party
	Bellechasse–Etchemins	Quebec	Bloc Quebecois → LP
2000	Champlain	Quebec	LP → Bloc Quebecois

NOTES

1. Although the notion of tactical voting has been primarily applied to plurality electoral systems, incentives to vote tactically may exist in countries with other electoral systems as well. Some recent studies indicate that such incentives exist in electoral systems with an ordinal ballot structure (voters order preferences among the candidates) where vote transfer is possible (such as, Ireland and the Australian Senate; see Bowler & Farrell, 1991; Jesse, 1995). An incentive to act tactically on the part of small-party

supporters arises in these countries as their party fails to meet the quota and they subsequently transfer their votes to big parties (which may not be their second most preferred party). Also see Tsebelis (1986) for potential incentives for tactical voting in proportional representation (PR) systems.

2. The difficulty is stemming from differences in the survey instruments that we discuss later in the paper.

3. Nevitte et al. (2000) describe the 1993 election as follows: '[b]y most accounts the 1993 federal election was a watershed election, producing one of the most stunning outcomes in Canadian electoral history. Never before had a major political party been so thoroughly defeated as the Progressive Conservatives were in 1993. Never before had a Quebec sovereignist party found itself the Official opposition in the House of Commons. And for the first time in recent memory a new political party, Reform, surged rapidly from obscurity to mount a vigorous challenge to the political status quo. Collectively, these dramatic events seemed to signify that the once stable Canadian party system had come adrift from its moorings' (p.1).

4. If this survey question existed consistently across surveys, those who responded by saying that their preferred party had no chance of winning would be identified as tactical voters. For a controversy over which survey items represent 'tactical voting' see Evans & Heath (1993) and Niemi, Whitten & Franklin (1992, 1993).

5. Absolute numbers of tactical votes may vary slightly depending on the procedure used to identify them in the absence of direct observations on voter motivations. We feel confident in comparing the rates of tactical voting because the same method of identifying strategic votes was applied to all elections in this study.

6. Because the voters do not have complete knowledge about the election outcome at the time they make their vote choice, ideally one should use individual pre-election expectations or poll results for the contextual variables. Unfortunately, reliable district-level estimates of pre-election expectations are difficult to obtain for all ridings, because the CES interviewed a few respondents only from a number of districts. For consistency, we use actual election outcomes to determine pre-election support for all four elections we study, following the tradition of Black (1978), Cain (1978), Niemi, Whitten, and Franklin (1992), and Kim and Fording (2001).

7. Our results for the CLOSENESS coefficients did not come out statistically significant

which actually corresponds to what Blais and his co-authors found in a previous study of the 1997 election (Blais et al., 2001, see footnote 8). Given this result, we attempted an alternative specification in which we drop CLOSENESS and the interaction term from the original model, and then perform all of the following steps. Our findings from the reduced model are almost identical to the ones obtained from the full model. Thus, we choose to present results based on the original fully specified model.

8. This is the probability for a given party not to receive the support of those voters for whom this party is most preferred but not expected to win the district (see the individual-level analysis above).

9. In the ideal case, we would prefer to use constituency-level data on vote flows from one party to another. Such information, however, is not available.

10. 1, 2 for the 1988 election since there were only three major parties.

11. They found 5 to 20 seat swings in the British elections they studied. The impact of tactical voting in Canada and Britain is comparable, considering the size of the British parliament, which is roughly twice that of the Canadian parliament.

12. The vote flows were calculated from a sample of 103 tactical voters, that is, about 3.6% of the group of 1993 survey respondents (2,875) included in the individual-level analysis of tactical voting.

13. As we stated above, Table IV presents aggregate figures based on the national-level (survey) data. We can observe an interesting phenomenon by looking at different regions in Canada in 1988. Namely, even under those propitious circumstances for generating a truly national debate along the free trade issue and common national choice for Canadians, anti-free trade voters in the West tactically chose the strongest opposition party in the region, the NDP, while in the East they did the same and moved to the Liberals. The end result was to deny both parties the claim to speak with a strong national voice (Bickerton, Gagnon & Smith, 1999: 13–14).

14. A caveat applies here: our study assesses the impact of the act of tactical voting on the day of election. However, the expectation of tactical voting can shape parties' pre-election electoral strategies, such as the choice of candidates for individual ridings, the amount of party support in each riding, the cooperation with other parties, and so on. Therefore this aspect of tactical voting, although largely unobservable and thus unmeasurable, can still have great impact on election outcomes.

08.

The Role of Media in the Repression-Protest Nexus: A Game-Theoretic Model.

Heemin Kim[*], Jenifer Whitten-Woodring[**] & Patrick James[***]

* Seoul National University, Seoul, Korea

** Department of Political Science, University of Massachusetts Lowell, Lowell, MA, USA

*** Center for International Studies, Dana and David Dornsife College of Letters, Arts and Sciences, University of Southern California, Los Angeles, CA, USA

Abstract. Idealized independent media function as "watchdogs." Indeed, human rights non-governmental organizations have argued that media freedom will improve human rights. This makes sense intuitively, yet recent formal and empirical studies show that the effect of independent media varies across regime types. We explore the relationship among media, government, and citizen protest movements and employ a game-theoretic model to investigate how the equilibria vary depending on regime type and media independence. In terms of equilibrium, we find that media watchdogging is most active in autocracies (and not in democracies), especially when the government' perceived capability to repress public protest is declining. Uncertainty about the government' ability to repress plays a central role in accounting for the manifestation of media watchdogging in conjunction with public protest. Illustrations from Tunisia and North Korea are provided to highlight equilibria derived from the formal model that vary as a product of perceptions about the government' ability to repress.

While the outcomes of the wave of pro-democracy uprisings in the Middle East and North Africa remain uncertain, it is clear that media, especially social media, played an important role in facilitating these protests. Yet, the nature of this role remains contested. Idealized media function as "watchdogs," keeping government honest and watching out for citizens' interests, through investigative reporting and challenging government frames.[1] It follows that independent media should collectively keep government responsive and responsible to citizens. Indeed, human rights non-governmental organizations (NGOs) have argued that media freedom will improve government respect for human rights. This makes sense intuitively, yet recent formal and empirical studies show that the effect of independent media varies across regime types (Whitten-Woodring 2009; Whitten-Woodring and James 2012). Moreover, what happens when media are not free? In January 2011, Tunisia, Egypt, Libya, and Bahrain lacked free media. Regardless of their medium, professional journalists, bloggers, and citizens who criticized the government in these countries experienced censorship, fines, imprisonment, harassment, physical attacks, and in some cases death (Reporters Without Borders 2010; Freedom House 2011; Committee to Protect Journalists 2012). Yet some journalists and citizens in these countries persisted in using media, especially social media, to spread news and mobilize opposition. And the people protested.

There is a perception that digital media are not subject to government censorship. But NGOs that monitor media freedom offer evidence to the contrary. Reporters Without Borders and the Committee to Protect Journalists document attacks on bloggers as well as attacks on journalists—ndeed many journalists blog and many bloggers are also journalists. In fact, Snider and Faris (2011) trace the origin of Egypt' revolution to 2004 and the emergence of "cooperation between digital activists and traditional media practitioners"as well as labor and opposition groups. Although digital media are more difficult to control than print and broadcast media, governments can erect virtual borders by controlling Internet service providers, as Egypt did on January 28, 2011. Governments can also limit content through regulations, filtering technologies, and old-fashioned threats and intimidation (Freedom House 2012a).

Moreover, the same content-tagging technology that makes the web more userfriendly can be used by governments to limit citizens' access (Mailland 2010). Thus, although new communication technologies, in particular the Internet and mobile phones, have made it easier and less expensive for news media to reach audiences all over the world, these options are not impervious to government control. As with their predecessors (the telephone, telegraph, radio, and television), predictions that the Internet and mobile phones would lead to a "borderless" and unregulated information landscape have failed (Goldsmith and Wu 2008).

We consider the role of news media, traditional and digital, in domestic conflict. We first review previous research on repression and dissent and identify media as a research priority, given its relevance to opportunity and willingness to act. Then we explore the relationship among media, government, and citizen protest movements and employ a game-theoretic model to investigate how the equilibria vary depending on regime type, media independence, and the probability that government repression will be effective. In terms of equilibrium, we find that media watchdogging is most active in autocracies (and not in democracies), especially when the government' perceived capability to repress protest is declining. As our model offers different equilibria depending on the government' perceived capability to repress protest, we investigate the implications of these results with case illustrations of Tunisia and North Korea, dictatorships with controlled media but different perceived capabilities to repress public protest.

Repression and Dissent: Where the Media Come In

Just as the events commonly labeled as the Arab Spring were largely unanticipated, so too was the rapid dissolution of the Soviet Union. Protests and revolutions, like all rare events, are difficult to predict. This difficulty stems from our tendency to overlook the long-term effects of repression and the interplay between government and dissenters (Rasler 1996). Events are contingent rather than easily determined, which suggests that the nexus of repression and dissent is a topic best handled through an approach guided by the framework of opportunity and willingness (Most and Starr 1989; Cioffi-Revilla and Starr 1995). This is the path followed by Poe (2004) in a synthesis of results from studies of government decision making about repression. The overarching categories of strength and threat are used to organize a wide range of factors that identify whether a sufficient degree of opportunity and willingness exists to cause a decision to repress; among the most relevant conditions are past repression, absence of democracy, lack of economic development, war involvement, threats and dissent, population size, and military involvement in government (Poe 2004). The present study extends the opportunity and willingness frame of reference to consider the three-way interaction involving the government with the public and media.

When work on repression and dissent is reviewed, the most frequent point of departure is Tullock (1971). His formal model of revolution created a rigorous foundation; key variables are the rewards and punishments from the regime and rebel movement, along with the risk of injury from fighting. While media can be expected to emphasize public goods when reporting dissent, it is also interesting to consider the unimportance of those considerations in determining whether support for a revolutionary movement will occur. Instead, free riding and a focus on personal gain are the default expectations for any collective action movement aimed at overturning a government (Tullock 1971). From this point of view, there should be a lack of willingness to participate in collective action against the government.

Research on protest movements converged on resource mobilization and the role of political opportunities, with various studies addressing elements of both. Resource mobilization theorists characterized social movements as rational reactions to inequities in institutional power relationships that came about when a shift in resources lowered the costs of mobilization and improved the chances of success (McCarthy and Zald 1977). The challenge with this approach was to define these resources and then identify their shifts (Jenkins 1983).

How, then, might some dissent be explained, even in the face of the powerful free rider effect against willingness toward dissent? Roeder (1982) develops and tests a multivariate model of how widespread participation might come about. Time allocated to revolutionary activity rises with the degree of profitability and other characteristics of the same nature (Roeder 1982). Yet, as Mason (1984) points out, the free rider effect and pure self-interest on which it is based cannot explain how certain types of behavior begin. Why, for instance, would rioting start in the first place? This question finds an answer through public goods provision, such as taking action against government discrimination on racial grounds (Mason 1984). Thus, some combination of public and private goods can tell a more complete story about how dissent begins and is sustained once in place.

Political opportunity theorists focus on the role of political opportunities and how their expansion or contraction influences protest movements (McAdam 1982). Kuran (1989) produces a formal model that focuses on how opposition can grow. Open trials and press freedom are significant variables in creating opportunity for dissent. Interestingly, Kuran (1989) also observes that revolutionaries can be expected to conceal their relatively selfish motives in order to attract followers to the public goods-related aspects of potential regime change. Thus, greater willingness to participate should result from a principled argument against government.

Interesting to ponder, as well, is Lohmann' (1994) theorizing and casework regarding the opportunity dimension vis-a`-vis a tipping point for protest activity. Consider the German Democratic Republic (GDR) in its final stages of existence. Once able to do so, media "ed public outrage"with reports against the corrupt and incompetent government (Lohmann 1994, 43-44; see also Lohmann 2000). A fairly nuanced finding emerges from this case regarding the endogeneity of political action vis-a`-vis information. Dissent picks up momentum (and vice versa) when the level of reported participation exceeds expectations (Lohmann 1994). Under such conditions, both opportunity and willingness are enhanced.

Among the preceding studies, political liberalization, including media freedom and the emergence of digital media, would be viewed as facilitating the formation and mobilization of protest movements. Likewise, a reduction in repression would be expected to increase the likelihood of dissent. Moore (1995) provides an interim report on modeling and testing with respect to rebellion and finds several patterns in place. Solutions to the free rider problem include selective incentives, social organization and tipping phenomena; the regime, by contrast, hopes to keep people poorly informed (Moore 1995). Moore (1995) correctly dismisses theories that predict either constant or nonexistent public participation; rebellion, instead, is contingent on any number of factors—opportunity and willingness in combination.

Beyond resource mobilization theory and the political opportunity model is the question of why increased repression is sometimes met with increased dissent. Lichbach (1987) and Rasler (1996) find that dissent is fueled when government repression and concessions are inconsistent over time. Based on simulation models, Hoover and Kowalewski (1992) find a lock-in effect for dissent and repression. Intensity of dissent is driven by grievances, while its scope is more a function of resources. Dynamic modeling is identified by Hoover and Kowalewski (1992) as a priority for further work. Goldstone and Tilly (2001) suggest that, rather than conceptualizing threat (especially in the form of repression) as the opposite of opportunity, the two actually work in conjunction with each other to mobilize and shape dissent. Thus, while repression in the short term might suppress or stop protest, in the long term, it has the potential to promote protest.

Studies on repression have found that democracy and development are negatively related to repression and that domestic threats—armed internal and international conflict and protests—are positively related to repression (Poe and Tate 1994; McCormick and Mitchell 1997; Poe, Tate, and Keith 1999; Davenport and Armstrong 2004; Bueno de Mesquita et al. 2005; Shellman 2006; Davenport 2007).[2] Thus, just as repression influences dissent, dissent influences repression. Studies of the repression–issent relationship indicate an interdependence that is influenced by the decision-making context for both government and dissident leaders. Moore (2000) develops a model of state response to protest and infers that states react strategically when dissidents protest, substituting accommodation for repression and vice versa when either action has been met with protest. Evidence from Peru and Sri Lanka confirms the anticipated substitutability effect (Moore 2000). Moore (2000, 121) concedes that this model is retrospective and suggests that "useful future direction" would be a game-theoretic approach. Carey (2006) finds that regime type makes a difference in preferred tactics: "governments in democracies were most likely to accommodate the opposition and, at the same time, were least likely to display continuous repressive behavior. Also, the level of hostile state actions was lowest in democracies and highest in semi-democracies" (Carey 2006). Shellman (2006) argues that when it comes to deciding whether to cooperate, both government and opposition leaders are influenced by context, in particular, their base of support and depth of resources.

One aspect of context that earlier studies overlooked is the role of media. Media provide information, and information shapes both opportunity and willingness in repression and dissent. Therefore, we add the media as an actor in the repression– dissent nexus, and our review now shifts to media vis-a`-vis opportunity and willingness in relation to repression and dissent.

Before we can study the role of journalism or news media in the repression–issent nexus, we must clarify what we mean by journalism and news media. Across cultures and over time, people have consistently sought information about events they have not witnessed (Kovach and Rosenstiel 2007). In the repression–issent nexus, access to this information or news is critical for both government and citizens. Journalism, according to the Merriam-Webster Dictionary (2013), is "he collection and editing of news for presentation through the media." Nip (2006) divides journalism into five types: traditional journalism (professional writers and editors determine content), public journalism (professional journalists determine most of the content with some citizen input), interactive journalism (professional journalists make most of the content decisions, but citizens interact and respond to the content), participatory journalism (citizens contribute to the news content, but professionals control the presentation of the content), and citizen journalism (citizens produce and publish the content). This classification begs the question, "ó'hat makes a journalist a journalist?"A limited definition would include only those who are licensed or those who are paid, but licensing journalists is considered a form of censorship, and constraining the definition to apply only to those who are paid minimizes the contributions of citizen journalists.

For example, the Rassd News Network began in 2010 in Egypt and consisted of contributions from volunteers that were verified and posted on Twitter and Facebook by the organization' staff (Faris 2013).[3] Consider also Global Voices, a nonprofit volunteer-led project that collects and translates citizen media and blogs—specially those that focus on places and issues that are often overlooked.[4] Neither of these organizations relies on professional journalists, yet both provide a wealth of news and information.

The examples of Rassd News Network and Global Voices raise the question of the relationship between journalism and activism. While these organizations blur the lines between activism and journalism, such boundaries have always been blurred. Before bloggers and digital activists, we had the pamphleteers (who were instrumental in both the French and American revolutions). Anderson (2010) proposes that journalists, bloggers, activists, and activist-journalists are "act entrepreneurs" who provide information and seek attention. While activism is not always journalism, activists often function as journalists by providing news and information. Certainly, digital media have "lowered the barrier" and made it possible for anyone with access to the Internet to distribute news (Tsui 2010).

In a world where almost anyone can provide information, how do people decide where to go for news, and how do news providers gain an audience? As Tsui (2010, viii) puts it, "he internet presents a unique opportunity as well as a radical challenge: in a world where everybody can speak, who will listen?"ó'Journalism requires an audience, which means journalists—whether professional or citizen, whether nonprofit or for-profit—must establish and maintain credibility. To establish credibility, the news producer, whether she tweets, or broadcasts on Cable News Network (CNN), must build a reputation by consistently providing reliable information and putting that information in context. Commentary and analysis are part of journalism because people rely on journalists not just to provide news, but to help them make sense of it. With the vast amount of information available through digital media, this aspect of journalism is arguably now more important. For every medium, there is a continuum of credibility (i.e., for newspapers, the continuum might range from The National Enquirer to The New York Times. Twitter ranking along the continuum will likely depend on the number of followers and the profession of the Tweeter).

Thus, we propose that anyone who gathers, produces, and presents news to an audience is, in effect, a journalist, regardless of the type of journalism he practices or the medium he utilizes. Kovach and Rosenstiel (2007, 2) define journalism in broad and flexible terms: "we need news to live our lives, protect ourselves, bond with each other, identify friends and enemies. Journalism is simply the system societies generate to supply this news." In keeping with this definition, we conceptualize news media as encompassing any medium used to communicate news and information. Thus, we prioritize the behavior of the news media rather than the medium employed. When it comes to the repression–issent nexus, a key behavior of news media is whether to watchdog, meaning to report critically about the actions of political and economic elites. We propose that news media will watchdog only when the benefits of doing so outweigh the costs. One potential benefit is increased audience attention. Thus, a primary motivation for watchdogging is the tendency of media to audience-seek. Yet watchdog reporting can draw harsh reprisals from political and economic elites. Consequently, the decision to watchdog is made only after careful calculation. Recent research on the role of media in the repression-dissent nexus suggests that the effect of media varies depending on regime type and media independence. One study finds that media freedom in a democracy is associated with improved human rights, but media freedom in an autocracy is associated with decreased human rights (Whitten-Woodring 2009). Another study employs a system of static equations that indicate protest is most likely when democracy reaches its highest level (regardless of the level of media independence) and least likely when democracy is not present and media are independent (Whitten-Woodring and James 2012). As expected, the model predicts that repression is at its maximum value when both democracy and media independence are absent (Whitten-Woodring and James 2012). We build on these studies and develop a game-theoretic model to explore the strategic interaction between and among government, protesters, and media.

Although research on repression and dissent often relies on news media accounts of these events to generate data, most studies overlook the role of media in these events.[5] This shortcoming has several consequences. Davenport (2010, 3) argues that not only do news media tend to under report both repression and dissent, but those who rely on news media tend to overlook the Rashomon Effect, which is that different sources will have "widely varying accounts of exactly who did what to whom."[6] In short, reports on repression and dissent will vary, depending on the type of source and medium.

Studies of mainstream media in the United States find that professional norms lead journalists to privilege official accounts over those of dissenters (Mermin 1999; Bennett 1990; Bennett, Lawrence, and Livingston 2007; Entman

2004). Bennett (1990) theorizes that journalists' reliance on official sources leads them to "index" or mirror the debates of these elites. When there is little or no debate among political and/or economic elites, there will be virtually no challenge to the government' characterization of the issue. A case in point is the failure of the US media to challenge the Bush Administration' rationale for invading Iraq (Bennett, Lawrence, and Livingston 2007). Entman (2004, 5) proposes a cascading network of frames which begins when elites "frame'r' stories for news media by 'r'electing and highlighting some facets of events or issues, and making connections among them so as to promote a particular interpretation, evaluation, and/or solution.'r'Both indexing and the cascading frames concept suggest news media in the United States are far less independent than the much idealized role of a watchdog press would suggest. Indeed, even Carl Bernstein and Bob Woodward, the reporters of the Watergate scandal that brought down President Richard Nixon, relied on leaks from official sources (Schudson 2003). Journalists work in competitive high-pressure environments where credibility is crucial, and official sources typically appear more credible to journalists and their audiences. Thus, although news media in the United States are considered among the most free in the world, they often fail to function independently.[7]

Just as media freedom does not guarantee that media will serve as a "4th estate" and keep government in line, a lack of media freedom does not always prohibit media from acting as watchdogs. Reporters in countries that lack media freedom have been known to risk their lives to provide information to their audiences. Consider Lasantha Wickrematunga, the Sri Lankan editor known for his critical reporting of the government, who in 2009 predicted his own murder in a posthumously published editorial. Also consider Russian journalist Natalya Estemirova who in 2009 was kidnapped and killed following her "relentless"reporting of government violations of human rights (Committee to Protect Journalists 2009). That same year, Orel Sambrano, a Venezuelan broadcast journalist, was gunned down in retaliation for his reporting on ties between drug traffickers and local businessman (Committee to Protect Journalists 2009). 2009 was a particularly deadly year for journalists because of the mass killing of fifty-seven people, thirty-two of whom were journalists or media support workers in the Philippines in November. Yet journalists are killed every year, and many of them are killed because they are trying to fulfill a watchdog role in countries where the media are not free.

Interestingly, in many of the attacks mentioned previously, journalists were not just watchdogging, they were giving voice to those in opposition to the government. This points to the possibility that sometimes the motivation to watchdog, in particular to criticize the government, stems from journalists bandwagoning with the opposition.[8] This conceptualization of media bandwagoning borrows from the Indexing hypothesis—he idea that any debate in the news media does not originate in the news media and is really just a reflection of the debate among elites—but in this case the opposition may not be from the elites. Instead, the opposition could represent a potentially large and receptive audience. And news media, whether they face commercial pressures or partisan pressure to mobilize, crave large audiences, because regardless of the type of journalism or the medium, journalists must attract an audience to gain influence and power.

The emergence of the Internet and other new technologies including smart phones gave rise to hopes that these media could circumvent government control. However, the same technologies can be used by government to control media (Lessig 2001; Benkler 2006). While social media and mobile phones can facilitate protest mobilization, governments can silence mobile phones, shut down Internet traffic, and employ social media to hunt down protesters. The first hint of the impending government crackdown on the 2011 protest in Bahrain came when cell phone signals were cut off in the area around Pearl Roundabout (Welsh 2011). On January 28, 2011, Internet traffic to and from Egypt came to an abrupt halt. Similarly, on September 29, 2007, the Burmese government completely shut down Internet connections to minimize communication during the Saffron Revolution. Following the protests in Bahrain, the government used Facebook to launch a witch hunt to track down and punish those involved in the protest and may have used a surveillance program to penetrate, control, and spy on dissenters'computers (Welsh 2011; O'rian 2012). In addition to technological controls, just like print and broadcast journalists, Internet journalists and bloggers are subject to legal threats, economic manipulation, harassment, intimidation, and attacks.

To a large extent, journalists in the United States and most other western democracies are capable of reporting critically on government policies and behavior, but they often fail to do so, perhaps (as mentioned previously) because of professional norms that encourage the privileging of official sources. Moreover, in these countries, levels of repression tend to be low, which might promote "fat-cat" media in which "a relative absence of repression can be anticipated to breed complacency into the media, leading to less watchdogging" (Whitten-Woodring and James 2012). Additionally, in both democratic and nondemocratic settings, when media are free from government censorship, they remain vulnerable to commercial pressures, which force journalists to cover stories that maximize audience size and do not antagonize advertisers or the stockholders of the corporations that own news media (Hamilton 2004). Therefore, we conceptualize media independence as the interaction of media freedom from government censorship and media freedom from commercial pressure.

Given this conceptualization, we recognize that there is no country in which media are perfectly free and no country in which media are perfectly controlled. News media are free to the degree that journalists are able to report without influence— whether that influence comes from government or market forces. Since all media must compete for audience and access to sources of information, news media are never completely independent. Self-published bloggers and established reporters for the British Broadcasting Corporation (BBC) must maintain relationships with their sources and credibility with their audience. While it is true that most independent media are in democratic countries, there are relatively independent media in nondemocracies (Mexico 1960 to 1996, Tanzania 1992 to 2007, Nepal 1980 to 1992), and democracies with media that lack independence (Colombia 2000 to 2005, Portugal 1976 to 1994, Poland 1991 to 1997, Mauritius 1970 to 1977, Thailand 1992 to 1997).[9]

Thus, we consider the influence of both media independence and regime type as we construct our model. The preceding factors, along with the likelihood of successful repression, combine to set the levels of opportunity and willingness for participant action in the game: media watchdogging (or not), public protest (or not), and government repression (or reform).

The Model

Given the uncertainty associated with pathways that include repression, we add a move by "nature" at the beginning of the game (we discuss this uncertainty subsequently). Nature decides the probability that government repression, if it happens, will succeed, say, p, before the regular players start the game. The media, people, and government do not know nature' choice, although they will possess some subjective beliefs about it. At each decision node, connected with dotted lines in Figure 1, players can update their beliefs (probabilities) based on the information, both endogenous and exogenous, accumulated up to that point, which we call Bayesian updating.

Our three-player game (portrayed in Figure 1) takes place in a state where we assume there is always some level of opposition. Because they have access to information, the media begin the game. They can watchdog (sometimes this watchdogging will mean bandwagoning with the opposition, but sometimes watchdogging is independently reporting on government wrongdoing) or not, with implications for opportunity and willingness among the public to protest. The media make this decision without knowing if the government will be successful in repressing protest, if it happens. Then the people can protest or not. They make this decision after watching the media' decision to watchdog or not, but without knowing the likelihood of success for government repression. Finally, the government can repress or reform. It makes this decision only if people choose to protest and without knowing if its repression will succeed or not. In this sense, we use the term repression in this article in a specific way in that it happens as a response to people' protest.[10]

Therefore, if the people do not protest, the government does not need to take any action, and the status quo will continue. Note that the status quo exists in two variants: SQA and SQB. These are distinguished on the basis of media watchdogging being present (SQA) or absent (SQB). While neither variant entails public protest, player payoffs can vary between them nonetheless.[11]

The government' action, labeled "repress,"and the resulting outcomes (repress 1 and repress 2) have a unique aspect. The fact that the government chooses to repress does not necessarily mean that the protesting people will be successfully repressed.[12]

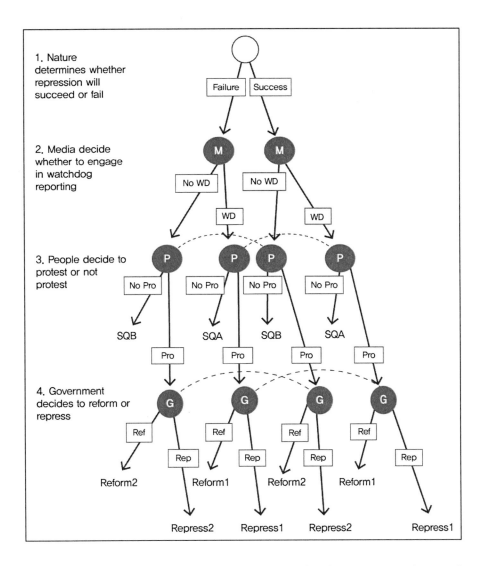

Figure 1. When the media join the game: watchdogging, protest, and repression

That is, the repression-related outcomes simply refer to whatever happens following the government' pursuit of repression. These outcomes may look quite different depending on whether the government successfully represses the protesting public.

Unsuccessful repression can mean anything in substantive terms—violence followed by reprisal or even system collapse—but obviously entails significant uncertainty. For example, the Mubarak regime in Egypt resorted to its usual repressive tactics against protesters from January 2011 onward. Conflict escalated and ultimately Mubarak lost power. However, given recent tensions involving the legislature and judiciary, uncertainty continues about leadership in Cairo. Uncertainty, in fact, would be the one constant feature of events in Egypt from the early days of January onward.

Because of this uncertainty, our players, the media, the people, and the government do not have complete information about whether the government' potential repression will succeed or not. The sources of this uncertainty can include government' resolve, whether the repressing forces (the military or the police) will stay loyal to the current regime, international environment, a triggering mechanism (an event or an accident) that will turn people more violent, the existence of a potential alternative to the current regime, the level of accumulated deprivation and anger among people, and the list can go on.

We first establish general principles about the preferences of our players: the media, people, and the government. Then we move on to specify ordinal preference orderings under different circumstances below. (More detailed information about the preferences of the players in various scenarios can be found in Tables A-X in the appendix, which is available at http://faculty.uml.edu/Jenifer_WhittenWoodring/ index.aspx.)

Consider first an expression for the government' utility:

$$U_{Gov} = P(\text{MPower}) \times B(\text{MPower}) - C(\text{Repression}).$$

That is, the payoff to the government is the probability of maintaining power multiplied by the benefit of maintaining power minus the cost of repression. For outcomes in which people do not protest or the government reforms, the second term drops out because the cost of repression is 0. The probability of maintaining power is high when people do not protest, but it goes down when people protest and the government reforms. The probability, benefit, and the cost change as the system moves from autocracy to democracy and from controlled to independent media. This variation is true for the media and the people as well and thus shapes the scenarios in the next section of this article.

Costs ensue from repression, even for the government itself. Potential losses are both material and ideational. Repression, in the material sense, damages or destroys human and physical capital. In addition, repression diminishes the level of social capital. This is significant because social capital is an important indicator of prosperity. When social capital—and especially its close associate, generalized trust—is reduced, the implications are negative for the performance of state and society (Uslaner 2002). Add to this the costs at the international level in terms of diminished standing, and repression can seem quite unattractive as a policy option. States will vary in sensitivity to the range of costs involved in use of repression, with only a few being relatively impervious to these considerations.

Utility for the media takes the following form:

$$U_{Med} = P(\text{MImpact}) \times B(\text{MImpact}) - C(\text{Watchdog}).$$

That is, the payoff to the media is the probability of making an impact (i.e., increased attention) multiplied by the benefit of making an impact minus the cost of watchdogging. When the media do not watchdog, then the second term drops out. The probability of making an impact is higher when the media watchdog than not and when the people protest (following the lead of the watchdogging media). As with the government, calculations shift as the system moves from autocracy to democracy and from controlled to independent media.

For example, the probability of making an impact goes up when the system moves toward independence because independent media have more credibility. Benefits to the media could take the form of prestige in society, along with pecuniary rewards that ensue from the news becoming more highly valued. This is interesting because, if we think of controlled media as wanting to move to become more independent (to break through the control and become more powerful), then it follows that payoffs from making an impact diminish as media become more free.

This plays in well with the concept of "at Cat Media" independent yet lazy media that fail to watchdog even though they are free to do so. Again, the lack of critical coverage by US media in the buildup to the Iraq War comes readily to mind. Another aspect is the "tabloidization" of media. In part because of market pressures, when the regime is relatively benign, news coverage will tend to focus on the trivial activities of celebrities rather than traditional hard news. Similarly, the potential benefits of making an impact are greater in a nondemocracy. This is because more autocratic states engage in practices that the majority of the public finds unappealing, such as corruption and unequal application of the law.

Utility for the people is calculated as follows:

$$U_{Peo} = P(\text{Reform}) \times B(\text{Reform}) - C(\text{Protest}).$$

That is, the payoff to the people is the probability of reform multiplied by the benefit of reform minus the cost of protest. When the people do not protest, the second term drops off. The probability, benefit, and the cost change as the system moves from autocracy to democracy and from controlled to independent media. For example, the cost of protest is higher in an autocracy than a democracy. Consider, for example, the respective fates of the Occupy movement in the United States versus the Saffron Revolution in Myanmar/Burma. Occupy experienced some limited coercion at the hands of the authorities, but its decline cannot be explained via repression. The demise of the antigovernment movement in Myanmar/Burma during 2007, by contrast, can be traced directly to massive retaliatory violence on the part of the government.

Scenarios

For now, let us assume that political systems are either democratic or autocratic and that the media can be either independent or controlled. Obviously, this is a simplification of reality, as there can be different intermediate levels of democracy and media independence. Nevertheless, we simplify the reality here as a first step to develop testable hypotheses. Once we test our propositions, we might be able to relax our assumptions and develop more nuanced treatments of situations that depart from the binary treatment of the political system and the media type.

Based on our simplification, we can develop four possible scenarios of political system/media type combinations:

(1) Scenario 1: Democracy + Independent Media
(2) Scenario 2: Democracy + Controlled Media
(3) Scenario 3: Autocracy + Independent Media
(4) Scenario 4: Autocracy + Controlled Media

For each of the four scenarios mentioned previously, we define ordinal preference functions for the three players in our model (a) when the perceived probability of successful government repression is high and (b) when it is low. (As mentioned previously, specific information on these preference orderings and justifications is in Tables A-X in the Appendix available at http://faculty.uml.edu/Jenifer_Whitten-Woodring/index.aspx.) We opt for ordinal preferences, because assigning numbers (adopting cardinal preferences) for individual outcomes would be too arbitrary.

A downside of this strategy is that it becomes nearly impossible to solve for precise Perfect Bayesian Equilibria (PBE) when the level of uncertainty about the likelihood of successful government repression is high, because we do not have numbers to rely on (unless we try to define ordinal preference functions for an infinite number of different levels of uncertainty). We can, however, make informed conjectures about the location of the PBE on the outcome space based on the patterns of solutions when the level of uncertainty is low.[13]

Now we solve for the equilibria of our game under four different scenarios. With the solutions in hand, we discuss what to expect when the players are uncertain about the likelihood of successful repression, that is, the probability is not close to 0 or 1. The preference ordering and justification for each scenario appears in the Appendix (available at http://faculty.uml.edu/Jenifer_WhittenWoodring/index.aspx).

Summary of Findings from the Formal Model

First, when it is nearly certain that the upcoming government repression will be successful, all four scenarios returned the same equilibrium, SQB. Whether you live in a democracy or not, and whether the media are independent or not, the media will not watchdog, and the people will not protest when they are certain that the government repression will be effective. In this situation, nothing happens, and the status quo is maintained.

Second, as the probability of successful repression approaches zero, the story becomes more interesting. In scenarios 1 and 2 (democracy-independent media combination and democracy-controlled media combination), the result is the same: SQB. That is, we do not expect to see reform, even if there is room for it, whether the media are independent or controlled in democracies. This may be because the marginal value of reform is regarded as low by both the public and media. With voting available as the mechanism to "how the rascals out," other means toward reform that would include collective action are just not worth the expenditure of resources. While opportunity may exist, willingness to act does not. Of course, this vision also includes a dose of complacency and even naivete'; can the electoral system really be counted upon to address all of society' ills?

But in scenarios 3 and 4 (autocracy-independent media combination and autocracy-controlled media combination), the outcome becomes reform 1. That is, the media watchdog, the people protest, and the government reforms, only when the government repression is perceived to be ineffective in autocracies.

Somewhat surprisingly, whether the media are controlled or independent does not make a difference in the outcome of our game under these scenarios. That is, it does not matter whether the media are currently controlled or independent; it is the future prospect of government' ability to suppress potential citizen protests that induces media to watchdog regardless of their independence. In sum, (1) perceived low probability of successful government repression and (2) the existence of autocracy combine to create the opportunity and willingness to reform the system. The independence of media does not matter.[14]

Third, our model predicts either status quo or reform. Yet, we actually see repression in the real world. Now let us go back to one of the points made earlier. The "repress" outcome simply means that it follows the government action of "repress" and does not guarantee successful repression. The government may try to repress and fail to subdue protesters. In many real-world situations, it is not clear whether the repression will succeed or fail. Our findings mentioned earlier are based on the assumption of near certainty of success or failure of government repression. As we also stated previously, it is difficult to find the PBE of our game when the uncertainty of successful repression is high because we adopt the ordinal scale of preferences. But the behavior of PBEs on the outcome space shows that repression happens in the real world only when the probability is not high, not low, and actually somewhere in the middle (and thus, people are uncertain). So, repression is not a product of power, but of uncertainty!

Fourth, neither SQA nor reform 2 results from the initial version of our model. These outcomes occur when there is watchdogging without protest, and protest without watchdogging that produces reform, respectively. Watchdogging and protest are intertwined in our model now. This accords with a certain sense of rationality under simplified, even extreme conditions. Watchdogging serves as a signal for the people in that it indicates the media are bandwagoning with the opposition. If it takes place and the people do not protest, that would point toward a failed assessment on the part of the media. Why take the risk of allying with the opposition unless there is a very high likelihood of the people' action in response, in particular mobilization of the opposition?

Thus, the absence of SQA as an outcome under simplified conditions of pure autocracy or democracy, along with completely free or constrained media and firm beliefs about the likelihood of successful government repression, seems appropriate. The fact that reform 2 never occurs also makes sense because the people would need to protest without a prior signal from media watchdogging and then experience a reward, via government reform, for their actions. This combination of action and inaction among the players emerges as very unlikely given the clear conditions, summarized a moment ago, regarding form of government, degree of media freedom and prospects for successful government repression.

The predictions of our game are in keeping with the findings of empirical studies of protest and of media watchdogging: both are rare events. Additionally, our results have important implications for the sampling of empirical studies of repression and reform. Our model predicts that when the likelihood of successful repression is low, government reforms; when it is high, people simply do not protest and accept the status quo. As empiricists have focused on reform (and repression), something they can observe, they are missing the important nonevent, status quo, a` la King, Keohane, and Verba (1994). We claim that the studies of repression and reform must include such non-events from now on in order to identify causal mechanisms.

Empirical Examples: Tunisia and North Korea

Case Selection

In order to examine our game' predictions in context, we employ the "most similar method" of case selection and focus on two states which have similar regimes (dictatorships) and media systems (controlled), but which had different perceived probabilities of successful repression: Tunisia and North Korea. According to Gerring and Seawright (2007), this method is appropriate for hypothesis generating and hypothesis testing. With the selection of these cases, we are testing the predictions of our model and identifying hypotheses about the causes of repression and protest for future empirical studies. At the beginning of 2010, both of these states had long histories of repression, marked by relatively little protest and little or no media watchdogging. But in 2010, several events may have encouraged the people of Tunisia to believe their leader was vulnerable (in other words, the perceived probability of successful repression had decreased). In contrast, in spite of a change of dictators with the death of Kim Jong-il in December 2011, the relationship between the people of North Korea and the government remains unchanged and we propose the perceived probability of successful repression remains high.

Tunisia

Writing just before the Arab Spring, Howard (2011) predicted that new technologies will not cause revolutions, but that revolutions, when they come, will be "digitized." He argues that "New information technologies do not topple dictators; they are used to catch dictators off-guard" (Howard 2011, 12). Indeed, this is pretty much what transpired in Tunisia in December 2010.

Since it gained independence from France in 1956, and prior to the uprising in 2010, Tunisia was a dictatorship, for the first three decades under Habib Bourguiba, and following a bloodless coup in 1987, under Zine el Abindine Ben Ali. In 2010, just before the Arab Spring, Tunisia was decidedly nondemocratic. Based on the study by the Center for Systemic Peace, Tunisia' Polity score was 4 in 2010. The Polity scale ranges from 10 [most autocratic] to 10 [most democratic] (Marshall, Gurr, and Jaggers 2010).

Media in Tunisia were not free to criticize government in 2010, and journalists who did so faced harassment, physical attacks, fines, and prison sentences (Freedom House 2011). Based on Freedom House' (2011) Freedom of the Press Index, Tunisia' Freedom of the Press score was 85 in 2010—he index ranges from 0 (completely free) to 100 (completely controlled). However, the Tunisian government did not have complete control of media. Almost all newspapers in Tunisia were privately owned, but newspapers and reporters that engaged in watchdog reporting faced threats and intimidation. During President Ben Ali' tenure, more than 100 journalists were exiled (Freedom House 2011). Although nearly 40 percent of Tunisians used the Internet in 2010, the government maintained control over Internet cafes and frequently blocked Internet sites.

In spite of the potential for harsh penalties, some Tunisian journalists and citizens used traditional and digital media to spread news that was critical of their government:

In January 2010, television correspondent Fahem Boukadous was sentenced to four years in prison for his 2008 coverage of violent labor demonstrations. Boukadous' trial lasted only 10 minutes, and he was convicted of "belonging to a criminal association" and "spreading materials likely to harm public order." His family expressed concern over prison authorities'failure to treat Boukadous' increasingly severe asthma attacks, and Boukadous himself protested this mistreatment with a hunger strike. (Freedom House 2011)

In 2004, Tunisian bloggers created Nawaat.org and used the website to document government corruption and social unrest (Center for International Media Assistance [CIMA] 2011). Among other expose's, in 2007, Nawaat blogger Riadh Guerfali (under the pen name Astrubal) uploaded a video on YouTube that documented the president' jet arriving at various destinations in Europe while Ben Ali was in Tunisia, and asked who was using the jet. It turned out Ben Ali' wife was using the jet for shopping.[15] As a result, the government blocked YouTube.

When WikiLeaks released the diplomatic cables, Guerfali established the website TuniLeaks to showcase the cables pertaining to Tunisia (Lyon 2011). WikiLeaks founder Julian Assange claimed these releases helped spark the uprising in Tunisia and some went so far as to call it the WikiLeaks revolution (Davis 2011). While these claims may be overblown, the cables did reveal to the people of Tunisia that Washington did not consider Ben Ali to be a "lose ally" of the United States. In addition, transmissions like the one below suggested that US diplomats shared some of the Tunisians'frustrations with Ben Ali:

President Ben Ali is aging, his regime is sclerotic and there is no clear successor. Many Tunisians are frustrated by the lack of political freedom and angered by First Family corruption, high unemployment and regional inequities. (Cable from Ambassador Robert F. Godec, quoted. in "US Embassy Cables: Tunisia— US Foreign Policy Conundrum" 2010)

Whether WikiLeaks, TuniLeaks, and Nawaat helped to pave the way for the revolution, frustration over government corruption, poverty, and unemployment was simmering in Tunisia. Things exploded soon after. On December 17, 2010, twenty-six-year-old fruit vendor Mohamed Bouazizi was so humiliated and angry after a confrontation with inspectors who confiscated his scale and fruit that he set himself on fire in front of a government building. Bouazizi' self-immolation set off awave of unrest that spread from his hometown of Sidi Bouzid to rest of the country as people posted videos of Bouazizi and the protests online. Then Al Jazeera picked up the story (Fahim 2011).Bouazizi died from his injuries on January 4. Ten days later, following massive protests, BenAli fled Tunisia.

Within the framework of our model, it appears that the Tunisian situation started when parties involved lacked certainty about the government' ability to suppress the potential protest. As the situation unfolded, the government failed to decrease this uncertainty (i.e., failed to convince the media and the people that it had resources, will, and the support of the allies), which led to more watchdogging, protesting, and eventual system collapse. This may have convinced people in Egypt (and beyond), to reassess their government' ability to successfully repress.

Of course, many autocracies exist with controlled media where watchdogging and protest do not occur. Our model tells us that people in these countries fail to protest due to belief in their government' ability to suppress potential action, not because their media are controlled.

North Korea

North Korea, officially the Democratic People' Republic of Korea, has been one of the most brutal autocracies in recent history since its inception in 1948. The Soviets brought in Kim Il-sung, a former anti-Japanese guerrilla leader, as their chosen instrument. Since then, no opposition is tolerated; most rights and freedoms are not guaranteed; and Kim and his successors have served without accountability. The leadership has remained in the same family. Long before his death, Kim Il-sung named his son, Kim Jong-il, as his successor and prepared the latter as the head of the second generation of this dictatorial regime. The same pattern of personal autocracy continued, and Kim Jong-il named himself as chair of the Military Affairs Commission of the North Korean Labor

Party. The world was somewhat surprised by the sudden death of Kim Jong-il. But the country quickly adapted to the succession by Kim Jong-il' son, Kim Jong-un. The latter seems to have consolidated his power without much resistance, and repressive government in North Korea continues. This continuity is reflected in North Korea' Polity score which started out as a 7 in 1948, was downgraded to 8 in 1957 and has been at -9 since 1967 (Marshall, Gurr, and Jaggers 2010).

The North Korean government maintains complete control over media and has "the most repressive media environment in the world" (Freedom House 2011).

Although the constitution theoretically guarantees freedom of speech, constitutional provisions calling for adherence to a "collective spirit" restrict all reporting that is not sanctioned by the government in practice. All journalists are members of the ruling party, and all media outlets are mouthpieces for the regime. Under the penal code, listening to foreign broadcasts and possessing dissident publications are "crimes against the state" that carry grave punishments, including hard labor, prison sentences, and the death penalty. (Freedom House 2011)

Freedom House (2012b) has consistently awarded North Korea a score of 96 or higher (where 100 denotes a complete lack of press freedom) in its Freedom of the Press Survey; Reporters Without Borders (2013) consistently has NorthKorea at the bottom of its Press Freedom Index, and in the 2011 to 2012 index, only Eritrea is below North Korea.

The North Korean regime has maintained tight control over its entire society through military, neighborhood group watch, and brutal punishment for (potential) dissidents, usually in the form of death or forced labor camps. Control by the North Korean Labor Party, or more precisely, one of the three Kims at any time, has rarely been in doubt. Thus, we can safely say that the probability of successful repression of (potential) public protest has been very near or at a value of one (i.e., near certainty) throughout the history of the Democratic People' Republic of Korea (DPRK).

Our model predicts that, under an autocratic regime with controlled media where the probability of successful repression is high, the equilibrium path is: no watchdogging, no protest, and thus, status quo. We have no documented record of massive protest for reform in North Korea, although its citizens are known to live very difficult lives. North Korean dissidents, if they have a chance, choose to flee the country instead of organizing public protest. Many North Korean refugees live in hiding in China. Some of them make it to South Korea, while others are captured and deported back to North Korea, where they face severe consequences. So, frustrated with the equilibrium of the game, status quo, some try to "exit" the game itself.

Conclusion

This study has developed a multiplayer, game-theoretic model of government repression, media watchdogging, and public protest. It therefore goes beyond comparative statics and identifies equilibria for a range of situations that vary in terms of democracy versus autocracy, presence or absence of media freedom and player beliefs regarding success or failure of potential government efforts at repression. What emerges is a general tendency toward the staying power of the status quo. Six of the eight scenarios result in a variant of the status quo with player inaction, while in two instances the government reforms after media watchdogging and public protest. Perhaps most interesting among all of the findings is that whether media are controlled or not does not seem to impact upon their watchdogging role; rather, it is the set of beliefs held about the government' ability to repress that matters. The relatively restrictive conditions, under which watchdogging and protest occur, moreover, are consistent with the general persistence of status quo conditions around the world. The combination of opportunity and willingness required for action to ensue against a government is not common in practice.

Future research should focus on (a) obtaining higher correspondence with real conditions; (b) possible selection issues, and (c) empirical work. Each idea is presented briefly in turn.

This study compares four ideal types. Imagine instead a unit square of combined probabilities, with media independence and democracy both ranging from 0 to 1. Thresholds within the square then could be identified where there is a transition from one equilibrium to the other. Given the need to define player preferences under different levels of democracy and media independence in a non-arbitrary fashion, this appears to be a daunting task for now. It might be more practical to initiate further theorizing with the refinement that media-with the need to seek an audience may be different than other outlets, that is, explore nuances within the current media phalanx.

There may be an unobserved selection issue in the current model. If watchdogging constitutes voicing the opposition, can it occur at all if either (a) regime opponents have found a voice in other ways or (b) critics are not seeking such an outlet? In a more general sense, what does a watchdog do when there is nothing to watch? In such cases, how would one know whether the media are watchdogging or not?

Finally, empirical work could explore the scenarios developed here. Obvious questions follow from the results of this study: How would the scenarios be detected empirically? What additional cases might be considered? Answers would include developing empirical strategies for assessing the media as actors within or across cases and so on. All of this, in turn, can be expected to inform the next generation of modeling.

Supplemental Materials

The online appendices are available at http://jcr.sagepub.com/supplemental.

Notes

1. Simply put, watchdog reporting lets people know about wrongdoing that those involved—usually elites—would prefer kept secret. See Waisbord (2000).

2. Certainly, there are other influences on repression. A number of studies have considered the effect of various types of international assistance on repression, but these findings are mixed (Barratt 2004; Hafner-Burton 2005; Abouharb and Cingranelli 2009). DeMeritt and Young (2013) argued that natural resources reduce the costs of repression and found that states with more oil resources are more likely to repress.

3. In 2013, the Regional News Network (RNN) was sold for $2 million USD to a con-

sortium of businessman.

4. For more on Global Voices, see Tsui (2010).

5. We are focusing on the role of domestic media in domestic repression and dissent; we are not focusing on international media or international conflict. Several studies investigate the role of media in international conflict (Van Belle 1997; Choi and James 2006) and foreign policy (Potter and Baum 2014).

6. The Rashomon Effect is named after the 1950 film Rashomon by Akira Kurosowa. Davenport (2010) explores this effect on news coverage of the Black Panther Party in the late 1960s.

7. Freedom House' Freedom of the Press Index has consistently coded the US media as "free" (Freedom House 2012b).The United States fell from twentieth place to forty-seventh place in the Reporters Without Borders (2011–2) World Press Freedom Index, largely due to the arrests of journalists covering the Occupy protests, but even so the United States was safely in the top half of the index, which plummets to 179 (Reporters Without Borders 2013).

8. Giving voice to the opposition is just one form of watchdog behavior. Other forms of watchdog journalism that do not require the participation of the opposition include investigative reporting of political and economic elites. We also assume that there is always some level of elite misbehavior that warrants watchdog reporting.

9. Whitten-Woodring (2009) posited that just as leaders in nondemocracies hold sham elections to gain legitimacy, they might also tolerate some media independence. Egorov, Guriev, and Sonin (2009) argued that dictators, who lack revenues from natural resources, in particular oil, might tolerate independent media as an inexpensive way to keep track of lower level bureaucrats.

10. We acknowledge that government can repress in the absence of protest, but we exclude this potential scenario from our model. State action to forestall mobilization—effectively raising the estimated likelihood of successful repression—would be at the center of such a scenario, explored in a recent study of the People' Republic of China (PRC). King, Pan, and Roberts (2013) "located, downloaded, and analyzed the content of millions of social media posts originating from nearly 1,400 different social media services all over China before the Chinese government is able to find, evaluate, and censor the subset they deem objectionable." Contrary to general expectations, "posts

with negative, even vitriolic criticism of the state, its leaders, and its policies are not more likely to be censored." Instead, the censorship program focuses on "curtailing collective action by silencing comments that represent, reinforce, or spur social mobilization, regardless of content. Censorship is oriented toward attempting to forestall collective activities" (2013, 326).

11. Preference orderings for Status Quo A and Status Quo B vary depending on regime type, media independence, and the perception of the likelihood that government repression will succeed. For example, in a democracy with media independence, when chances of successful repression are high, media will prefer SQB over SQA because in the case of SQA media will have watchdogged (and that is costly), but the people choose not to protest, meaning they have basically not paid attention to the media. In contrast, in this same scenario, the people will prefer SQAover SQB because they will have gained information from the media watchdogging. More information regarding these preference orderings can be found in Tables A-X in the Appendix, available at (http://faculty.uml.edu/Jenifer_WhittenWoodring/index.aspx).

12. This also allows for the possibility of contrasting short-term and long-term effects of repression. In particular, the game allows that there may be an eventual backlash and increased mobilization even if repression is successful in silencing protesters in the short term—what Francisco (2005) terms the "dictator' dilemma."

13. The description of this process is available upon request from HeeMin Kim at recount01@snu.ac.kr.

14. One possibility for media making a difference is to report that government repression is likely to fail. That way the media may indirectly help to bring about reforms in autocracies.

15. This video is available at http://www.youtube.com/watch?v¼XRW2BJOewcc.

09.

When Meritocracies Fail

Heemin Kim & Glenn R. Parker

Department of Political Science, Florida State University, Tallahassee FL 32306-2049, USA

Abstract. We contend that a democratically-operated organization is normally unable to sustain a meritocracy (i.e., organization with a reward structure based on academic and/or professional achievement) because of rational behavior on the part of organization members. Briefly, rewards in democratic meritocracies tend to be based on the preferences of the median member rather than the best employees. As a result, these highly productive members either reduce their level of output ("shirk") - trading work for leisure - or exit the organization. This dynamic process mediocratizes the meritocracy by reducing the supply of highly productive employees, and the incentives to be productive within the confines of the organization.

Introduction

An historically important question in the study of all types of organizations, ranging from public bureaucracies to legislatures, is the most productive form or structure. Many considerations enter the arguments but the work of Alchian and Demsetz (1972) suggests a concern that has not received much theoretical or empirical attention: the ability of organizations to adequately meter the performance of their employees. Simply put, every effective organization must develop reward structures that correlate with employee performance. Even organizations incorporating reward structures based upon objective standards of achievement and productivity are susceptible to systematic declines in organizational performance due to the rational behavior of utility-maximizing employees. We intend to build upon this insight by Alchian and Demsetz to demonstrate that democratic organizations have a difficult time maintaining meritocracies.

A meritocracy is defined as an organization with a reward structure based on professional achievement; a democratic organization is one in which members determine the organization's policies or select those who do. We confine our attention to those organizations where majority voting is crucial - a rather simple version of democracy. Democratic meritocracies have a rather exalted place in our normative view of organizations: they purportedly sustain employee morale, install a sense of self-worth, and enhance organizational productivity. Such attributes, if true, are certainly admirable but can democratic organizations incorporating reward structures based on merit alleviate the problem of metering?

Briefly, rewards in democratic meritocracies tend to be based on the preferences of the median member rather than the best employees. As a result, these highly productive members either reduce their level of output ("shirk") -trading work for leisure-or leave the organization. Shirking on the part of the most productive members of the organization reduces organizational output. Eventually these individuals exit the organization for other organizations they believe will distribute organizational resources in a closer proximity to individual effort. Two mechanisms assure that replacements will generally be less productive than those they replace. First, since the method of organizational resource distribution is insufficient to hold a productive member, potential recruits equally productive as exiting members will not consider the organization a viable employment alternative. Second, the benefits available for attracting another productive member are likely to shrink as the remaining members of the organization establish property rights to the unclaimed resources made possible through exits. The result of this process is that the meritocracy gradually loses its best people, and attracts individuals who are normally less productive when compared to those departing. This dynamic process mediocratizes the organization by reducing the supply of highly productive members, and the incentives to be productive within the confines of the organization.

A Formal Exposition

We assume that organizations require a certain number of workers to function, that individual productivity can be measured along a one-dimensional continuum, and that each member of the organization is an individual utility maximizer. We also introduce the following assumptions.

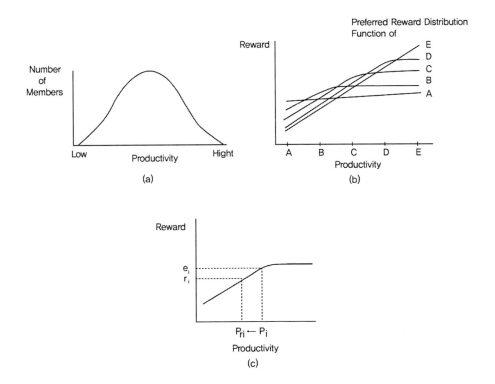

Fig, 1,
(at t=1)
(a) Distribution of the members along the quality dimension
(b) Hypothetical reward distribution functions
(c) Member i's exit and production decision based on i's preferred reward distribution function.

Assumption 1: Complete information. Members of the organization know who are the best workers and who are the poor workers. That is, each worker knows everybody else"s place on the productivity dimension as well as his own place on it.

Let us assume that members of a certain organization are normally distributed at t = 1 [Fig. 1(a)]. We assume a normal distribution for the purpose of illustration, but our argument does not depend upon this assumption. At t = 1, members determine how the (limited) budget should be distributed among them. Each worker has his own idea about how the budget should be distributed among all the members of the organization, given individual levels of productivity and a limited budget. This information is represented by an individual's preferred reward distribution function (hereafter PRDF). We make the following assumptions about the individual PRDFs.

Assumption 2: (i) Workers at the same level of the productivity dimension share the same PRDFs. That is, workers at the same level expect the same amount of rewards and have the same perceptions about the amount each productivity level should receive; (ii) the individual PRDFs are monotonically increasing. That is, all members of the organization recognize that more productive members deserve greater rewards, but those at different productivity levels may not agree as to how much more productive members deserve to be rewarded; (iii) for any individual I, the person who is most generous to i is i himself; (iv) workers are more generous to those who are close to themselves on the productivity dimension (see below).

Assumption 2 leads to hypothetical PRDFs of workers at different levels of the productivity dim5ension in Fig. 1(b). As Assumption 2(iii) states, of all the PRDFs, member D"s PRFD provides the highest reward to D. The same is true for all other members. As Assumption 2(iv) states, workers at D think those at A should get more rewards than the workers at E think they should get. Similarly, workers at D are willing to allow those at E to receive more rewards than workers at A are willing to allow those at E.

Assumption 3: There is not only a very limited job market for those at the lowest productivity levels, but their market price is extremely low. This assumption may not be off the target when we consider the fact that those with low productivity levels rarely enter the job market.

Member i's exit and production decisions can be defined in the following manner:

1. If $r_i < \Theta_i$, i exits
2. (i) If $\Theta_i < r_i < e_i$, I reduces his effort level from P to P [see Fig. 1(c)].
   (ii) IF $\Theta_i < r_i$ and $e \leq r_i$, i maintains his current productivity (effort) level P_i.

Where r_i=i's actual or relized reward; Θ_i=i's opportunity cost of statying in the organization; e_i=the reward level that i thinks he deserves for his present productivity level, P_i, namely the point on his PRDF corresponding to the productivity level, P_i; and P_{ri}=the productivity level that i perceives to be commensurate with the reward level r_i, namely the point on his PRDF corre-sponding to the reward lever r_i.

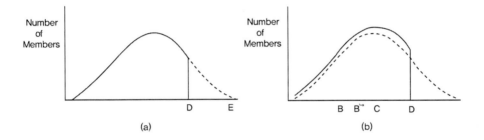

(a)

(b)

Figure 2.

(a) Membership distribution at the end of t = 1
(b) Member distribution at the end of t = 1' (With the initial distribution at t = 1 in dotted line)

Assumption 4: For most of the members of the organization (with the exceptions noted in Assumption 3), e_i is a certain indicator of i's market price (or i's opporttunity cost, Θ_i); e_i and i's actual market price need not be the same or even close. Assumption 4 simply stated that the greater the difference between e_i and $r_i(e_i > r_i)$, the more likely i will find alternative employment that offers rewards greater than r_i. This assumption in adopted here only to illustrate our argument in a simple straightforward fashion.

Say the PRDF of the worker at C [in Fig. l(b)] was chosen at t = 1. For those between the production level E and slightly below, the difference between what they think they deserve and the actual reward is so large that they enter the job market, find jobs, and exit the organization. For those just below, either the difference is not so large, or if it is, they cannot find jobs that pay more; hence, they stay. For those at production level A, the difference between what they think they deserve and the actual reward is considerable. But since the market for them is so small, and their market price is so low (Assumption 31, they remain in the organization. Therefore, after the reward distribution decisions of the organization and the exit decisions of its members at t = 1, the distribution of its members along the productivity dimension looks like the one depicted in Fig. 2(a).

Since some members have left the organization, they need to be replaced by new members. At t = 1', the organization recruits new members. Potential recruits learn about the reward distribution scheme adopted by the organization, and those workers at the margin (say beyond the production level of D) do not seek employment in the organization because they can do better elsewhere. No matter, those in the organization do not have any incentive to recruit those at the production level of D or above because their individual rewards are maximized by not having such highly productive members around.[1] Therefore, at the end of the recruitment process at t = 1', the membership distribution of this organization along the productivity dimension looks something like the one described in Fig. 2(b). One can see that the median member point along the productivity dimension shifts to the left (from C to B'), to a lower productivity level, unless all the recruitment made at t = 1' occur between C and D.

At t = 2 (say next fiscal year), members of the organization determine how the budget should be distributed. Since some of the most heavily rewarded members have left the organization and have been replaced by those who are rewarded less, surplus rewards exist in the budget which the remaining members expect to divide among themselves. That is, individual PRDFs tend to shift upward at t = 2 [Fig. 3(a)].[2]

Say the PRDF of the worker at B was chosen at t = 2. For those between the production level of D and slightly below, the difference between what they think they deserve and the actual reward is so large that they enter the job market, find jobs, and leave the organization. At t = 2', only those who are less productive than those who just left the organization are hired. Therefore, after the exit decisions at t = 2 and the recruitment process at t = 2', the median member point along the productivity dimension has shifted further to the left.

Our formal exposition illustrates an important point: if an organization consistently adopts a budget distribution scheme which coincides with the PRDFs of those other than its best members (including the median member or those close to him as in the illustration above), the median quality point of the organization will keep shifting to the left, ultimately reducing the overall quality of the organization. This process of organizational exit continues until outside employment opportunities for productive, dissatisfied members of the organization disappear. At this point, we expect those rewarded below their expected levels to begin or intensify their shirking.

Suppose those at C are now the most productive members and those at B are median members. Then those at C will be rewarded r_c although they think they deserve e, in Fig. 3(b). Suppose there are no outside employment opportunities that pay those at C greater than r_c. Then those at C will reduce their productivity (i.e. effort level) to P_{rc}. Likewise those between B and C will reduce their productivity since they are not rewarded as much as they think they deserve. The net effect is that those who used to be between B and C are now packed between B and P_{rc}, and the organizational output again declines.

The process of organizational deterioration does not end here. Since the best members (who used to be at C) are now less productive workers, their PRDF tends to shift and the new reward function provides greater reward to those at P_{rc}, than any other PRDF [Assumption 2(iii)]. The median member's reward distribution function may also shift as a result of the more productive members' reducing effort. Since the best members are simply less productive than before, there again is a gap between what those at P_{rc}, think they deserve (a point on their new reward function) and what they actually receive (a point

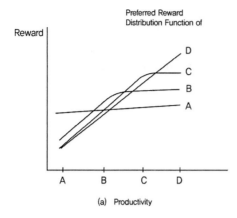

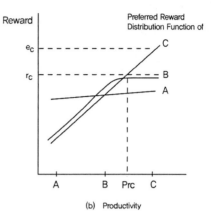

Figure 3.

(a) Reward distribution function at t=2

(b) Reward distribution function at t=3

on the median member's reward function). Thus they shirk further, and the position of the best members in the organization shifts farther to the left. This process of deterioration continues until the increase in the best members' utility from less effort equals the reduction in reward on the median member's reward distribution function. We expect that the best members eventually will look more and more like the median member in terms of organizational performance. In sum, at the equilibrium point the opportunity cost of staying in the organization is equal to (or smaller than) the present reward for each member of the organization, and the best members' position converges toward the median member position on the productivity dimension. The above assumptions, and the formal exposition, lead to the following proposition:

Proposition: In democratically-run meritocracies with an organizational budget constraint, (i) the median member position on the productivity dimension keeps shifting to a lower level through the exit of their best members; and (ii) the productive members' productivity level converges toward the median. (i) and (ii) combine to reduce organizational output and mediocratize meritocracies.[3]

It is important to distinguish the median member position in Proposition (ii) from the initial median position of C. As soon as the deterioration of a meritocracy begins, the median member position keeps shifting to the left, and so does the best member position, possibly passing the initial median position. Therefore, the convergence toward the (shifted) median member position in our model indicates a real mediocratization in quality, and not necessarily the convergence toward the center as is typical in unidimensional studies of voting. Unlike the median voter position in voting games, the median member position in our model is a moving target!

Discussion

Since each worker's position on the productivity dimension determines his behavioral disposition in our model, the comparison of our analysis with Robert Frank's analysis of positional competition is compelling (Frank 1985). According to Frank, people care more about the relative standing of their incomes among their peers than about their absolute incomes. Since people care about relative status, productive workers accept a salary lower than the value of what they produce in return for high status; and less productive workers are compensated for their low status with a wage more than the value of what they produce. If indeed people are so status concerned as Frank argues, the process of the organizational decline in our model may slow down since the most productive workers now find it tolerable to stay in the organization due to the high status they enjoy. But the pace of organizational decline will depend on how much people are more concerned about status than about absolute rewards. Even so, organizational decline will still occur because now members in democratic organization disagree not only about the worth of individual members' productivity but about the value of the high status that productive members enjoy!

Not all meritocracies are destined to disintegrate. After all, for our model to be valid, productive members exiting the organization for other meritocracies must have places to go. Several factors can keep meritocracies functioning. First, some organizations have been blessed with a large majority of very talented members, thereby assuring that the distribution of resources favor the best members of the organization. In formal terms, the positions (on the productivity dimension) of the best members and the median members are very close in the initial stage in these organizations and there is little impetus for the best members to converge toward the median member. Second, some organizations have non-democratic rules that skew resources to the best members of the organization. For instance, an organizational head with autocratic powers may be imposed on an organization with a mandate to reward the best members. Finally, some organizations simply have more resources than others and they can successfully expand the resource base to better accommodate the expectations of their best members (violation of the assumption of a limited budget).

Notes

1. One may go a step further and argue that those at C, the median members, would not approve of replacements more productive than themselves; hence all the recruitment at t = 1' occurs at or below C. If that happens, the process of organizational deterioration simply accelerates.

2. It is possible that, as the productivity of the organization declines, the total budget (or revenues) falls as well. Then individual reward functions may not shift upward at t = 2. As the rest of this section will show, our argument of organizational deterioration is valid whether the budget remains fixed or shrinks, as long as it does not grow fast enough to make all the productive members happy (see the last section of this paper).

3. We do not contend that our argument is true for all meritocracies. We only are interested in democratic meritocracies with an organizational budget constraint.

10.

Signaling and Tariff Policy: The Strategic Multi-stage Rent Reduction Game

Michael Lusztig[*], Patrick James[**] & Heemin Kim[***]

* Southern Methodist University

** University of Missouri

*** Florida State University

Abstract. This study uses a game-theoretic analysis to suggest that governments can minimize the political risks associated with significant liberalization of trade by employing a multistep process in the reduction of state-supplied rents. The model argues that when governments precede significant reductions in state-supplied rents with a smaller reduction, or with a reduction that can be portrayed credibly as externally imposed, they may be in a position to evaluate, and hence mitigate, costs associated with significant trade liberalization. Substantive implications are explored in the context of United States trade policy and the still-curious ability of the Franklin Roosevelt administration to engage in strategic rent reductions without suffering meaningful political backlash.

Résumé. Cette recherche utilise une approche formelle, fondée sur la théorie des jeux, pour suggérer que les gouvernements sont parfois en mesure de minimiser les risques politiques associés à une libéralisation substantielle du commerce international lorsqu"ils emploient une stratégie qui réduit graduellement les allocations gouvernementales (statesupplied rents). Ce modèle démontre que lorsqu"un gouvernement précède à une réduction significative de ses allocations aux groupes privilégiés par une réduction de moindre importance, ou du moins une réduction qui puisse être expliquée d"une façon plausible par des forces externes, il est en mesure d"évaluer les coûts politiques réels associés à une libéralisation importante de commerce international. Ces propositions sont appliquées aux politiques commerciales américaines, avec une attention toute particulière portée à l"habileté de l"administration de Franklin Roosevelt de s"engager dans une réduction stratégique des allocations gouvernementales aux groupes privilégiés, sans toutefois subir des coûts politiques importants pour des telles actions.

Well established within international political economy and public choice theory is the principle that policies of significant trade liberalization constitute acts of potentially considerable aggregate economic benefit, but typically involve severe political risk (Baldwin, 1989; Rowley and Tollison, 1988; Tullock, 1967). While trade liberalization provides marginal benefits to a large number of consumers, it imposes substantial costs onto a comparatively small number of producers who typically mobilize to pressure governments to retain state-supplied rents. Such pursuit of wealth transfer (typically through the form of import protection and/or subsidies) is known as rent seeking. Given the potentially high political costs associated with alienating domestic rent seekers, it is interesting to consider conditions under which governments might mitigate the risks of trade liberalization. Moreover, the trend toward the removal of barriers to commerce throughout Europe and Asia over the last decade makes the question of trade liberalization elsewhere especially salient.[1]

This study uses a game-theoretic analysis to build upon the "limits of rent seeking" model (Lusztig, 1998; 2003) to suggest that governments can minimize the political risks associated with significant liberalization of trade by employing a multistep process in the reduction of state-supplied rents. It argues that when governments precede significant reductions in state-supplied rents with smaller reductions, or with a reduction that can be portrayed credibly as externally imposed, they may be in a position to evaluate, and hence mitigate, costs associated with policies of significant trade liberalization. More specifically, initial reductions in state-supplied rents force rent seekers to signal to what degree they are able to compete in world markets, thus giving governments an accurate profile of the competitiveness of the producer population—a profile that domestic producers may try to hide from governments. At the same time, these rent reductions also signal the rent seekers" ability to mobilize and engage in opposition.

Substantively, this article focuses on explaining and prescribing means by which governments can engage in significant reductions in state-supplied rents while limiting the political backlash associated with defying protectionist rent seekers. The case of the United States during the Great Depression of the 1930s constitutes an excellent illustration of the argument. It also is the basis for an enduring puzzle in the history of US political economy: How was the administration of Franklin Roosevelt able to engineer a sea change in US trade policy without suffering the political backlash anticipated by public choice theory? To the extent that our study answers this question, it contributes to a rich literature that seeks to address this puzzle (see Ferguson, 1984; Frieden, 1988; Gilligan, 1997; Goldstein, 1993a; Haggard, 1988; Hiscox, 1999).

The Limits of Rent Seeking

The central argument of this article builds upon the limits of the rent seeking model. Consider an environment in which producers have two means of earning returns on factors of production: they can dedicate resources to successful competition in world markets (call this competitive production), or they can expend resources in the preservation or extension of state-supplied rents (call this rent seeking). Competition and rent seeking are obviously ideal types; in the real world most producers will rely on some combination of the two.

As a rule, producers who select production points involving a greater commitment to competition will support government initiatives to liberalize trade. Freer trade facilitates competitive production by lowering the costs of factor inputs (both imported and, by the logic of free-market pricing, indigenous). Moreover, the implied reciprocity associated with trade liberalization should provide expanded access to export markets.

Within the rent-seeker population, consider a further dichotomy. In an environment that has featured significant levels of state-supplied rents, there will emerge a class of producers who, by virtue of competitive and comparative disadvantage, could not possibly survive free market competition. For an extreme, but illustrative, mythical example think of olive growers in Finland. Given sufficient subsidies for greenhouses and electricity, as well as import barriers that would protect them from less costly and higher quality competitors in warmer climes, such producers could prosper. However, should state-supplied rents be significantly reduced, these producers would be unable to continue operations. Such producers are styled inflexible rent seekers. A minimal level (variant by producer), or critical threshold, of state-supplied rents is necessary for economic survival.

The second category of rent seeker consists of producers who prefer rent seeking to competition, but given a sufficient reduction in state-supplied rents– that is, below the critical threshold–could restructure operations to compete in world markets. These are flexible rent seekers. Ironically, upon such a change in the environment in which they operate (which, of course, could even be stimulated by exogenous factors such as technological innovation), flexible rent seekers ultimately may join non-rent seeking producers as supporters of, or even advocates for, further trade liberalization initiatives.[2]

If they are internationally competitive, why do flexible rent seekers continue to rely on import protection? There are at least two reasons. First and most obviously, it is easier to accept oligopoly rents in the form of import protection or subsidy than it is to capture profits in a more competitive market. Even if economies of scale could be enhanced through liberalization, there is still the risk factor to consider. Second, the costs of adjustment for industries that have benefited from oligopoly rents (particularly if they have done so for a long period of time) can be steep; investing in adjustment, then, is something that flexible rent seekers will avoid if possible (Dixit and Londregan, 1995).

Upon realizing that a government appears to be committed to rent reduction, however, flexible rent seekers will dedicate fewer resources to punishing (operationalized as sanctioning electorally, perhaps even by seeking to defeat and replace) leaders who liberalize trade. Because an alternative exists to all-out resistance, the preponderance of resources will be instead dedicated to restructuring operations to withstand import competition. Such restructuring includes product and service innovation, rationalization of product lines and personnel, and perhaps most importantly, seeking new markets to replace market shares lost at home. This last imperative minimizes the punishment that flexible rent seekers will inflict on governments. Indeed, such rent seekers will rely on governments to create market opportunities abroad, and will seek to influence them.

For inflexible rent seekers, the choices are not terribly compelling. First, if they believe that a government is strongly committed to rent reductions, they may shift from production of a particular good to importation, or they may move operations offshore to more protected environs (of course, such an option exists for flexible rent seekers as well). In any case, these non-committed inflexible rent seekers voluntarily exit the marketplace without much resistance. Demonstration of commitment on the part of the government, then, is important to the extent that it may persuade some inflexible rent seekers to go quietly. Second, committed inflexible rent seekers, inclined to fight, will lobby for restoration of the status quo. Politically speaking, committed inflexible rent seekers will be disposed toward inflicting severe punishment on governments that reduce rents. Inflexible rent seekers that retaliate against governments reducing rents below the critical level face few opportunity costs; such rent reduction is a "death sentence" for inflexible rent seekers. (For them, the critical level of rents is the minimum required for survival of the firm or industry.) On the other hand, the demise of inflexible rent seekers is not instantaneous across the board. These rent seekers may be expected to dedicate resources to the cause of punishing the government electorally as a means toward reversing the policy decision. Of course, governments that survive the wrath of inflexible rent seekers often find themselves in a stronger position. The most inefficient segment of the producer population is culled, providing greater flexibility with respect to trade policy in the future.[3]

The death of inflexible rent seekers as producers does not translate into their expiration as political players. Voting and other forms of political action are still available. However, to use a play on words related to Robert Axelrod"s (1984) concept formation, these former workers and owners are expected to have a very short "shadow of the past." The decline or even disappearance of an industry is unlikely to create a long memory among its former participants. The final victory of the passenger automobile, for example, did not produce voting blocs that tried to punish political leaders who refused to stand in the way of its proliferation. Those employed in "horse and buggy" industries moved on to other economic activities. The underlying point, which holds for both the preceding example and dislocation caused by trade liberalization, is that employment is not identity related in the same way as, for example, occupation of a particular territory. Short-term economic losers adapt and change relatively quickly, all other things being equal. Thus political "life after death" for those experiencing dislocation should not be a major worry for a government considering trade liberalization.

The game-theoretic analysis below provides greater insights into the conceptual relevance of flexible and inflexible rent seekers.

Forcing Signals and the Question of Rent Reduction

The dichotomy between flexible and inflexible rent seekers constitutes a refinement of standard public choice theory. Rent seekers axiomatically are committed to the retention of state-supplied rents. However, not all feature the same degree of commitment. Intuitively, governments undertaking significant reductions of rent in a community dominated by flexible rent seekers will absorb less punishment than those that reduce rents in a community dominated by inflexible rent seekers. Yet this begs the fundamental question of how governments are able to determine the extent to which their society is made up of flexible or inflexible rent seekers. Without this knowledge, they will have difficulty in assessing the political risk associated with significant liberalization of trade. Indeed, it is this paradox that has made shifts towards free trade comparatively rare phenomena, given the inherent economic benefits.

Of course, governments can make objective assessments about the ability of their producer populations to survive increased import competition. They will have some a priori knowledge about the international competitiveness of domestic industries, and thus will be able to estimate, with a degree of accuracy, the extent to which industries can withstand the reduction of state supplied rents. It is a standard assumption in the literature on strategic trade theory, however, that firms will know more than governments about costs, demands and other traits within an industry (Brander, 1995: 1423; Herander and Kamp, 1999: 61). Asymmetric information can distort the ability of governments to determine accurately the extent to which various industries are flexible or inflexible rent seekers. All rent seekers have an incentive to portray themselves as inflexible. Producer groups rarely (if ever) admit that high tariff or subsidy levels are necessary to ensure high profits. Rather, state-supplied rents tend to be portrayed as necessary for firm or industry survival. In other words, flexible rent seekers have an incentive to mimic inflexible rent seekers.

Given the difficulty that governments have in determining the makeup of the rent-seeker population, and given that the benefits of free trade tend to manifest themselves over a longer time horizon than the short electoral cycle, governments" default position is typically inertia in the realm of trade politics. We argue, however, that this need not be the case. Governments committed to trade liberalization may seek an identification or screening mechanism that allows them to distinguish largely flexible rentseeking populations from those less flexible.

A clue about the nature of this identification mechanism is found in the literature on international crisis bargaining. One of the problems facing negotiators in a crisis is that those who are irrevocably committed to their position often cannot distinguish themselves from those less committed but with an incentive to mimic committed negotiators: since there is "nothing a nonbluffer can do that a bluffer would not have the ability and incentive to imitate, the recipient of a threat can never be completely convinced that the threatener is not bluffing" (Wagner, 1989: 189). Both the nonbluffer and the recipient have an incentive to deter the bluffer. One method that nonbluffers use to distinguish themselves from bluffers is to send signals that are costly to communicate as a means of demonstrating commitment to their position (see Schelling, 1960; Spence, 1973). By this logic, bluffers can be distinguished from nonbluffers because the former are unlikely to be willing to bear the price of costly signals.

Another means of separating bluffers from nonbluffers is for the purveyor of the threat to create conditions under which the former are forced to take actions that distinguish themselves from the latter. In such circumstances, the purveyor may be said to force signals. It is the concept of forced signals that is of interest at present. Flexible rent seekers represent bluffers (insofar as they mimic inflexible rent seekers) when lobbying for retention of state-supplied rents, while a government interested in liberalizing trade—the recipient of the bluffs—must find a way to force a signal. Put differently, before a government can make an accurate assessment of the risks involved in liberalizing trade, it must accurately assess the proportion of flexible rent seekers within the rent-seeker population.

One means by which the government can force signals is to reduce rents, observe the behaviour of the rent-seeking population, and then make its calculations accordingly.[4] Provided that rents are reduced below the critical level threshold for most of the rent-seeking population, and governments demonstrate sufficient commitment to the rent reduction, the reduction of rents forces a discernible separation in the behaviour of flexible and inflexible rent seekers. The obvious flaw, of course, is that while this constitutes an effective identification mechanism, it is no better (and indeed, no different) than the government's original objective. What is required is a means of reducing rents in a relatively costless way as a prelude to a more significant reduction that might be undertaken after the government evaluates the costs by observing the behaviour of the rent-seeking population. The government can utilize this identification mechanism through at least two means without absorbing significant countervailing punishment. First, it can take advantage of circumstances under which the decision to reduce rents can be portrayed initially as structurally imposed. The second, more risky course of action is when the government's decision is wholly strategic—that is, the government weighs the risks of alienating rent seekers against a set of anticipated benefits (see Lusztig, 1996; Verdier, 1994).

Governments occasionally may be forced to reduce the supply of rents due to circumstances beyond their control. A severe economic crisis, such as the ones faced by many Latin American countries during the early to mid-1980s, constitutes one example. In such cases, governments are relatively invulnerable to the rent-seeking population both because these threats pale in comparison to the larger crisis, and crises undermine commitment to the status quo.[5] While a crisis does not wholly mitigate risk (see Nelson, 1989), skilful government leaders can take advantage of the fact that the decision to reduce rents may be portrayed as structurally imposed. They subsequently can gauge the make-up of the rent-seeker population, and if conditions are favourable, further reduce the level of import protection without forfeiting the political support of the flexible rent-seeker population.

Another means by which rent reductions can be structurally imposed is through the mandate of international regimes such as the World Trade Organization (and its predecessor, the General Agreement on Tariffs and Trade), the World Bank, or the International Monetary Fund (see Przeworski and Vreeland, 2000). Governments often try to represent membership in such organizations as leaving them no choice but to comply with regime-mandated rent reductions.[6] The demonstrable costs of noncompliance— including a loss of face internationally and potential exclusion from the benefits of the regime— provide governments with a credible claim that they "had" to reduce state-supplied rents.

For example, both Canada and Mexico found themselves subjected to pressure from international regimes to reduce rents, in the 1970s and 1980s, respectively (see Lusztig, 1998, forthcoming). Such structurally imposed rent reductions provide governments with "plausible deniability" about other options. Each creates circumstances where the status quo is no longer as attractive as before. Moreover, in both countries structurally imposed rent reductions forced flexible rent seekers to signal their activities to adjust to global competition. In turn, this allowed the governments of Canada and Mexico to enter into bilateral trade agreements with the United States relatively secure in the knowledge that there would be limited political backlash from formerly protectionist producer groups. More interesting, however, are circumstances where the government does not enjoy the camouflage of structurally imposed rent reductions. It is for cases of strategic rent reductions that the following game-theoretic analysis becomes important. The basic question is this: Can a gradual approach to reform be used effectively as a screening mechanism?

A Rent Reduction Game

The strategic multistage rent reduction game in Figure 1 illustrates a risky but potentially effective means for governments to undertake significant reductions in rents (T), while absorbing limited costs.[7]

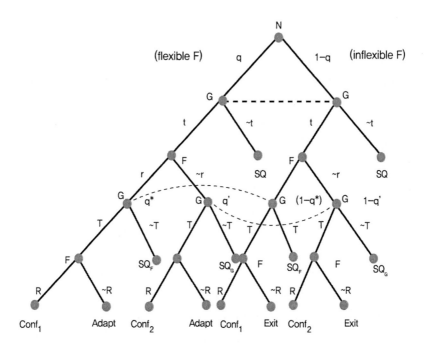

Figure 1. Multistage Rent Reduction Game with Asymmetric Information

Figure 1 illustrates the multistage rent reduction game that the government plays against each member of the rent-seeker population. In this game, the government, G, actually plays against the rent-seeker population in a given industry. The game begins with a chance move by Nature regarding the probability (q or 1-q) that the government is playing against a flexible or inflexible rent seeker, F. The information sets provide data about F's type. Since F is assumed to know its own type, all of F's information sets contain singleton decision nodes (no dashed lines), while G's information sets contain multiple nodes reflecting G's uncertainty about F's type.

An initial reduction in rents, t, represents a small, not very controversial reduction. This stage of the game, with G choosing between t and ~t, may be repeated a number of times. The logic is that each small reduction has the potential to change the behaviour of only the portion of the rentseeker population that falls below the threshold of the critical level of rents. However, the cumulative effect of a number of small reductions should separate flexible and inflexible rent seekers. Over time, the government should be in a position to determine the makeup of the rent-seeker population. Moreover, because a number of inflexible rent seekers are culled along the way, the producer population should be increasingly receptive to trade liberalization (see Milner, 1988). In short, this game not only allows the government to determine the size of q, but also permits it to increase q's magnitude. (Put differently, the size of q presumably is increased with each iteration.)

For G, the basic quest is for political capital, understood in the general sense of preserving or even enhancing the prospects of remaining in office. Office holding is assumed to confer a continuing stream of benefits, which will vary in terms of type and magnitude with the political system at hand. In all electoral systems, however, the central decision maker–designated as the Chief of Government (COG) in Robert Putnam's (1988) useful frame of reference—is regarded as self-interested. Thus, all other things being equal, the COG is likely to make choices that are perceived to maximize political capital. For this reason alone the risky path of rent reduction can be expected to remain a relatively uncommon choice among the options available to governments in office.

While it would be beyond the scope of this study to offer a detailed specification of even a generic utility function for a COG (although see Grossman and Helpman, 2002), at the very least the main components and tradeoffs between and among them can be identified:

Let $u_G = f(Q)$, $Q = g(1,)$, $du_G/d\,Q > 0$, $d\,1/d\, < 0$,

where Q is the level of political support for government,
1 is economic efficiency; and
is the degree of rent.

The dynamic tension involving pursuit of political capital through both macro-economic management intended to please the general public and targeted provision of rent to potentially influential groups is clear in the preceding expressions. Utility for the COG is a monotonically increasing function (f) of political support, which is taken as the indicator of the likelihood of ongoing enjoyment of benefits from office holding.[8] This connection is conveyed by the first of the two derivatives that appear just above. Political support, in turn, consists of both breadth and depth. The former is regarded as depending primarily on economic efficiency, whereas the latter is enhanced by provision of rents. As noted by the second of the two derivatives from above, efficiency and rent provision are at odds with each other. This is the essence of the dynamic tension facing the COG in setting policy: keeping key interest groups at bay while maintaining a sufficiently positive macro-economic performance to sustain overall welfare.

All things being equal, governments prefer that rent seekers adapt, because this obviates the dead-weight costs associated with rent seeking and therefore improves the economy's aggregate performance. Governments enjoy a "halo effect" from a strong economy. On the other hand, as mentioned, there is a strong potential for a political backlash (at least in the short term) against governments that reduce rents.

For our game with a limited number of potential outcomes, it is not necessary to define the government's utility function in detail. Rather, it is sufficient to derive the government's preference ordering of potential outcomes based on the relationships defined above. Thus we assume the following preference ordering for G:

$$u_G(\text{Adapt/Exit}) > u_G(\text{SQ}) > u_G(\text{SQ}_G) > u_G(\text{SQ}_F) > u_G(\text{Conf}_2) > u_G(\text{Conf}_1)$$

We assume that Adapt or Exit is the best outcome for G. It is one in which G incrementally reduces rents (that is, t, followed by T) and F chooses to adapt/exit either with or without minor resistance.[9] We further assume that the three status quo outcomes rank next.[10] Least desirable among the outcomes are Conf$_2$ and Conf$_1$, which respectively refer to outcomes in which rent seekers retaliate once and twice against G. The choice of all-out retaliation by F suggests potential political disaster for G.

Based on the discussion in the second section of this article, we let $u_F = h(C, R)$, where C is the level of competitive production and R is the level of rent seeking.

A flexible rent seeker prefers to adapt rather than resist. An inflexible rent seeker prefers to resist rather than exit. Then we assume the following preference orderings for flexible and inflexible rent seekers:

$$u_F(SQ) > u_F(SQ_F) > u_F(SQ_G) > u_F(Adapt) > u_F(Conf_1) > u_F(Conf_2)^{11}$$
$$u_F(SQ) > u_F(SQ_F) > u_F(SQ_G) > u_F(Conf_1) > u_F(Conf_2) > u_F(Exit)^{12}$$

We provide solutions for the multistage rent reduction game in the Appendix. As the Appendix shows, the game has a number of equilibria, and solving them is quite a technical endeavour. The solution concept used for signalling games is Perfect Bayesian Equilibrium (PBE) (see Gibbons, 1992). It is interesting to observe that, even with just two players and one-sided incomplete information, the game produces more equilibria than might have been intuitively anticipated.[13]

From the PBEs in the Appendix, we can derive the following propositions:

Proposition 1a: The government can induce the Adapt outcome (that is, induce flexible F to adapt) by first introducing a small reduction in rents when the government believes that the probability of industry being flexible is sufficiently high. Proof: See [1] (i) (a) and [2] (i) in the Appendix.[14]

Proposition 1b: The government is more likely to achieve the reduction in rents when it values Adapt highly($u_G(Adapt)$)and/or when the value of the status quo to the government is low $(u_G(SQ); u_G(SQ_G))$.
Proof: See [1] (i) (a) in the Appendix.

Proposition 2: Under all other conditions, the government never introduces even a small reduction in rents and the status quo prevails.[15]
Proof: See [1] (ii), [2] (ii), and [3] in the Appendix.

The government's and rent seekers' decision making under Proposition 2 may not be empirically observable. The absence of tariff reductions, however, does not necessarily mean non-action or non-consideration on the part of the government. Rather, governments calculate the benefits and costs of their actions, and under the conditions of Proposition 2, their equilibrium behaviour is the action of non-introduction of tariff reductions. Obviously the game in Figure 1 presents a somewhat simplified snapshot of reality, with each actor having only two moves. In the real world, the situation identified in Proposition 1a above can be fortified with more dynamic and repeated interactions between players. That is, through the repetition of small rent reductions by the government, a number of inflexible rent-seekers are culled along the way, and the rent-seeker population becomes increasingly flexible. This way, the player behaviour described in Proposition 1a tends to reproduce itself. And the end result is greater free trade.[16]

A drawback to the multistage game from G's point of view is that the game can become a drawn-out process. Indeed, the greater the number of iterations in the game, the safer the ultimate, large-scale reduction in rents (T) becomes, but the longer it takes for free trade to emerge,

Substantive Implications

A familiar but still controversial example should help to illustrate the logic of the substantive implications. When President Franklin D. Roosevelt came to power in 1933, he was determined to stay the nationalist, Hoover, and that was strongly advocated by his "Brains Trust" of close economic advisers, the bulk of the business and agricultural community, and indeed, the American public. His First New Deal, in fact, constituted a corporatist alliance of nationalist business and agriculture, anchored by initiatives such as the National Industrial Recovery Act (NIRA, that mandated government-mediated collusion in numerous industrial sectors as a means of maintaining prices), and the Agricultural Adjustment Act (AAA, that was dedicated to the maintenance of agricultural price supports). Neither initiative was market-based, and thus both were inconsistent with the liberalization of trade (see Burns, 1956; Schlesinger, 1958; Skocpol and Finegold, 1982).

By 1934, however, there were signs that FDR's First New Deal coalition was beginning to fragment. The American Liberty League emerged as a big business lobby group dedicated to undermining what it saw as the principal threats to the American way of life: communism, trade unionism, liberal Democrats in Congress, social welfare policies and, above all, the Roosevelt administration (Rudolph, 1950; Wolfskill, 1962). Cognizant of the threat to his First New Deal coalition, Roosevelt quietly began to lay the groundwork for a replacement: what was to become his Second New Deal coalition. The new coalition consisted of labour, the urban underclasses, internationalist business and financial interests, and the agricultural sector.[17]

While by no means committed to jettisoning his First New Deal coalition in the spring of 1934, Roosevelt took steps to ensure that option existed. To that end he sent the Reciprocal Trade Agreements bill to Congress. However, it was not until December 1935 that he committed to a policy of unconditionality—whereby a concession to one most-favoured nation was a concession to all such countries—and could be said to have abandoned the nationalist course that characterized the early years of his presidency.[18]

Roosevelt's initial reluctance to embrace internationalism is explicable, in large part, by the protectionist nature of the American business sector in the first three decades of the century. Indeed, the Smoot-Hawley Tariff (1930) had illustrated graphically the hegemony of rent seekers in the trade policy arena. Although as Jeff Frieden (1988) points out, the effects of the Depression forced some conversion of what we have called flexible rent seekers to free trade while rationalizing others out of the market, the majority of the industrial sector that survived the Depression thus far was still nationalist and isolationist (Ferguson, 1984; Hull, 1948).

Even upon his conversion to internationalism in 1935, however, Roosevelt did not commit to radical liberalization. Indeed, wary of provoking the wrath of rent seekers, the Roosevelt administration recognized the importance of a gradual and incremental reduction of rents under the Reciprocal Trade Agreements Act (RTAA) (Hull, 1948: 177). The obvious secondary advantage to Roosevelt, a cautious reformer, was that gradual rent reductions gave him ample opportunity to determine any economic ill effects from preceding reductions.

Under the RTAA, the Roosevelt administration signed 23 reciprocal trade agreements between 1934 and 1940. Eight more were signed between 1940 and 1947. Between 1934 and 1939, ad valorem duties fell by about one third (Brenner, 1978: 157). Thus, in the vernacular of the rent reduction game, the government played strategy t multiple times. Given this fact, according to the logic displayed in Figure 1, we should expect to see rent-seeker behaviour changing incrementally as well. Which, in fact, we do. Inflexible rent seekers exited the market; flexible ones not only signalled their status as flexible rent seekers, but became supporters of a further liberalization of trade.

This claim is supported by two indirect but collectively compelling measures. First, the tenor of submissions before the House ways and means committee and the Senate finance committee reflects changes in the preferences of a small but axiomatically committed segment of the producer population. In hearings on the RTAA in 1934, and on its renewal in 1937, a majority of those submitting depositions did so in opposition to the RTAA. In 1940, for the first time, and by a rate of more than two to one, non-labour and non-agricultural interests supported renewal of the RTAA.

Second, while survey data are limited, those that exist support the claim that flexible rent seekers shifted their preferences. As early as 1939, the largest manufacturers (presumably, due to opportunity costs, those most sensitive to decreases in the marginal rate of rents) appear to have abandoned protectionism. Indeed, while a 1939 Roper poll suggested that US business in general supported higher tariffs, large manufacturers (those producing $50 million dollars in goods per year) were largely opposed (Fortune, 1939: 96). While 42 per cent of small producers (those that produced less than $1 million in goods per year) advocated higher tariffs in 1939, only 7 per cent of large manufacturers did so. By the postwar era, with continued reductions in rents under the RTAA, small manufacturers began to conform to the pattern observed by large manufacturers. As Bauer, et al. (1972: 113-16) found in response to practically the same question as the Roper poll, by 1954 only 5 per cent of small manufacturers favoured higher tariffs. These findings were replicated in other polls. The April 1955 edition of Fortune, for example, showed that over the previous 15 years, the number of executives favouring a lowering of the tariff almost doubled, while the percentage advocating an increase fell from 31.5 per cent to 5 per cent. Similarly, a poll of 500 business and labour leaders in the Saturday Review (January 23, 1954) conducted by the Research Institute of America found in response to the question "Do you favor further lowering of our tariffs?" that 60.4 per cent answered yes, and 20.9 per cent answered no. Similar findings were reported in the March 1962 issue of Dun's Review and Modern Industry.

The conversion of flexible rent seekers took place gradually. However, the twin mechanisms of RTAA renewal and the numerous iterations of rent reduction gave the Roosevelt administration (as well as subsequent governments) ample opportunity to gauge the reaction of the rent-seeker community. By the postwar era, free trade in industrial goods was well entrenched as US policy, with only a few sectors (most notably textiles and, later, steel) fighting rearguard battles. Best of all from a prescriptive stance, there was no meaningful political backlash against the government–a fact that can be contrasted to other instances of radical trade liberalization (see Lusztig, 2003)

Moreover, while it is impossible to demonstrate counterfactual evidence of how postwar US industrial trade policy would have unfolded in the absence of the shift from the First New Deal to the Second, and hence without the RTAA, inter-sectoral comparison bolsters the case that the logic of the rent reduction game had a decisive impact. While the industrial sector in the United States was subjected to the rigours of market rationalization under the RTAA, the agricultural sector was not. Recall that agriculture was the sole holdover from the First New Deal to the Second. As such, the farming sector was rewarded with the continuation of agricultural subsidies throughout the Depression and the Second World War. By the postwar era, when the international trade regime that was to become the GATT was constructed, powerful rent seekers still existed within the agricultural sector. Thus, even though US farmers were competitive by world standards in the early postwar era, agricultural interests were sufficiently powerful to ensure that agriculture was excluded from the trade regime (Goldstein, 1993b). US industry, by contrast, offered no such resistance.

Conclusion

Building on the "limits of rent seeking" model that distinguishes two basic categories of rent seeker, it has been demonstrated formally that governments can rely on circumstance, as well as political strategy, to effect policies of significant rent reduction without suffering severe political costs. Although the examples have been drawn from the realm of trade policy, the logic of the argument is applicable to other policies of rent reduction as well.

The model accepts one of the key tenets of the international political economy and public choice literature—that rent-seeking producer groups tend to be more successful at influencing trade policy than are free traders. However, unlike the extant literature, the article suggests that where rent-seeker populations are largely flexible, governments that liberalize trade can avoid many of the political costs associated with such a policy. Of course, a significant problem is that because flexible rent seekers have no incentive to reveal their true nature, governments are unwilling to risk large rent reductions.

For governments to gauge whether or not it is politically safe to reduce rents, they require a screening mechanism for forcing flexible and inflexible rent seekers to signal their true positions. One means of doing this is to effect a significant reduction in rents and then observe the behaviour of rent seekers. However, such a strategy buys the government no security against political retaliation. On the other hand, governments may employ two alternative methods to force signals from flexible rent seekers. First, where an initial, substantial reduction in rents can be demonstrably portrayed as structurally imposed, governments may take advantage of the opportunity to observe separation between flexible and inflexible rent seekers, while absorbing limited political costs. Indeed, under such circumstances, flexible rent seekers actually may take the initiative in advancing a further liberalization of trade. More prescriptively, in cases where rent reductions are not structurally imposed, governments may reduce rents gradually and incrementally as a means of gauging the make-up of the rent-seeker population, without absorbing significant political costs. The experience of the Roosevelt administration demonstrates this point.

While the general benefit of the model is that it allows us to understand better how governments may avoid the political costs of free trade, a specific objective of the article is to provide a complement to existing theories as to why the United States shifted its trade policy after 1934. Existing explanations tend to fall into three categories (Ikenberry et al., 1988). Systemic-level explanations, the most prominent being hegemonic stability theory, suggest that US dominance of the world system motivated it to act in the national (and indeed international) interest (see Keohane, 1984; Kindleberger, 1973). The problem here, as Putnam (1988) has pointed out, is that such explanations tend to be insensitive to domestic politics. Indeed, they cannot explain why protectionists no longer were able to exert much influence over US trade policy after 1934. State-level theories maintain that the crisis of the Depression stimulated power plays within the administrative branch and that this constitutes the dominant explanation for the shift in US foreign economic policy (see Goldstein 1993a; Haggard 1988). Finally, societal-level explanations posit that one pressure group—advocating internationalism—defeated the heretofore dominant nationalist pressure group, which had been weakened by the prevailing crisis (Ferguson, 1984; Frieden, 1988). Like state-level explanations, most societal-level theories are compelling, but fail to account for why there was no reversion to the status quo ante in the postwar years, when the effects of the crisis had passed.[19] Our argument, consistent with Milner (1988), is that the business sector, formerly protectionist and now global and free-trading, represents an important force resisting the reimposition of protectionism.

Three directions for further theory and research pertain to the dimensions of variations in a given industry, the range of player preference orderings, and the number of players involved.

One obvious direction for future research is to relax the assumption of only one dimensional variation in a given industry. The current model allows for the presence of flexible and inflexible rent seekers in some probability distribution (that is, q, $1q$). Factors such as industry structure and relative capabilities are certain to create other dimensions along which choices will vary. Relative concentration, for example, will affect the likelihood of potentially menacing collective action among rent seekers, flexible or otherwise (Olson,

1965). Variation in the timing of rent reduction and a choice regarding whether or not to resist also could be expected. Thus a model resembling the repeated Chain Store Game, in which a single large player confronts a series of challengers (rent seekers), might be used in further developing the rent reduction game (James, 1999; Selten, 1978). Such a specification would include estimates of G's "toughness" (that is, willingness to follow through), which would allow the possession of private information by all players. While a model of this kind lies beyond the scope of the present study, it would be a natural project for further research.

In this article, we assume one specific set of preference orderings (for government, flexible, and inflexible rent seekers). We believe our choice of preference orderings describes the most common preferences in reality. However, given the number of potential outcomes in the model, there are a number of possible preference representations even within the confines of the ordinal preference structure. Obviously different preference orderings would lead to different solutions for the strategic rent reduction game. Then, a more general model could incorporate these possible preference orderings by introducing more extensive sets of inequality conditions than we do in this article.

Finally, the number of players in the game could also be expanded to heighten its connection with the intricacies of rent reduction as a political enterprise. In a democratic political system where trade restrictions are a political issue, neither the government nor the rent seekers constitute a single actor. A two-person game, therefore, should be regarded as a starting point when it comes to modeling the complex interactions among the branches of government, interest groups and the general public. For example, in the current game the COG decides on a strategy for inducing rent seekers to reveal their true preferences, but it is also known that legislators who represent constituencies dominated by rent seekers will participate in the determination of government policy. This process, among others not included in the present game, could have an impact on how it is solved. For instance, the politics of energy—perhaps the most fundamental sector of the economy—cannot be understood without an assessment of the legislature's role in the United States and other countries (Uslaner, 1989).

Another example concerns the opening up of the game to participation by foreign governments and firms: How would the game change if a foreign government, along with G, had to be modelled in terms of its tariff policies? Could the actions or reactions of foreign firms alter the equilibria? These and other questions are receiving attention from economists in the context of somewhat different substantive issues, such as the use of export subsidies to signal (un)competitiveness of domestic producers to those abroad as a result of varying motivations (Brainard and Martimort, 1996; Brander, 1995; Collie and Hviid, 1994, 1999; Herander and Kamp, 1999; Kolev and Prusa, 1999). Thus the potential to build further upon modeling efforts elsewhere already exists. The present study is an example of that spirit in action because it incorporates both screening and signaling mechanisms in an effort to portray more accurately the interactions of governments and firms with respect to economic rents from protectionism.

Each of the three preceding suggestions is sufficient to generate an ambitious agenda for further research. These ideas, when taken together, indicate that the game-theoretic model presented in this study can provide a solid foundation for learning more about trade liberalization and rent seeking in the context of democratic politics.

Appendix

To present the solutions to the strategic multistage rent reduction game in a clear fashion, we simplify Figure 1 as follows. On the left side of the extensive form (when F is flexible) in Figure 1, F's decision to resist or not on its last move (R or ~R) leads to the outcomes of Confrontation and Adapt, respectively. From flexible F's preference ordering above (u_F[Adapt] > u_F [$Conf_1$] > u_F[$Conf_2$]), not resisting constitutes a "dominant" action at these decision nodes. By backward induction, then, we can eliminate the "Resist" option and "trim the tree." On the right hand side of the extensive form (when F is inflexible), F's decision on its last move leads to the outcomes of Confrontation and Exit. From inflexible F's preference ordering (u_F[$Conf_1$] > u_F[$Conf_2$] > u_F[Exit]), resisting constitutes a "dominant" action at these decision nodes. So, we eliminate the "Not Resist" option. This leads to Figure 2.

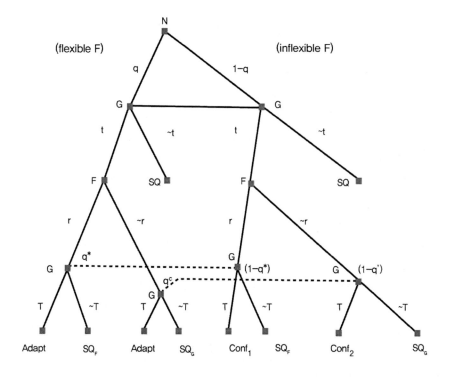

Figure 2. The Reduced Multistage Rent Reduction Game

Then we solve the PBE for the multistage rent reduction game in Figure 2. In doing so, we examine strategies available to F, and G's optimal responses to them. Each of F's strategies is composed of a pair of actions, chosen by flexible and inflexible Fs. With regard to notation, F's strategy of, say (r, r), should read "F chooses r when it is flexible; F chooses r when it is inflexible." G's strategy is composed of "G's initial action; G's response to F's action, r; and G's response to F's action, ~r." For example, G's strategy of (t, T, T) should read "G chooses t in its first move; in its second move, G chooses T if F chooses r; and G chooses T if F chooses ~r."

[1] F chooses (r, r), that is, pooling on r.

G's information set corresponding to r is on the equilibrium path. So G's belief $(q^*, 1 - q^*)$ at this information set must be determined by Bayes' rule and F's strategy. Since F is pooling, G learns nothing new about F's type: q^* = q. Given G's belief of $q^* = q$, what is G's optimal response to (r, r)? We first calculate

$$EU_G(r,T) = q \cdot u_G(Adapt) + (1-q) \cdot u_G(Conf_1)$$
$$EU_G(r, \sim T) = u_G(SQ_F).$$

We can then summarize G's optimal strategy as follows:

(i) (a). (t, T, T) and $(t, T, \sim T)$ are optimal iff $EU_G(r, T) t EU_G(r, \sim T)$.
∘ $q \cdot u_G(Adapt) + (1-q) \cdot u_G(Conf_1) tu_G(SQ)$.

Solving it for q gives,

$$q t \frac{u_G(SQ) - u_G(Conf_1)}{u_G(Adapt) - u_G(Conf_1)}.$$

So (t,T,T) and (t,T,~T) are optimal when the above inequality condition holds. That is, G introduces t, followed by T when it believes that the probability of F being flexible is high.

(i) (b). (t, ~T, T) and (t, ~T, ~T) are never optimal since $u_G(SQ) > u_G(SQ_F)$. That is, if F always resists t, G is better off not introducing t (which leads to SQ) than introducing it and backing down later (which leads to SQ_F).

(ii) (~t,X) is optimal when
$$q < \frac{u_G(SQ) - u_G(Conf_1)}{u_G(Adapt) - u_G(Conf_1)}.$$

where X is any pair of G's responses to F's action. That is, when F always resists the initial t, and if G believes that the probability of a flexible F is sufficiently low, G might as well not introduce t in the first place. The next question is whether F's pooling strategy (r, r) is optimal given G's strategy of (t,

T, T), (t, T, ~T), and (~t, X).

(i) (a). When F chooses (r, r) and G chooses (t, T, T) or (t, T, ~T), then Adapt becomes the outcome if F is flexible, and Conf1 is the outcome if F is inflexible. Can F do better by moving away from (r, r)? We first check how G would respond to ~r. If G's response to ~r is T, then $EU_F(\sim r) = u_F(\text{Adapt})$ when F is flexible and $EU_F(\sim r) = u_F(Conf_2)$ when F is inflexible. If G's response to ~r is ~T, then $EU_F(\sim r) = u_F(SQ_G)$. Since $u_F(SQ_G) > u_F(\text{Adapt})$ and $u_F(SQ_G) > u_F(\text{Conf1})$ for flexible and inflexible F respectively, it is in F's interest to switch to ~r if G responds with ~T.

Therefore, if there is an equilibrium in which F's strategy is (r, r), G 's response to ~r must be T. Then G's strategy of (t, T, ~T) cannot be part of an equilibrium. So, $EU_G(\sim r, T) t EU_G(\sim r, \sim T)$ must be satisfied. Then q' · u_G (Adapt) + (1 − q') · u_G(Conf2) $t u_G(SQ_G)$.

Solving it for q' gives,

$$q' t \frac{u_G(SQ_G) - u_G(Conf_2)}{u_G(\text{Adapt}) - u_G(Conf_2)}.$$

F's strategy of (r, r) is the optimal response to (t, T, T) when the above condition is satisfied. Then a pooling PBE for the game is:

$$\left\{ (t, T, T), (r, r), q^* = q\, t\, \frac{u_G(SQ) - u_G(Conf_1)}{u_G(\text{Adapt}) - u_G(Conf_1)}, \quad q'\, t\, \frac{u_G(SQ_G) - u_G(Conf_2)}{u_G(\text{Adapt}) - u_G(Conf_2)} \right\}$$

[2] F chooses (~r, r), that is, separation with flexible F playing ~r.

(i). We can find a PBE similar to the one found in [1] (i) above. If F chooses (~r, r) (and G chooses (t, X)), then both of G's information sets are on the equilibrium path: $q^* = 0$ and $q' = 1$. Given these beliefs, i's best response is (t, ~T, T), which guarantees the outcome Adapt when F is flexible and SQ_F when F is inflexible. Given (t, ~T, T), F's optimal strategy is (~r, r). Therefore, there exists a separating PBE, {(t, ~T, T), (~r, r), $q^* = 0$, $q' = 1$}.

(ii). (~t, X) guarantees the outcome SQ. It is easy to show that {(~t, X),

(~r, r), q* = 0, q' = 1} is a separating PBE (process not shown).

[3] F chooses (r, ~r), that is, separation with a flexible F playing r, or (~r, ~r), pooling on ~r.

Under these conditions (q* = 1 and q' = 0; and q' = q, respectively), G chooses ~t in all PBEs (process not shown). (~t, X) guarantees SQ, which is F's most preferred outcome.

Notes

1. See, for example, Brawley (1993); Conybeare (1987); Dombrowski (1998); Grieco(1990); Meadwell and Martin (1996); Sandler (1997).

2. In New Zealand, a reforming government after 1983 imposed severe rent reductions on the agricultural sector. While there was a great deal of economic dislocation on the part of farmers over the short term, within two to three years the agricultural sector was strongly committed to further liberalization of trade and pressured the government to retain low agricultural rents while at the same time lowering state-supplied rents to the industrial sector (Douglas, 1993; Johnston and Frengley, 1994). Governments also can offset the dislocation costs associated with trade liberalization by providing trade adjustment packages to producers. This strategy was employed in Great Britain, for example, in the legislation that repealed the Corn Laws (see Lusztig, 2003: chap. 2).

3. Staiger (1995) makes a similar argument, suggesting that even modest liberalization of trade will induce some rent earners within import competing sectors to relocate out of that sector. It also should be noted that the position in the economic cycle can affect the calculations made by flexible rent seekers, but that factor is treated as exogenous in the current version of the model. It would be interesting in future research to endogenize the role of the economic cycle.

4. In this sense the model is separate from so-called "cheap talk," in which the signaling takes the form of discussion rather than action (Odell, 2000: 133-34).

5. There is a large literature on the impact of crisis in providing policy manoeuverability for political innovators; see Goldstein (1993a), Gourevitch (1986) and Krasner (1984).

6. Sandholtz (1993) suggests that this "hand-tying" explains why most European govern-

ments were willing to sacrifice a degree of national sovereignty by agreeing to a monetary union at Maastricht. The union would permit the political costs of monetary discipline to be transferred from democratically elected governments to the more insulated regime. This is not to suggest, of course, that there are not domestic costs associated with regime compliance. Moreover, such costs are variant across countries.

7. The rent reduction game that appears in Figure 1 is related to models from the vast literature on strategic trade policy but differs significantly from the many treatments that originate in economics. Three prominent issues explored in recent economic literature, in each instance through game-theoretic models with asymmetric information, are (a) strategic trade policy regarding public contracts (Brainard and Martimort, 1996); (b) optimal tariffs or export subsidies as signals of (un)competitiveness (Collie and Hviid, 1999; Herander and Kamp, 1999); and (c) setting tariffs in relation to a foreign monopolist (Collie and Hviid, 1994; Kolev and Prusa, 1999). (The literature on strategic trade policy is reviewed authoritatively by Brander [1995].) While insights from these works will be noted subsequently, the substantive issues and associated game-theoretic models are fundamentally different from those of the present study. To cite one example, the studies from economics are more concerned with (in)efficiencies in domestic production and trade as a result of varying export subsidies and tariffs that might be confronted by a foreign monopolist, whereas the focus of the present investigation is on the politics of trade liberalization.

8. For a COG with a fixed term in office, the goals substituted for lengthening service would appear obvious. The ability to control policy making for either direct personal benefit or to reward important support groups is enhanced through more autonomy, which logically should correlate with political support for the government. Thus the ability to procure benefits more effectively over each time interval (that is, intensity) would come into play as a consideration rather than extension of time served (that is, frequency).

9. Player F imposes a cost on G when minor resistance occurs, but F's ultimate success in that scenario creates an offsetting benefit. The persistence of G in the face of minor resistance creates a demonstration effect for other firms and even industries. Thus, the equivalence of the absence and presence of minor resistance recognizes that "costly signalling" by a player can create potentially important external benefits (Fearon, 1994).

10. The pure status quo ranks ahead of the one marginally adjusted by G (that is, through t, but not T) because the latter, which does not include even a minor act of retaliation by F, might encourage observers to think that G is lacking in resolve. Even worse is the status quo adjusted by F (that is, t followed by r and no further actions) because it suggests that F's minor act of retaliation discouraged G from reducing rents any further. (In the intermediate case of SQG there might at least be some other plausible explanation for why G decided to go no further.)

11. All rent seekers hold identical preferences over the first three alternatives. SQ is best, by definition, because rent seekers continue to collect profits without confronting the risks posed by change. The next best alternative is a minor adjustment to the status quo, in which F engages in a minor act of retaliation against G and the latter takes no further action. After that, a change in the status quo by G (that is, t), with no further action, is the next most preferred (that is, no major reduction in rents). Adapting to G's major rent reduction ranks next among the alternatives. The confrontation outcomes appear last in the ordering, with two acts of resistance being preferred to one. If F follows this path, it must be assumed that it is at electoral "war" with G and derives additional utility from attacking at each stage.

12. One can imagine a second type of inflexible rent seeker who prefers exit to confrontation, described earlier as a noncommitted inflexible rent seeker. To maintain simplicity of presentation, we do not consider this possibility. Since our goal is to show that the government can reduce rents and still survive in the multistage game, if we can show that the government can do that against a "tougher" adversary—that is, the committed inflexible rent seekers, who prefer confrontation—then it follows that the same can be achieved against the adversary who is not inclined to resist.

13. One question that might be raised about the game's specification is whether a single probe or "trial balloon," in the form of a limited rent reduction (that is, t), truly represents the process of gradualism as described earlier in more impressionistic terms. In a compelling review of research on strategic trade policy, Brander (1995: 1422) warns that, if anything, more is likely to be learned from a model such as that appearing in Figure 1 than one with many stages, because the "folk theorem" intervenes in the latter instance. To be more precise, repeated interactions in strategic trade games will produce a wide and even unwieldy range of feasible outcomes, consistent with the folk theorem as invoked elsewhere.

14. The second scenario (scenario [2] (i) in the Appendix) presents an interesting case, as the government updates its belief about the industry's type from the latter's response to government's small reduction in rents.

15. Obviously, the propositions above hold when public officials understand the logic of the multistage rent reduction game.

16. Although not shown in the Appendix, it obviously would be much easier to induce trade liberalization in the PBEs with the type of inflexible rent seeker described in footnote 12. In this manner, the process of culling inflexible rent seekers would be much less painful to the government.

17. For an expanded discussion of the Second New Deal coalition see Lusztig (1996: chap. 3); for more on Roosevelt's desire to ensure the support of internationalist business interests pending full-scale defection of conservatives see Roosevelt's speech to the Bankers' Convention in Washington, October 24, 1934 (Roosevelt, 1938: 435-40).

18. Most pertinently, the RTAA provided the administration with the power to negotiate bilateral trade deals that were not subject to congressional oversight. The logic was that Congress was far more susceptible to rent-seeking interests than was the more insulated Department of State.

19. The most compelling recent account of trade outcomes, which shows how the distribution of political authority, electoral structures, and institutional foundations exert influence on trade policy outcomes for the United States and Canada, appears in Bennett and Duchesne (2000).

11.

Changing Cleavage Structure in New Democracies: An Empirical Analysis of Political Cleavages in Korea.

Heemin Kim, Jun Y. Choi & Jinman Cho.

Abstract. Cleavage structure cuts across the members of a state and affects the electorate' choice of parties and candidates. Social cleavage structure can be stable or go through changes depending on on-going social change as well as political parties'electoral strategies. With the collapse of communism and the advent of the third wave of democracy, many countries in Eastern Europe, Latin merica, and Asia have experienced rapid social change. New political parties have formed, and democratic elections have been introduced in most of these countries. With rapid social change and the resulting shifts in party strategies, do we also expect rapid change in social cleavage structure in these countries? Or does cleavage structure change only gradually and remain stable over a short-term period? In this paper, we attempt to answer these questions by examining the relative importance of three cleavages commonly claimed to have relevance to politics in the 2000s dregionalism, ideology, and generational differencesdin voters, choices in Korea. We analyze the voting behavior of the electorate in the 16th and 17th National Assembly elections, in 2000 and 2004, respectively, by employing multinomial logistic analyses of voter survey data. Our analysis indicates that the relative importance of various cleavages changed during the early 2000s: the influence of regionalism remained strong, but its intensity declined; the importance of ideology grew; and a new cleavage of generational differences appeared. Our study shows that the cleavage structure is fluid even in a short-term period, especially in new democracies, as citizens and elites adjust their behaviors in response to changing social situations. Political parties may also introduce a particular electoral strategy to induce change in the cleavage structure.

Introduction

Cleavage structure cuts across the members of a state, affecting the electorate' choice, and thus, the resulting party system (Schattschneider, 1960; Lipset and Rokkan, 1967; Rae and Taylor, 1970). Examples of such cleavages include class, religion, ethnicity, and language, among others. Party systems are the institutions designed to link citizens and leaders, aggregating the electoral resources of the citizens (McDonald and Budge, 2005 Kim et al., 2006). Party system configurations open up some possibilities for representation and constrain others. On one hand, they tend to have great continuity across elections (Lipset and Rokkan, 1967) because of the weight of voter images and organizational structure, yet they are also capable of undergoing sharp changes as new issues emerge or new electoral strategies are chosen (or eschewed; see Kitschelt, 1994). In the end, social cleavage structure can be stable or go through changes depending on on-going social change and parties'electoral strategies.

With the collapse of communism and the advent of the third wave of democracy, many countries in Eastern Europe, Latin America, and Asia have experienced rapid social change. New political parties have formed, and democratic elections have been introduced in most of these countries. With rapid social change and the resulting shifts in party strategies, do we also expect rapid change in social cleavage structure? Or does cleavage structure change only gradually and remain stable over a short-term period? These are intriguing questions for political scientists, but until now, few studies have looked at changing or stable cleavage structures in new democracies. In this paper, we attempt to analyze cleavage structures utilizing data from one of those new democracies, South Korea (Korea hereafter).

Korea has a relatively homogeneous population, sharing ethnicity, language, and historical traditions. The authoritarian rule imposed on the Korean people, first by General Park Chung-hee (1961–1979), then by General Chun Doo-hwan (1979–1987), suppressed the emergence of truly social cleavages; the single most dominant issue in Korean politics was the authoritarianism-democracy divide until 1987, when the transition to democracy began.

With democratic opening and free elections came regionalism as the dominant cleavage in Korean politics. This was especially the case in the rivalry between the southeastern region of Youngnam and the southwestern region of Honam, due to the electoral strategies of political parties.

Political leaders who emerged as alternatives to authoritarian rule were perceived as representing certain regions of Korea without nationwide appeal and with their party support firmly entrenched in those regions. It is widely agreed among observers of Korean politics that since the democratic opening, electoral competition has been used as an expression of regional frustration and animosity, with regionalism playing the decisive role in the choices the Korean electorate made (Chung, 1993; Park, 1993; Choi, 1995 Lee, Nam Young, 1998, 1999). Table 1, which shows the percentage of National Assembly seats obtained by each of the major parties since the 13th National Assembly elections in 1988, exemplifies the importance of regionalism for the party support of the electorate.

However, for various reasons, it was largely expected that the impact of regionalism would decline in the 17th National Assembly elections scheduled for 2004: first, three key charismatic leaders who single-handedly controlled their own regionally-based parties had retired from politics by this time (two of them after having served as President). This led to adjustments in each party' electoral strategy to maintain the same level of political support under different circumstances; second, candidate Roh Moo-hyun of the New Millenium Democratic Party (NMDP) won the presidential election in 2002. The NMDP was a regional party representing the Honam region, but Roh himself came from the rival Youngnam region, thus diluting the effect of regionalism in politics; third, it was widely viewed that Roh Moo-hyun was elected with support primarily from the younger generations and the more progressive elements of Korean society, thus paving the way for ideology and generational issues to play greater roles in Korean politics.

Table 1. Regional nature of the major party support in Korea[a]

Region	13th NA (1988)			14th NA (1992)		15th NA (1996)			16th NA (2000)			17th NA (2004)	
	DJP	DPP	DPRP	DLP	DP	NKP	NCNP	ULD	GNP	NMCP	ULD	GNP	Woori Party
Seoul–Gyonggi	42%	23%	12%	47%	42%	56%	31%	5%	41%	58%	1%	30%	70%
Choong chung	33%	0%	56%	57%	9%	11%	0%	86%	17%	33%	46%	4%	79%
Young nam	55%	21%	3%	75%	0%	67%	0%	13%	98%	0%	0%	88%	6%
Honam	0%	97%	0%	5%	95%	3%	97%	0%	0%	86%	0%	0%	81%
Other	47%	0%	6%	47%	0%	75%	0%	13%	33%	58%	0%	55%	45%

[a] Each cell entry represents the percentage of seats in the region the party acquired in that election. Entries for Youngnam and Honam regions (highlighted in bold and italic) show extreme nature of regional support of individual parties

Since the National Assembly elections in 2004, many students of Korean politics have debated the impacts of newfound cleavages of ideology and generational differences, as well as the potentially declining role of regionalism on Korean politics. However, there is little agreement among scholars, and the existing studies seem to have methodological deficiencies (Kang, 2004; Lee and Leem, 2004). There were more than two major parties competing in the National Assembly elections in Korea from which voters could choose. Therefore, in order to properly delve into what determined the electorate' choice among several candidates, it is crucial to employ a statistical method that can deal with multiple choices. In this paper, we attempt to do so by employing multinomial logistic analysis, a statistical method designed to accommodate nominal dependent variables with more than two categories. We will specifically state and test our hypotheses using appropriate data. By doing so, we will examine the relative importance of regionalism, ideology, and generational differences in voters'choices and investigate the possibility of changing cleavage structure in Korea.

In the following section, we identify the factors impacting the electorate' decisions in Korea and develop hypotheses based on our identifications. Then, we present statistical models to test our hypotheses with the description of the data, methodology, and the measures we use. We analyze the voters'choices in the 16th and 17th National Assembly elections in 2000 and 2004, respectively, using multinomial logistic models. We conclude the paper by summarizing our findings about Korea and by discussing their implications for the stability or fluidity/volatility of cleavage structure in new democracies.

Hypotheses

In this section, we discuss cleavages and events that are believed to have affected election outcomes in Korea. Based on this discussion, we present eight hypotheses about the factors which affected voting behavior at the time of the 16th and the 17th National Assembly elections. We start with the important cleavage of regionalism in Korea.

Regionalism

Conventional wisdom asserts that regionalism has driven the outcomes of elections in the post-democratization period in Korea (Park, 1993; Choi, 1995; Lee, Kapyoon, 1999; Yang, 2001). However, regionalism in Korea had, in fact, affected the outcomes of elections prior to Korea' democratization. For example, when Park Junghee ran against Yoon Bo-sun in the 5th presidential election in 1963, support for each candidate was polarized between the Northern and Southern regions of Korea. Such a regional divide was again witnessed in the 6th presidential election when Park Jung-hee vied with Kim Dae-jung in 1971: The electorate of the Youngnam and the Honam regions were diametrically opposed.

However, there exist the following qualitative differences in regionalism before and after Korea' democratization. First, regionalism prior to democratization shows polarizing differences between rural and urban regions caused by the industrialization, urbanization, and agricultural policies of the government (Yoon, 1981, 1987). On the other hand, regionalism after democratization has been driven by a particular region' preference for a candidate/party of its own region. This was manifested in the regional political conflicts between the Youngnam and the Honam regions. Second, regionalism before democratization tended to emerge and become politicized in the presidential elections while, in the post-democratization era, regionalism has driven elections at all levelsdpresidential, National Assembly, and local. In essence, the regionally-based political parties manipulated the rise of regionalism as part of their electoral strategies in the post-democratization period. Third, regionalism before democratization tended to be less persistent, more temporal, and less influential in electoral outcomes. However, regionalism in the post-democratization era has been persistent and more influential in electoral outcomes.

Cha (1988) points out that the regionalism variable was the single most important factor affecting the choices of the Korean electorate in the 13th presidential election in 1987, the first democratic election in Korea; other variables such as age, education, and gender did not have a significant impact on the outcomes of the election. Park (1993) also proposes that the voters'8 places of birth (i.e. their regions) were the key drivers for their choices in the 14th National Assembly elections in 1992. In addition, Lee, Nam Young (1998, 1999) finds that regionalism generated emotional voting behavior that resulted in the blind casting of votes for candidates from the same region as the voters, as the regional chasm between the Youngnam and the Honam, and the Honam and Non-Honam electorates intensified.

As we mentioned before, however, after Roh Moohyun won the presidential election in 2002, political circumstances in Korea took a new turn. In this context, some argued that the importance of regional cleavage, which had dominated the outcomes of the Korean elections since democratization, might decline. For example, Kang (2003) asserts that ideological differences had a significant impact on the outcome of the 2002 presidential election. Lee and Leem (2004) find that ideological cleavage and generational cleavage had significant effects on electorate voting behaviors in the 17th National Assembly elections in 2004. They also argue that the influence of regional cleavage in the Youngnam region declined.

Relying upon the discussion above on regionalism in Korea, we hypothesize that regionalism was a decisive factor for voters'decisions in the National

Assembly elections prior to 2004, and that the impact of regionalism declined substantially in 2004 when the 17th National Assembly elections were held.

The left-right ideology

There has been a common perception among observers of Korean politics that the left-right ideology did not play an important role in the choices the electorate made, mainly because there was no meaningful ideological distinction among political parties. Practically all the parties formed since the democratic opening in 1987 have been conservative parties reflecting Korea' history in the war with the North and Korea' subsequent role as the front between the East and the West during the cold war era. As political development continued, many practitioners and observers of Korean politics emphasized the desirability of policy-oriented (that is, more ideologically-oriented) political parties, which further implied that there was no meaningful ideological distinction in Korea (Sohn, 1995; Lee, Kapyoon, 1999; Choi, 2002; Cho, 2003).

There have been some empirical analyses showing the significance of ideological positions of voters in their choices of parties/candidates at the time of the National Assembly or presidential elections in the 1990s. These studies, however, were marred by methodological problems: primarily the failure to control for other important factors (such as regionalism), resulting in specification errors (Lee, 1992, 1996; Kang, 2003). Therefore, the evidence that the left-right ideology did influence the choice of the Korean electorates is, if at all, very weak, at least up until 2000.

However, there has been change. Some scholars have reported that ideological differences among generations did affect the electorate' choices in a significant manner in the 2002 presidential election (Kang, 2002, 2003). Then, shortly before the scheduled National Assembly elections in 2004, a progressive party representing Korean workers, the Democratic Labor Party (DLP), was born. This new party without any regional base performed rather well and became the third largest party in terms of seat share in the Korean National Assembly. It is safe to assume that those who voted for the DLP were ideological voters.[1] Given that the left-right ideology played an important role in the choice of the electorate in the 2002 presidential election and that a sufficient number of voters voted in accordance with their ideologies in 2004, we hypothesize that the left-right ideology had a significant impact on the choice of the voters in the National Assembly elections in 2004, while it did not in 2000 (and before).

Generational Differences

The presidential election of 2002 is viewed as the first national-level election in the history of Korea in which generational differences played a critical role in the election outcomethe old primarily supported Lee Hoi-chang, the Grand National Party candidate, while the young preferred Roh Moo-hyun. This new generational cleavage can be traced back to several different roots. The first has to do with economic, or the lefteright, ideological division. Lee Hoi-chang, with his nobleman' image and conservative stands on various issues, was supported by those who were well-to-do and who preferred stability, many of them happening to belong to the older generation. On the other hand, Roh Moo-hyun, a high school graduate without a college education, became a human rights lawyer by passing a difficult bar exam on his own. He was the epitome of the self-made man and a champion of the weak and poor, an image that appealed to the younger generation. The year 2002 was also a period when many South Koreans went through a transformation in their beliefs about the optimal place of South Korea between the U.S.A. and North Korea. The acquittal in a U.S. military court of two U.S. soldiers who accidentally caused the deaths of two Korean girls by running them over with a military vehicle enraged Korean citizens and led to countless candlelight vigils and violent demonstrations in front of the U.S. embassy throughout the year. The Bush administration' tough stance against North Korea as part of the 'axis of evil'also added fuel to the debate over what North Korea meant to South Koreans. Many South Koreans believed that the Bush administration' North Korea policy not only undermined former President Kim Dae-jung' 'Sunshine' policy (engagement policy), but unnecessarily heightened tensions in the Korean Peninsula, from which, if anybody, South Koreans would suffer.

Under these circumstances, the older, so-called 6-25 (the Korean War), generation was quite suspicious of the true intentions of North Korea and placed greater weight on maintaining the traditional military alliance with the U.S. Lee Hoi-chang had continuously stated his preferences for a North Korean aid policy based on 'reciprocity' and called for the cessation of all monetary aid to the North that could be subverted to funding its nuclear programs. Naturally, Lee was a favorite among the older, established generations in South Korea. On the other hand, Roh Moo-hyun advocated continued cooperation with the North to prevent heightened tension in the Korean Peninsula, which could lead to a U.S.-North Korea clash. Further, he indicated that under his presidency, he would establish an equal relationship between the U.S. and Korea. His seemingly independent position was extremely popular among the younger, so-called post-6-25 (or post- Korean War), generation (Joong-ang Ilbo, 2002, various dates).

Table 2 shows the split between the old and the young in the presidential election of 2002. As we can see, voters in their twenties and thirties over-whelmingly supported Roh Moo-hyun. On the other hand, voters in their fifties and above overwhelmingly voted for Lee Hoi-chang. Those in their forties con-stitute some sort of boundary between the two contending generations.

Since a new cleavage of generational differences clearly played an im-portant role in the 2002 presidential election and there is no reason to believe that it dissipated after 2002, we hypothesize that generational differences had a significant impact on voters'choice in the National Assembly elections in 2004, while they did not in 2000.

Exogenous shock I: The 'Blacklist' movement in 2000

Oftentimes, some important political or economic events immediately before or during the electoral campaign affect the choices of the electors. Examples in-clude the oil shock and the Iranian hostage crisis in the 1980 U.S. presidential election. Similarly, the 'lacklist'movement of the Korean NGOs at the time of the 16th National Assembly elections is purported to have affected election out-comes in 2000 (Cho, 2001; Cho and Kim, 2002).

Since the democratic opening of 1987, personalistic and paternalistic politi-cal parties developed based on regional support (see Kim, 1994, 1997). This meant that political parties'nomination processes were in the hands of a few key party leaders, and as a result, a group of the same candidates returned to the electoral arena every four years. The general public in Korea desired fresh blood and political reform at a fast pace, but prospects were bleak as long as the nomination process was controlled by an elite few.

Feeling hopeless, an alliance of 412 NGOs in Korea directly challenged all political parties by publishing a 'lacklist'of corrupt politicians who they thought should not be elected for the upcoming 16th National Assembly elections in 2000. Despite the controversy over its legality (Cho, 2000), the electorate responded to this movement. Out of 86 prominent politicians on the list, 59 failed to return to the National Assembly. The Korean media portrayed this as a show of citizen power. Given the proportion of candidates adversely affected by this movement, we hypothesize that the 'lacklist'movement at the time of the 16th National Assembly elections had a significant impact on the choice of the electorate.

Exogenous shock II: The presidential impeachment in 2004

On March 12, 2004, a stunning political event occurred in Korea as its National Assembly impeached President Roh Moo-hyun, only a year into his term as President. The opposition parties with over two-thirds of the seats in the Assembly decided to use their numerical strength only one month before the next National Assembly elections. As a result of the impeachment, the case was sent to the Constitutional Court for a final decision according to the Korean constitution. Roh' presidential powers were immediately suspended, and Prime Minister Koh Gun became acting head of state. The opposition' motivation for the impeachment was the President' public expression of support for the governing Woori Party for the upcoming National Assembly elections (which oddly enough was a violation of election law in Korea; see historical background below) and his refusal to publicly apologize for his conduct as the opposition demanded (Hankuk Ilbo, 2004, various dates).

Roh Moo-hyun, when elected President in 2002, not only faced a majority opposition party in the GNP, but a significant portion of his own party which had not supported him at the time of the nomination process. With or without signals from the Blue House, the presidential mansion in Korea, those within the governing New Millennium Democratic Party (NMDP) who were loyal to President Roh defected from it to establish a new governing party. The result was the founding of the so-called Woori ('Our' Party in 2003.)

Table 3 shows the seat distributions in the National Assembly in Korea. The middle column shows the seat distribution among political parties after the National Assembly elections in 2000. The far right column shows the seat distribution as of January 2004 after the founding of the Woori Party. As we can see, even after the establishment of the de-facto governing Woori Party, the Roh government' base of power was quite weak within the National Assembly. Further, Roh supporters'defection from the NMDP ultimately turned it into a hostile opposition since the NMDP' remaining members felt betrayed by the Roh supporters.

Table 3. Seat distribution in the National Assembly in Korea

Political parties	After the 16th General election in 2000	As of January 2004
Grand National Party	133	148
New Millennium Democratic Party	115	60
United Liberal Democrats	17	10
Woori Party	N/A	47
Others	8	6
Total	273	271[a]

[a] A death and a conviction reduced the number of assembly persons by two

In a press conference in early 2004, President Roh stated that he hoped the governing Woori Party would acquire as many seats as possible in the up-coming National Assembly elections scheduled in April. This remark enraged the opposition, since under Korean election law, public officials are prohibited from openly supporting a particular political party (although the law itself sounds rather unrealistic). The National Election Commission formally warned the President against further similar remarks. In addition, the opposition demanded a public apology by the President for the remark. Otherwise, it threatened to push for the impeachment of President Roh as the GNP and the NMDP combined had more than the requisite two-thirds of the seats in the National Assembly to pass the impeachment motion.

In a nationally televised press conference in March, President Roh refused to apologize regarding the violation of election law. This further goaded the opposition assembly persons, and many who had been reluctant to vote for the impeachment were now inclined to vote for it. On March 12, the historic impeachment vote was taken. The governing Woori Party assembly persons, lacking the necessary one-third vote to block the impeachment, occupied the assembly president' podium to prevent the vote itself, but were dragged off the floor by assembly security. In a subsequent vote cast only by the opposition, 193 out of 195 voted for the impeachment, exceeding the necessary two-thirds majority (181) by 12 votes. As a result, the President was impeached. As a final measure, the case was sent to the Constitutional Court for a final decision. Roh' presidential powers were immediately suspended, and Prime Minister Koh Gun became the acting head of state (Hankuk Ilbo, 2004, various dates).

To the opposition' amazement, reactions to the impeachment were a near universal condemnation. Virtually all NGOs, labor organizations, student groups, scholars, and lawyers' associations denounced the vote and declared civil disobedience. Massive demonstrations ensued (Hankuk Ilbo, 2004, various dates).

The National Assembly elections were held on April 15, as scheduled. The outcome of the National Assembly elections, along with the seat distribution just before the elections, is shown in Table 4. The elections resulted in the new Assembly whose composition was quite different from the previous one. For our purposes, we cannot overlook the demise of the opposition, especially of the NMDP, and the political victory of the governing Woori Party. The GNP also lost a significant proportion of seats considering the increase in the total number of seats in the Assembly to 299. This was the first time in 19 years that the governing party acquired a simple majority of seats (which requires 150 in a 299-seat assembly) in the National Assembly in Korea.

Table 4. Seat distribution in the National Assembly in Korean.

Political parties	As of January 2004	After the 17th General election in 2004
Grand National Party	148	121
New Millennium Democratic Party	60	9
United Liberal Democrats	10	4
Woori Party	47	152
Democratic Labor Party	N/A	10
Others	6	3
Total	271	299[a]

[a] The new electoral law enacted just before the elections increased the number of seats in the National Assembly to 299

Surveys of the electorate indicated that the impeachment was the over-whelming criterion for its choice of parties/candidates. In the 2004 National Assembly elections, politics clearly were not 'ocal.'Voters paid little attention to the candidates, but looked primarily at their party labels (Joong-ang Ilbo, 2004, various dates). Obviously, the electorate did not approve of the impeach-ment vote by the opposition and punished it accordingly.[2] Based on the dis-cussion above, we hypothesize that the presidential impeachment in 2004 had a significant effect on the choices of the electorate in the National Assembly elections in 2004.

A series of observations made above lead to the following set of hypotheses:

Hypothesis 1: Regionalism was the single most important cleavage that de-termined voter choice prior to 2004.

Hypothesis 2: Political ideology did not affect voter choice in the National Assembly elections prior to 2004.

Hypothesis 3: Generational differences did not affect voter choice in the National Assembly elections prior to 2004.

Hypothesis 4: The 'Blacklist'movement significantly affected voter choice at the time of the 16th National Assembly elections in 2000.

Hypothesis 5: The impact of regionalism declined in the 17th National Assembly elections in 2004.

Hypothesis 6: Political ideology affected voter choice in a significant manner in the 17th National Assembly elections in 2004.

Hypothesis 7: Generational differences played an important role in the 17th National Assembly elections in 2004.

Hypothesis 8: The presidential impeachment significantly affected voter choice at the time of the 17th National Assembly elections in 2004.

Data, methods, and the model

In order to test the hypotheses proffered in the previous section, we employ multinomial logistic models. This method is appropriate when the dependent variable is nominal and has more than two categories. The multinomial logistic model can be regarded as an extension of the binary logistic model in that it is "simultaneously estimating binary logits for all possible comparisons among the outcome categories" (Long, 1997, p. 149). Relying on this method, we analyze the factors affecting the outcomes of the 16th and 17th National Assembly elections. The data for both elections are based on voter surveys conducted by the Korean Social Science Data Center (KSSDC). We focus only on the 16th and 17th National Assembly elections because the voter surveys conducted by the KSSDC prior to the 16th National Assembly elections did not include questions regarding ideology, which is a crucial variable for the purpose of this study.

The model for the 16th National Assembly elections is:

$$Model\ 1:\ V_1 = \alpha + \beta_1 Ideology + \beta_2 Generation$$
$$+ \beta_3 Blacklist + \beta_4 Choongchung$$
$$+ \beta_5 Honam + \beta_6 Gangwon$$
$$+ \beta_7 Youngnam + \varepsilon$$

The dependent variable (V1) has multiple discrete categories: the electorates'choices for the parties running in their districts. The Ideology variable is based on responses to the ideological tendency item, coded 1 for 'liberal,'2 for 'moderate,'and 3 for 'conservative.' The Generation variable is based on the respondents'ages, coded 1 for those in their twenties, 2 for the thirties, 3 for the forties, and 4 for those in their fifties and older.[3] The Blacklist variable measures the impact of the 'Blacklist' movement on the respondents'choices of parties/candidates, coded 1 for 'Strongly influenced choice,'2 for 'Moderately influenced,'3 for 'Influenced a little,'and 4 for 'id not influence at all.'The rest of the variables are regional dummy variables based on the respondents'places of residence. The Seoul-Gyunggi region is used as a baseline.

The model for the 17th National Assembly elections is essentially the same as model 1 above, except the 'lacklist'variable is replaced by the presidential impeachment variable.

$$Model\ 2:\ V_2 = \alpha + \beta_1 Ideology + \beta_2 Generation$$
$$+ \beta_3 Impeachment + \beta_4 Choongchung$$
$$+ \beta_5 Honam + \beta_6 Gangwon$$
$$+ \beta_7 Youngnam + \varepsilon$$

Like model 1 above, the dependent variable (V2) has multiple discrete categories reflecting parties running in respondents'districts. The Ideology variable is based on the responses to the ideological tendency item, coded 0 for 'Very liberal'to 10 for 'Very conservative.'[4] The Generation variable is based on the respondents' age, coded 1 for those in their twenties, 2 for the thirties, 3 for the forties, and 4 for those in their fifties and older. The Impeachment variable measures the respondents' attitudes towards the presidential impeachment, coded 1 for 'Strongly for the impeachment,' 2 for 'Moderately for,' 3 for 'Moderately against,'and 4 for 'Strongly against.'The rest of the variables are regional dummy variables based on the respondents'places of residence. The Seoul-Gyunggi region is again used as a baseline.

Findings

The results of our multinomial logistic analyses appear in Tables 7 and 8. As we discussed above, the multinomial logistic model estimates the effects of the independent variables for all possible pairs among the categories (political parties in our study) of the dependent variable. Readers will notice that not all possible pairs of political parties are presented in Tables 7 and 8. As one can see in Tables 3 and 5, for all practical purposes, the electoral competition was between the GNP and the NMDP at the time of the 16th National Assembly elections in 2000. So, we grouped all other and minor parties (including the ULD) and independents together in a single category.[5]

Likewise, the electoral contest for the 17th National Assembly elections was, for all practical purposes, between the GNP and the Woori Party, as Tables 4 and 6 attest. Therefore, all possible match-ups (pairs or dyads) including the GNP and/or the Woori Party are presented in Table 8. We also present the match-ups including the DLP, since the creation and the performance of the Party have been viewed as evidence of ideological cleavage by some scholars. We also include the NMDP in Table 8, since it was a regional party representing the Honam region, and was one of the two culprits of the presidential impeachment in 2004 (the other one, of course, was the GNP). This means only the ULD and independents (combined representing 7 out of 299 seats in the National Assembly) are excluded from the presentation in Table 8.

The positive sign of the coefficients in Tables 7 and 8 indicates that the probability of the respondent voting for the first party in the pair increases as the value of the independent variable increases. For example, the coefficient of the Honam region (variable) for the pair of the NMDP and the GNP in Table 7 has a positive sign. This means, the respondent' probability of voting for the NMDP instead of the GNP increases if the respondent comes from the Honam region. On the other hand, the negative sign of the coefficients indicates that the probability of the respondent voting for the first party in the pair decreases (the probability of voting for the second party in the pair increases) as the value of the independent variable increases. For example, the coefficient of the ideology variable in the pair of the NMDP and the GNP has a negative sign in Table 7. This means, the respondent' probability of voting for the NMDP instead of the GNP decreases as s/he becomes more conservative.

We begin our discussion of the impact of the independent variables in our model with the exogenous shocks influencing the electorates'voting decisions. We hypothesized that the 'Blacklist' movement had significant impacts on voter choice for the 16th National Assembly elections. Contrary to our expectations, however, the coefficients for the Blacklist variable fail to reach statistical significance, indicating that the 'Blacklist'movement did not play an important role in the voting behavior of the electorate. Thus, Hypothesis 4 is not empirically supported. One possible reason the Blacklist variable was insignificant is that many politicians included in the 'Blacklist'were weeded out by the political parties (or party leaders) at the nomination stages, thus never reaching the general election contests.

Table 6. The results of the 17th National Assembly elections in 2004 by regions[a]

Region	GNP	NMDP	Woori Party	ULD	Others/ Independents
Seoul–Gyonggi	33	0	76	0	0
Choongchung	1	0	19	4	0
Youngnam	60	0	4	0	4
Honam	0	5	25	0	1
Others	6	0	5	0	0
Total	100	5	129	4	5

[a] The values in each cell represent the number of district seats won by each party in each region. Since the do not include PR seats (based on the new election law), they are smaller than those reported in Table 4. The Democratic Labor Party won only one district seat and was included under 'Others'. Due to its widespread (not concentrated) support throughout the country, however, it won 9PR seats (see Table 4)

On the other hand, all other things being equal, at the 17th National Assembly elections, the presidential impeachment had a clear-cut impact on the voters'decisions. According to Table 8, when one of the parties that impeached the president, the GNP or the NMDP, is matched up with one of the other parties, the Woori Party or the DLP, the chances that voters, who were against the impeachment, would cast their votes for either the GNP or the NMDP are found to be remote. And when the Woori Party and the DLP are matched up with each other, the coefficient for the impeachment variable becomes statistically insignificant, which makes sense in that the former was a victim of the impeachment and the latter was not involved at all. When the GNP and the NMDP, the partners in the impeachment process, are matched up against each other, the results indicate that the lesser evil, the NMDP, became the choice of the voters opposing the impeachment. Based on these results, we can conclude that Hypothesis 8 is empirically supported.

Table 7. Multinomial logistic analysis of the 16th National Assembly elections

	Variables	Coefficients		Exp (B)
NMDP vs. GNP	Intercept	0.206	(0.503)[a]	
	Generations	0.061	(0.107)	1.063
	Ideology	−0.364**	(0.163)	0.695
	Blacklist	0.010	(0.307)	1.010
	Gangwon	0.014	(0.493)	1.014
	Choongchung	0.919***	(0.332)	2.506
	Honam	1.896***	(0.347)	6.662
	Youngnam	−1.698***	(0.313)	0.183

Others[b] vs. GNP	Intercept	−1.962**	(0.844)	
	Generations	−0.110	(0.168)	0.895
	Ideology	−0.086	(0.248)	0.917
	Blacklist	0.724	(0.577)	2.063
	Gangwon	0.618	(0.659)	1.855
	Choongchung	1.567***	(0.455)	4.793
	Honam	0.712	(0.608)	2.039
	Youngnam	−1.733***	(0.594)	0.177
Others[b] vs. NMDP	Intercept	−2.186***	(0.839)	
	Generations	−0.171	(0.168)	0.842
	Ideology	0.278	(0.248)	1.320
	Blacklist	0.714	(0.579)	2.043
	Gangwon	0.604	(0.697)	1.830
	Choongchung	0.649	(0.438)	1.913
	Honam	−1.184**	(0.563)	0.306
	Youngnam	−0.035	(0.638)	0.966
N		492		
−2 log likelihood		327.970		
χ^2		178.950 (p=0.000)		

** $p < 0.05$; *** $p < 0.01$
[a] Numbers in parentheses are standard errors
[b] 'Others' include minor parties

The Generation variables behave as we expected. The results of the 16th National Assembly elections reveal that generational differences did not affect voter choice since all of the coefficients for the Generation variable turn out to be statistically insignificant. On the other hand, generational differences played an important role for the 17th National Assembly elections, especially when the GNP is matched up with either the Woori Party or the DLP. In the 17th National Assembly elections, while the younger voters preferred the Woori

Party or the DLP to the GNP, the older firmly supported the GNP over the other two parties. We need to remember that the Woori Party and the GNP combined acquired over 90 percent of the seats in the National Assembly, and the DLP became the third largest party in 2004. Hence, we can say that the Hypothesis 3 and Hypothesis 7 are supported empirically.

Table 8. Multinomial logistic analysis of the 17th National Assembly elections[a]

	Variables	Coefficients		Exp (B)
GNP vs. Woori Party	Intercept	2.28***	(0.53)	
	Generations	0.17*	(0.09)	1.186
	Ideology	0.29***	(0.05)	1.352
	Impeachment	−1.48***	(0.13)	0.225
	Honam	−3.33***	(1.04)	0.036
	Youngnam	0.50**	(0.22)	1.672
NMDP vs. Woori Party	Intercept	0.98	(0.79)	
	Generations	0.02	(0.14)	1.012
	Ideology	0.14**	(0.07)	1.164
	Impeachment	−1.10***	(0.19)	0.330
	Honam	1.31***	(0.34)	3.984
	Youngnam	−1.70***	(0.62)	0.185
DLP vs. Woori Party	Intercept	−0.10	(0.95)	
	Generations	−0.23)	(0.15	0.799
	Ideology	−0.18**	(0.07)	0.845
	Impeachment	−0.33	(0.23)	0.722
	Honam	−0.69	(0.57)	0.525
	Youngnam	0.23	(0.36)	1.289

GNP vs. NMDP	Intercept	1.30	(0.80)	
	Generations	0.14	(0.15)	1.172
	Ideology	0.15**	(0.07)	1.162
	Impeachment	−0.39**	(0.19)	0.681
	Honam	−4.64***	(1.05)	0.009
	Youngnam	2.20***	(0.62)	9.031
DLP vs. NMDP	Intercept	−0.88	(1.14)	
	Generations	−0.25 x	(1.20)	0.790
	Ideology	−0.32***	(0.10)	0.726
	Impeachment	0.76***	(0.27)	2.187
	Honam	−2.00***	(0.63)	0.132
	Youngnam	1.92***	(0.70)	6.962
GNP vs. DLP	Intercept	2.18**	(0.97)	
	Generations	0.39**	(0.17)	1.484
	Ideology	0.47***	(0.08)	1.600
	Impeachment	−1.15***	(0.24)	0.311
	Honam	−2.64**	(1.17)	0.069
	Youngnam	0.27	(0.39)	1.297
N		906		
−2 log likelihood		874.889		
χ^2		549.632 (p=0.000)		

* $p < 0.10$; ** $p < 0.05$; *** $p < 0.01$.

[a] Coefficients for the control variables, Gangwon and Chongchung, were excluded from the table to save space

Next, we discuss the impact of the ideology variable. When 'thers' (minor parties) is matched up with either the GNP or the NMDP in the 16th National Assembly elections, the ideology variable becomes statistically insignificant, as we expected. However, when the two major parties, the NMDP and the GNP, are matched up with each other, the Ideology variable becomes statistically significant, indicating that, other things being constant, conservative voters tended to vote for the GNP. As the main competition was between the GNP and the NMDP (see Tables 3 and 5), it appears safe to say that Hypothesis 2 is rejected, albeit with mixed results. On the other hand, Hypothesis 6 is strongly supported empirically as all the coefficients of the Ideology variable in Table 8 turn out to be statistically significant and have the sign that we anticipated. In sum, political ideology did have some impacts on voter choice even prior to 2004, but its influence seems to have become much more significant in the 2004 elections. Next we examine the impact of regionalism on the choice of the electorate in Korea. Table 7 shows significant regional elements in the support of both of the regionally-based parties, the NMDP in Honam and the GNP in Yougnam, at the time of the 16th National Assembly elections in 2000. We see the same regional influence in the choices of all major party supporters in the 17th National Assembly elections in Table 8, except those of the DLP, probably the only party in Korea without a regional base. In short, we can say that regionalism had a significant effect on the voting behavior of the electorate in both the 16th and 17th National Assembly elections. These results in Tables 8 and 9, however, do not tell us much about the relative importance of regionalism and the possibility of its declining influence on voter decisions in 2004, which Hypotheses 1 and 5 refer to. In order to test these hypotheses, we perform the following analysis.

Table 9. Discrete changes in the probability of party support, The 16th and 17th National Assembly elections

16th National Assembly elections				
Variable	Change	GNP	NMDP	Others
Honam	0 → 1a	−0.399	0.419	−0.020
Youngnam	0 → 1	0.381	−0.314	−0.068
Ideology	1 → 3[b]	0.155	−0.163	0.008
Generations	1 → 4[b]	−0.023	0.052	−0.029

17th National Assembly elections					
Variable	Change	GNP	NMDP	Woori Party	DLP
Honam	$0 \rightarrow 1$	−0.337	0.101	0.239	−0.004
Youngnam	$0 \rightarrow 1$	0.113	−0.044	−0.071	0.002
Ideology	$0 \rightarrow 10^{b}$	0.552	0.009	−0.489	−0.073
Generations	$1 \rightarrow 4^{b}$	0.101	−0.001	−0.077	−0.024

[a] $0 \rightarrow 1$ is a discrete change from 0 to 1 in a dummy variable.

[b] This represents a change from the minimum to the maximum value of a given independent variable

Each entry in Table 9 represents the change in the probability of voting for a given party candidate for a change in an independent variable X (Honam, Youngnam, Ideology, or Generation), from Xminimum to Xmaximum, while holding other independent variables constant at their means.[6] One can say that the larger the absolute value of the change, the bigger the impact of the independent variable on the electorates' voting decision.

From Table 9, we can conclude that the Hypothesis 1 is empirically supported. In the 16th National Assembly elections, the largest change in the probability of voting for a given party candidate was caused by the change in the variables representing regionalism, Honam and Youngnam, which means that, among the factors we discuss, regionalism had the biggest impact on the choices of the electorate. Other entries in the upper half of Table 9 confirm our previous analysis: the influence of ideology did exist prior to 2004 but its impact was limited; the impact of generational differences on voters'd choice in the 2000 elections was virtually non-existent.

The results of our analysis of the 17th National Assembly elections in the bottom half of Table 9 tell quite different stories. The impact of regionalism appears to have declined in the 17th National Assembly elections compared to the previous elections, which supports Hypothesis 5. In contrast, the influence of ideology has grown, especially when the voter' choice was between the GNP and the Woori Party. The impact of generational differences in 2004 seems to have increased from 2000, especially among the supporters of the GNP.[7]

Discussion

Several scholars claim that the social cleavage structure in Korea has gone through changes in the 2000s, as political parties adjust their electoral strategies in the post-democratization era. The authoritarian rule imposed on the Korean people (1961e1987) suppressed the emergence of truly social cleavages until 1987, when the democratic transition began. With the arrival of the democratic opening and free elections came regionalism as the dominant cleavage in Korea. As we discussed above, this occurred due to the electoral strategies of political parties. However, it was largely expected that the impact of regionalism would decline in the scheduled National Assembly elections in 2004 as political parties adjusted their electoral strategies again for the period after the retirements of charismatic regional leaders. Also, it was widely anticipated that ideological and generational issues would play greater roles in Korean politics due both to changing social situations and the resulting adjustment of party strategies.

In this paper, we attempted to examine the relative importance of regionalism, ideology, and generational differences in voter choice and investigate the possibility of changing cleavage structure in Korea. We analyzed the choices voters made in the 16th and 17th National Assembly elections in 2000 and 2004, respectively, by employing multinomial logistic analyses. The idea was to see if the cleavage structure remains stable or can change within a relatively short time period in countries with rapid social change. This is important because many countries have gone through similar social changes on their way to democracy, and what we find may have a bearing on them, as well. We further investigated the impact of unanticipated political events, one-time shocks, so to speak, on the choice of the electorate, the 'Blacklist' movement in 2000 and the presidential impeachment in 2004.

Our results show, contrary to common perception, the 'Blacklist' movement did not play an important role in voter choice during the 2000 National Assembly elections. One possible reason why the Blacklist variable was found to be insignificant is that many politicians included in the 'Blacklist' were weeded out by the political parties (or party leaders) at the nomination stages, thus never reaching the general election contests. On the other hand, the presidential impeachment had a clear-cut impact on the voters'decisions in 2004. When one of the parties that impeached the president, the GNP or the NMDP, was matched up with one of the other parties, the Woori Party or the DLP, the chances that voters who were against the impeachment, would cast their votes to either the GNP or the NMDP were found to be remote.

We also found that generational differences did not affect voting behavior in 2000. On the other hand, they played an important role in 2004. While the younger voters preferred the Woori Party or the DLP to the GNP, the older firmly supported the latter over the other two parties. This change from 2000 to 2004 is consistent with our expectations, as well as claims made by some scholars of Korean politics. Concerning the impact of ideology on voter choice, our results show that political ideology did have some impact even prior to 2004, but its influence seems to have become much more significant in the 2004 elections. Until now, conventional wisdom was that ideology began to affect voter choice after 2000. Our analyses also show that regionalism had a significant effect on the choice of the electorate in both the 2000 and 2004 National Assembly elections.

To see the relative importance and the changing influence of political cleavages in 2000s, we performed a more sophisticated analysis in Table 9. It turned out that in 2000, regionalism was the single most important factor determining the choices the electorate made. The influence of ideology did exist in 2000, but its impact was limited. The effect of generational differences on voters'choice in 2000 was virtually negligible. The impact of regionalism appears to have declined in the 2004 elections compared to the previous elections. In contrast, the influence of both ideology and generational differences has grown since 2000.

As we discussed above, with the analyses in this paper, we have attempted to investigate whether the cleavage structure remained stable or has gone through changes in Korea in the early 2000s. We would be the first ones to admit that it is impossible to make a definitive judgment about the stability/fluidity of the cleavage structure of a nation based on the data from two elections. Our efforts were hampered by the unavailability of common survey questions in the voter surveys of Korean elections we discussed above. Based on our analyses of limited data, however, it appears that the relative importance of various cleavages has changed in the early 2000s: the influence of regionalism remained strong, but its intensity has declined; the importance of ideology has grown; and a new cleavage of generational differences has appeared.[8]

Our study shows that the cleavage structure is a fluid concept even over a short-term period. To the extent that Korean example can 'travel' across countries, we may see changing cleavage structure, especially in new democracies with rapid social change, as citizens and elites adjust their behaviors in response to new social situations. Political parties may introduce particular electoral strategies to induce changes in the cleavage structure. When a new set of cleavages emerge, whether they are 'cumulative'(e.g., Northern Ireland) or 'cross-cutting'r (e.g., the Netherlands) will have an important bearing on the stability of party and political systems and can contribute to or hinder democratic consolidation in these new democracies, as many political scientists have argued (e.g., Almond et al., 2006).

Our study shows that the cleavage structure is a fluid concept even over a short-term period. To the extent that Korean example can 'travel' across countries, we may see changing cleavage structure, especially in new democracies with rapid social change, as citizens and elites adjust their behaviors in response to new social situations. Political parties may introduce particular electoral strategies to induce changes in the cleavage structure. When a new set of cleavages emerge, whether they are 'cumulative' (e.g., Northern Ireland) or 'cross-cutting' (e.g., the Netherlands) will have an important bearing on the stability of party and political systems and can contribute to or hinder democratic consolidation in these new democracies, as many political scientists have argued (e.g., Almond et al., 2006).

Appendix. Analyses of the Presidential elections, 1997 and 2002

The results of our analyses of the two most recent presidential elections appear in Tables 10e12 in this Appendix. We included the 'Blacklist' movement and the presidential impeachment in our models for the 16th and 17th National Assembly elections respectively, as control variables (exogenous shocks influencing the electorates'voting decisions). Likewise there were important political events, one-time shocks, which influenced the electorate heavily at the time of the recent presidential elections. They were the 1997 financial crisis and the controversy surrounding a SOFA (Status of the Forces Agreement) with the U.S. in 2002. They were both statistically significant, just as we expected.

Table 10. Multinomial logistic analysis of the 15th Presidential Election (1997)

	Variables	Coefficients[a]		Exp (B)
Lee Hoi-chang vs. Kim Dae-jung	Intercept	−1.797***	(0.643)	
	Generations	0.216**	(0.099)	1.241
	Ideology	0.416***	(0.090)	1.516
	GNP Responsible for Financial Crisis[b]	−1.772***	(0.200)	0.170
	Gangwon	0.617	(0.378)	1.853
	Choongchung	−0.208	(0.264)	0.812
	Honam	−3.734***	(0.540)	0.024
	Youngnam	1.432***	(0.258)	4.187
Lee In-jae vs. Kim Dae-jung	Intercept	−0.408	(0.665)	
	Generations	−0.213**	(0.102)	0.808
	Ideology	0.004	(0.089)	1.004
	GNP Responsible for Financial Crisis[b]	−0.545**	(0.211)	0.580
	Gangwon	0.322	(0.465)	1.380
	Choongchung	0.416	(0.286)	1.586
	Honam	−0.946***	(0.287)	0.388
	Youngnam	1.370***	(0.290)	3.937

	Intercept	−1.389**	(0.683)	
	Generations	0.430***	(0.106)	1.537
	Ideology	0.412***	(0.095)	1.819
Lee Hoi−chang vs. Lee In−jae	GNP Responsible for Financial Crisis[b]	−1.228***	(0.207)	0.440
	Gangwon	0.294	(0.447)	1.342
	Choongchung	−0.669**	(0.302)	0.926
	Honam	−2.788***	(0.580)	0.192
	Youngnam	0.062	(0.259)	0.812
N	922			
−2 log likelihood	1372.854			
χ^2	479.782 (p=0.000)			

** p < 0.05; ** p < 0.01

[a] Number in parentheses are standard errors

[b] This question asks whether the GNP, the governing party at that time, was responsible for the worst financial crisis in the history of the country in 1997 (coded 1 for 'yes' and 0 for 'no').

Generational differences played an important role for both the 1997 and 2002 presidential elections, since all of the coefficients for the Generation variable turn out to be statistically significant. This result is somewhat different from that of the National Assembly elections, since the variable was significant only in the 17th National Assembly elections in 2004. It appears that individuals, i.e., presidential candidates, seem to be more divisive forces among generations than political parties. When the two major party candidates (Lee Hoi-chang and Kim Dae-jung) are matched up with each other in the 1997 presidential election, the Ideology variable becomes statistically significant, indicating that, other things being constant, conservative voters tended to vote for Lee Hoi-chang over Kim Dae-jung. The coefficient of the Ideology variable in Table 11 (the 2002 presidential election) also turns out to be statistically significant.

Table 10 shows significant regional elements in the support of both of the major party candidates, Kim Dae-jung in Honam and Lee Hoi-chang in Youngnam, at the time of the presidential election in 1997. We see the same regional influence in the choices of both Roh Moo-hyun and Lee Hoi-chang supporters in the 2002 presidential elections in Table 11. In short, we can say that regionalism had significant effects on the voting behavior of the electorate in both presidential elections.

Table 11. Binary logistic analysis of the 16th Presidential election (2002)[a]

Variables	Coefficients[b]		Exp (B)
Intercept	4.197***	(0.517)	
Generations	−0.332***	(0.076)	0.718
Ideology	−0.723***	(0.078)	0.485
SOFA[c]	−0.142**	(0.057)	0.867
Gangwon	−0.318	(0.292)	0.728
Choongnam	0.079	(0.217)	1.083
Honam	2.529***	(0.323)	12.543
Youngnam	−0.901***	(0.168)	0.406
N	1187		
−2 log likelihood	1141.149		
χ^2	377.536 (p= 0.000)		

** $p < 0.05$; *** $p < 0.01$

[a] There were only two viable candidates in 2002. Roh Moo-hyun was coded 1, and Lee Hoi-chang was coded 0

[b] Number in parentheses are standard errors

[c] This question asks whether Korea needs to modify the United States–Republic of Korea SOFA (Status of Forces Agreement) even if doing so may damage its relationship with the U.S. Strongly agree=1, Strongly disagree=5

Table 12. Discrete changes in the probability of candidate support, the 15th and 16th Presidential elections (1997 and 2002)

15th Presidential election				
Variable	Change	Kim Dae–jung	Lee Hoi–chang	Lee In–jae
Honam	0 → 1[a]	0.4168	−0.3769	−0.0399
Youngnam	0 → 1[a]	−0.276	0.205	0.0714
Ideology	1 → 5[b]	−0.2	0.3258	−0.1258
Generations	1 → 4[b]	−0.0123	0.179	−0.1667
16th Presidential election				
Variable	Change	Roh Moo–hyun		Lee Hoi–chang
Honam	0 → 1[a]	0.3371		−0.3371
Youngnam	0 → 1[a]	−0.2215		0.2215
Ideology	1 → 5[b]	−0.5954		0.5954
Generations	1 → 4[b]	−0.2214		0.2214

[a] 0 → 1 is s discrete change from 0 to 1 in dummy variable

[b] This represents a change from the minimum to the maximum value of a given independent variable

Notes

1. The DLP was established out of the Korean Democratic Labor Confederation. It intends to represent workers, peasants, urban poor, women, and conscientious intellectuals, and endeavors to overcome problems created by capitalism. It desires limits on private property and the nationalization of means of production for essential goods and services (excerpts from the DLP platform, 2004). Due to its thinly spread (instead of regionally concentrated) support base, it acquired only two district seats, in the industrial centers of Woolsan and Changwon in 2004. However, it secured 8 party list seats based on 13 percent of the nationwide party list votes, primarily from the working class and progressive college students.

2. On May 12, 2004, the nine-member Constitutional Court announced its decision, by a majority vote, to overturn the impeachment, reinstating President Roh to office. It

ruled that, although some minor election law violations had occurred, they were not serious enough to warrant a presidential impeachment. This verdict was widely accepted by the Korean public. His new political lease on life, coupled with control of the National Assembly, was expected to allow Roh Moo-hyun to pursue a more activist agenda (CNN, 2004, May 13; New York Times, 2004, May 14).

3. One may think that it is more appropriate to treat the generational differences as a continuous variable rather than a categorical one. In this article, we do not claim that there is a linear relationship between voter age (say from early twenties to seventies or eighties) and voting patterns. Rather, we claim that blocks of voters in a similar age group (which we call 'enerations' share similar voting patterns because of the life experiences they share. The so-called '86 generation'would be a good example. This term acquired prominence when those born in the 1960s and were in their thirties as a group voted for more progressive candidates/parties than their older peers in the elections in late 1990s and early 2000s. Since we try to pick up shared voting patterns of similar age groups rather than a linear relationship, we believe a categorical variable we use in

4. This is one survey item for which the KSSDC changed the scale of possible responses between the 16th and the 17th National Assembly elections. While the surveys for the former adopted a three-point scale for respondents'ideological tendencies as we discussed above, those for the latter adopted an eleven-point scale.

5. Further, there were many missing values in the survey data for the 16th National Assembly elections, and we had to exclude the cases with missing values from our multinomial logistic analysis. It decreased the number of the respondents who voted for the ULD significantly, which caused a bias in the results when the votes for the ULD were used as a separate category for the multinomial logistic analysis.

6. For information about how to calculate the discrete change in the predicted probability, see Liao (1994) and Long (1997).

7. It would be interesting to study factors impacting the electorate' vote decision for the presidential elections in Korea and compare their relative importance with what we found in this manuscript. We went ahead and executed the same type of analyses for the two most recent presidential elections, of which the results appear in Appendix. Looking at the results of our analyses of recent National Assembly elections and the

presidential elections together, we conclude that they were influenced by nearly identical factors with comparable relative importance. See Appendix for details.

8. We treated regionalism, ideology, and generational differences as 'cleavages' in this study, as previous studies of Korean politics did (e. g., Kang, 2002, 2003, 2004; Lee and Leem, 2004) they cut across the members of a state and affect the electorate' choice, and thus, the resulting party system (Schattschneider, 1960; Lipset and Rokkan,1967; Rae and Taylor, 1970). On the other hand, one may argue that we are dealing with 'Issues' that determined the election outcomes in 2000 and 2004 National Assembly elections in Korea. In that sense, our broader theoretical question can be re-framed as whether these short-term election issues can develop into long term political cleavages 'hat systematically affect political allegiances and policies'(Almond et al., 2006).

12.

A New Approach to a Territorial Dispute Involving a Former Colonizer-Colony Pair: The Case of the Dokdo/Takeshima Dispute between Japan and Korea*

Heemin Kim & Jinman Cho

Abstract. Given that most states in the international system were once ruled as colonies or other dependencies of at least one foreign power, many scholars have examined the ongoing repercussions of colonialism. We study one such topic, that of territorial dispute between a former colony and its former colonial ruler. Specifically, we look at one such pair, Korea and Japan, and at the territorially disputed islets of Dokdo/Takeshima. Hitherto, policymakers and scholars alike have emphasized the importance of history and international law in this dispute.

In this paper, we argue that plausible historical and legal arguments are not adequate tools to explain the current deadlock or predict the future outcome of the dispute, an important element of social-science research. In this paper, we see the territorial dispute as a strategic issue based on the utilities/preferences of the citizenry in the disputant nations. With that in mind, we introduce two different types of utilities possessed by Korea and Japan in relation to Dokdo/Takeshima and show

* This research was partially funded by a 2008-2009 grant from the Northeast Asian History Foundation to the first author. The authors retain full responsibility for all content here in and our analyses and conclusions may not necessarily represent the views of the Foundation. We thank Seok-ju Cho, Paul Hensel, Seung Ho Joo, and Emerson Niou for their helpful comments. Hee Min Kim is Professor of Social Studies Education at Seoul National University in Seoul, Korea and a Professor Emeritus of Political Science at Florida State University, U.S.A. Jinman Cho is Research Professor of the Center for International Studies at Inha University, Korea.

how the disputed islets can be valued differently depending upon the weights of these two types of utilities. Utilizing two utility functions and a bargaining model, we predict the most likely outcome of the dispute, which is (very close to) the status quo. Given the current relative importance of the two utilities in Korea and Japan, any kind of negotiated settlement between the two countries is unlikely. Successful bargaining on the issue of the islets will only be possible when the preferences of the citizens of these countries undergo a fundamental change regarding what is and is not considered important. We conclude by discussing some scenarios in which the preferences of Korea and/or Japan over the disputed islets may change.

Introduction

Most states in the international system have at some time been ruled as colonies or other dependencies of at least one foreign power,[1] so if colonial legacies do affect events after independence, much of the world seems likely to be affected. Recognizing this, scholars have examined the effects of colonialism on such topics as economic development, trade, democratic stability, ethnic conflict, and territorial claims either between former colonies or between a former colony and its former colonial ruler (Blondel, 1972; Valenzuela and Valenzuela, 1978: 535-557; Bollen, 1979: 572-587; Huntington, 1984: 193-218; Bollen and Jackman, 1985: 438-457; Lipset et al., 1993: 155-175; Blanton et al., 2001: 219-243; Athow and Blanton, 2002: 219-241; Bernhard et al., 2004: 225-250).

In this paper, we will look at a territorial dispute over the islets of Dokdo/Takeshima[2] stemming from the colonial legacy between Korea and Japan. This is a much-studied dispute. Previous case studies on the disputed islets have almost exclusively relied on historical and legal arguments. Further, most were done by either Japanese or Korean scholars and support the sovereignty rights of the authors' home country over the islets. In this paper, our focus and approach are different. Instead of making a normative argument about the ownership of the islets, we explore (i) why the neighboring countries of South Korea and Japan have not been able to resolve the Dokdo/Takeshima issue for so long and (ii) what conditions need to be met for the resolution (or settlement) of this dispute.

In the next section, we will discuss the current state of affairs between South Korea and Japan regarding these small islets situated between the two countries in the East Sea (the Sea of Japan). In the following section, we review existing studies of the Dokdo/Takeshima dispute and contend that historical and legal approaches are not sufficient to analyze the dispute between the two countries. To better understand the nature and future of the Dokdo/Takeshima dispute, we use a bargaining model derived from game theory and introduce two different types of utility, one emotional and one substantive. We conclude by explaining our findings and discussing the potential implications of territorial disputation between the two (historically A New Approach to a Territorial Dispute Involving hostile) states in general and of the Dokdo/Takeshima dispute in particular.

Current State of the Territorial Dispute over Dokdo/Takeshima between Korea and Japan

Recently, the territorial dispute over the islets between (South) Korea and Japan again became a hot issue when the Japanese government announced in July 2008 that Dokdo/Takeshima would be claimed as Japanese territory in a teaching guidebook for middleschool teachers (Kyunghyang Sinmun, July 17, 2008). At about the same time, the Japanese Ministry of Foreign Affairs (MOFA) website declared "Japan's inalterable position on the sovereignty of Takeshima" officially, to the effect that "[...] it is apparent that Takeshima is an inherent part of the territory of Japan [...] The Occupation of Takeshima by the Republic of Korea is an illegal occupation undertaken on absolutely no basis in international law. Any measures taken with regard to Takeshima by the Republic of Korea based on such an illegal occupation have no legal justification" (MOFA, 2008). The conflict between Korea and Japan sharpened as the U.S. Library of Congress held a meeting on the viability of changing the name of the island from "Dok Island" (the English translation of the Korean Dokdo) to "Liancourt Rocks."[3] In the midst of the earthquake and nuclear-leakage crisis in Japan in March 2011, tempers flared up once again when the Japanese government approved middle-school geography and civics textbooks that stated that Dokdo/Takeshima belonged to Japan and Korea was occupying it illegally.

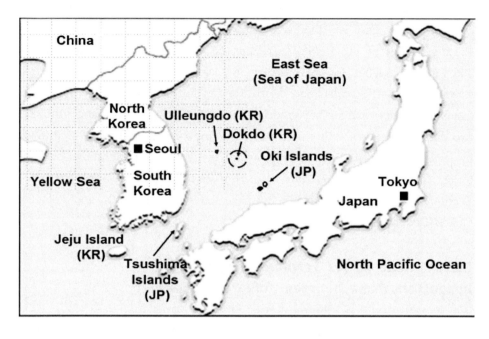

Figure 1. Map of Dokdo/Takeshima

Throughout contemporary history, Koreans have felt very strongly about Dokdo/Takeshima.[4] A recent survey of public opinion regardingDokdo/Takeshima shows that 98.2 percent of Koreans considered it to be their territory (Research News, August 12, 2008). Koreans accuse Japan of practicing legal trickery when Japan calls the islets Takeshima or Liancourt Rocks. This belief further strengthens the existing anti- Japanese sentiment in Korean society. The Korean position is that there is no reason to negotiate with Japan over this territory, and Korea is unwilling to accept any proposal that deprives it of absolute sovereignty and control over Dokdo/Takeshima (Yuji, 2006: 104-128). Korea intends to hold permanent sovereignty and control over Dokdo/Takeshima, while completely eliminating negotiations with Japan and ignoring the occasional global media coverage of the issue.

Before 2001, Dokdo/Takeshima was labeled as Korean territory in Japanese textbooks. Since then, however, Dokdo/Takeshima has been included in Japan's exclusive economic zone (EEZ) in Japanese history, geography, and civics textbooks (Chosun Ilbo, July 11, 2008). The dispute further intensified on March 16, 2005, when the Shimane Prefectural Assembly in Japan publically announced that it had voted to designate a "Takeshima Day,"[5] and the Takeshima Problem Research Association was established later that year to study the Dokdo/Takeshima issue and make its findings known to the public (Hankook Ilbo, July 18, 2008). Furthermore, since 2000, Japan has taken active measures to see the islets listed as Liancourt Rocks in the publications of foreign governments and international organizations. As a result, currently the U.S. CIA World Factbook, Wikipedia, and the Netsaber website all use the term Liancourt Rocks, to refer to Dokdo/Takeshima.

The Japanese government's actions have increased public awareness of the issue in Japan, as is shown in a survey jointly conducted by the Sankei and Fuji news networks in which 73.7 percent of Japanese who previously had not been even aware of Dokdo/Takeshima now consider it to be part of Japan, and 75.0 percent said that Japan should take more aggressive measures in pursuing its sovereignty over the islets (Korea Daily, August 10, 2008).

The Korean government's unresponsive attitude regarding the issue of territorial sovereignty over Dokdo/Takeshima in recent years has met with public criticism in Korea. The government has not been vocal about the issue because it believed that this might result in Dokdo/Takeshima becoming internationally recognized as a disputed area, when Korea has actual physical control over it.

But a recent survey conducted in Korea shows that 79.4 percent of respondents stated that strong actions must be taken regarding the Dokdo/Takeshima issue, even if it has a negative impact on relations with Japan (Seoul Sinmun, July 14, 2008). In August 2008, the Korean government established the Dokdo Research Institute to direct research about the Dokdo/Takeshima issue at the governmental level, and has held many academic events regarding Dokdo/Takeshima.

There has also been a growing demand among Korean people to exercise sovereign rights, for instance of building an ocean hotel, developing a settlement, and exploring seabed resources. As Japan will object to these actions, the dispute between Korea and Japan over the territorial sovereignty of Dokdo/Takeshima will likely continue.[6]

Territorial Dispute over Dokdo/Takeshima: Historical and Legal Arguments

Previous studies of sovereignty over Dokdo/Takeshima have been mainly conducted by historians (J. Yoo, 1996: 117-138; Y. Yoo, 1996: 55-74; Lee, 1997: 389-421; Shin, 1997: 333-358; Choe, 1998: 187- 203; Hyun, 1998: 93-120; Choi, 2005: 177-195; Choi, 2007: 401-428; Han, 2007: 318-352; Koo, 2007: 353-383) and legal scholars (Kim, 1996; Lee, 1998: 423-475; Jhe, 2005: 177-195; Choi, 2006: 295-329; Jhe, 2006: 201-228; Kim, 2006: 184-211). They have focused on examining the historical record on Dokdo/Takeshima and logical reasoning under international law.

At the same time, governments and scholars in Korea and Japan have taken positions over the territorial sovereignty of Dokdo/Takeshima based on their own respective historical and legal viewpoints. A brief summary of Korea's position over Dokdo/Takeshima is as follows: a passage from the oldest extant Korean historical text, Samguk Sagi ["History of the Three Kingdoms"], published in the 12th century, states that Kim Isabu of Silla, one of the three kingdoms in the Korean peninsula, conquered the state of Usan-guk in 512 A.D. Further, it is clearly stated in two geography texts, Sejong-Sillok Jiriji ["Annals of King Sejong," 1454], and Dong'guk Yeoji Seungnam ["The Geography of Chosun," 1531] that "Usan-guk" refers to the present-day Ulleungdo and Dokdo/Takeshima. These records came approximately 200 years before any historical records of the islets in Japanese documents, the earliest of which are from a report written for the Japanese Foreign Ministry in 1667, Onshu Shicho Goki ["Records of Observations on Oki"]. Towards the end of the 17th century, Korea's An Yongbok received a document from Japan's Tokugawa bakufu (the de facto central government was run under a shogun, the Emperor's military deputy and actual ruler of Japan at that time), which confirmed that Dokdo/Takeshima belonged to Korea.

The expanding Japanese empire forcibly took Dokdo/Takeshima under its sovereignty while curtailing Korea's diplomatic rights in 1905. Japan eventually annexed the whole Korean Peninsula in 1910. After Japan was defeated in World War II, however, an order by the Supreme Commander of the Allied Powers — Pacific, Douglas MacArthur, declared the suspension of Japanese administrative control over Dokdo/Takeshima. The first president of South Korea, Syngman Rhee, announced the "Presidential Declaration on the Territorial Waters" in 1952; with this document, he drew the so-called "Peace Line," which included Dokdo/Takeshima on the Korean side. Since then, Korea has exercised its territorial sovereignty over Dokdo/Takeshima through various actions such as constructing a territorial monument in 1953; building a lighthouse in 1954; allowing common citizens to settle on the islets in 1980; building a helicopter landing facility in 1981; installing a radar facility in 1993; and building an anchorage in 1996. As far as Koreans are concerned, Dokdo/Takeshima is so clearly Korean territory that there is no need to give in to Japan's demand to take the issue to the International Court of Justice.

So far, we have looked at the historical development from the Korean point of view. Japan's position regarding territorial sovereignty over Dokdo/Takeshima is very different (Ryoichi, 1968; Hori, 1997:477-523; Kajimura, 1997: 423-475; Seitsu, 2000; Hara, 2001: 361-382; Masao, 2005; Akaha, 2008: 156-188; Embassy of Japan in Korea, 2011). The historical records Korea claims as evidence of its sovereignty do not clearly state that they are referring to the present-day Dokdo/Takeshima. Similar to how Korea argues that Dokdo/Takeshima is subsidiary to Ulleungdo, Japan claims that Dokdo/Takeshima is subsidiary to Oki Island.[7] While Korea abandoned the uninhabited Dokdo/Takeshima during the 17th century, Japan exercised its control over Dokdo/Takeshima by allowing fishing off its shores.

In 1905, Japan lawfully gained sovereignty over Dokdo/Takeshima, as far as the Japanese government was concerned (Niksch, 2007). The Japanese government does not consider the order by the Supreme Commander of the Allied Powers, issued after the Japanese defeat in World War II, a binding treaty determining which territories belong to Korea. It was the San Francisco Peace Treaty of 1951 that determined which territories belong to Korea, and this treaty did not mention Dokdo/Takeshima specifically. Therefore, many Japanese believe, Japan attained control over Dokdo/Takeshima through this Peace Treaty. Syngman Rhee's declaration of the Peace Line and the steps Korea has taken to exercise territorial sovereignty over Dokdo-Takeshima are considered nugatory because they go against the international law of open seas. Japan has continuously objected to Korean actions through official channels on the grounds that they were a breach of territorial sovereignty. By agreeing to place Dokdo/Takeshima in the neutral zone through the New Japan-Korea Fishery Treaty of 1998, goes the argument, Korea in fact abandoned the exclusive zone surrounding Dokdo/Takeshima. The fact that Korea does not respond to Japan's demand to take the issue to the International Court of Justice is a reflection of Korea's weakness in its claim, so Japan argues.

When we examine Japanese and Korean arguments about the territorial sovereignty of Dokdo/Takeshima, we can see that there are large discrepancies in the interpretation of the same historical evidence or international laws and each country adopts the version that serves its own interest.

In this section, we have briefly shown that previous studies tended to focus on historical and international legal approaches, which led to normative judgments about which country Dokdo/Takeshima must belong to. These approaches, however, are not sufficient to (i) explain why the two countries have failed to reach a negotiated settlement in he over half a century since Korea's independence from Japan in 945, and (ii) make predictions about the outcome of the dispute, an mportant element of social-science research. In this paper, we view he Dokdo/Takeshima dispute as more of a strategic game played by he two countries and adopt a bargaining model for illustration. To etter understand the present and predict the future of the dispute, e first need to know why Japanese and Koreans care about these mall islets so much. In the next section, we discuss the benefits of having control over the disputed islets.

Why is Dokdo/Takeshima Important?
Two Different Types of Utility of the Disputed Islets

Why do Japanese and Koreans care about these small islets enough to risk long-term damage to the relationship between the two countries? The value of

Dokdo-Takeshima for Japanese and Koreans is decided by various factors that are hard to compare, quantify, or aggregate, including economic/military factors as well as sovereign/ emotional factors. We apply the utility theory from the economics literature to represent the perceived value of the islets to Korea and Japan. It is assumed that each country will choose a policy that maximizes its utility.

A. Type I Utility: Emotional Utility Based on Historical and Sovereignty Issues

Why is it so important for Japanese and Koreans to gain sovereignty over Dokdo/Takeshima? First, it can be noted that the anti-Japanese sentiment among Koreans dating back to Japanese colonization in the early 20th century can still be found in the Dokdo/Takeshima dispute today. Koreans believe that Japan's claim over Dokdo/Takeshima is completely unfounded and a shameless act of subconscious colonialism.

In this context, Korea's claim over Dokdo/Takeshima is fundamentally based on national pride. Japan's taking even an inch of Dokdo/Takeshima would be considered a second national humiliation. Therefore, in reality, Korea's emotional utility over Dokdo/Takeshima is satisfied only when its claim over Dokdo/Takeshima is absolute. If the result were not an absolute claim over Dokdo/Takeshima, there would be a significant drop in Korea's emotional utility.

On the other hand, Japan believes there is a problem with Korea's unilateral decision to call Dokdo/Takeshima its territory, especially when it was controlled by Japan by means of fishing practices and exclusive development rights after the 17th century and later transferred to its formal sovereignty in accordance with international law. In other words, when Japan returned Korean territories through lawful means after being defeated in World War II, Dokdo/Takeshima was not included, and any disagreement should be settled by international law.[8]

Japan's sovereignty/emotional utility of Dokdo/Takeshima is probably lower than of its other disputed territories, such as the Northern Territories (Kuril Islands) and Senkaku/Diaoyu Islands (Koo, 2005: 24-35). Japanese feel that

Russia is unlawfully claiming the Northern Territories even though they were historically Japan's territory, and they do not want the Senkaku Islands to be disputed territory with China or Taiwan, because Japan is currently exercising sovereign rights there (Yuji, 2006: 116-126). As previously mentioned, hardly any Japanese people were aware of Dokdo/Takeshima in the past, making it a low-priority disputed territory for Japan.

Considering what we have discussed above, we can probably say that the emotional utility of Japan in Dokdo/Takeshima is different from that of Korea. If it loses the current claim over Dokdo/Takeshima, its sovereignty-based emotional utility will decrease, but not as drastically as it would have for Korea. At the same time, Japan's sovereign/emotional utility over Dokdo/Takeshima does not need to be fixed at this level. Recent trends show that Japan's sovereignty-based sentimental utility may increase considering that its right-wing politicians (especially before the end of Liberal Democratic Party rule in 2009) have taken an active role in sensitizing the public to the issue of territorial sovereignty over Dokdo/Takeshima, which the international media has increasingly picked up.

B. Type II Utility: Utility Based on Non-emotional, Substantive Factors

Although Koreans have a very strong belief that Dokdo/Takeshima belongs to Korea, they may not be able to name anything other than "national pride" as a reason to defend Dokdo/Takeshima from Japan. Therefore, it is useful to go beyond the simple argument that Dokdo/Takeshima "undoubtedly" belongs to Korea and understand the substantive value of the islets.

At the time of the establishment of diplomatic relations between Korea and Japan in 1965, the records of which were made available to the public in August 2005, the value of Dokdo/Takeshima was unclear to both the Japanese and Korean delegations (Yuji, 2006: 104-128; Choi, 2008: 133-147). This can be seen from the fact that Iseki Yujiro, the head of the Asia division of the Japanese foreign ministry at the time, stated at the fourth preparatory meeting in September 1962 that "Takeshima has no value. It is as large as Hibaya Park, and it would make no difference even if we bomb and get rid of it." Korea rejected this idea not based on the practical value of Dokdo/Takeshima but based on anti-Japanese sentiment.

There are some studies that have explored the substantive value of Dokdo/Takeshima and the surrounding area. They can be summarized as follows (Park, 2005: 6-27; Cyber Dokdo, 2011): First, Dokdo/Takeshima has value for its fisheries. The territorial waters surrounding Dokdo/Takeshima are where the cold current from the north and the warm current from the south meet, and therefore these waters have abundant plankton and plenty of migratory fish. Second, the territory has ecological value. Dokdo/Takeshima's marine plants are different from those of the Yellow Sea or Jeju Island and have a unique ecosystem that has characteristics similar to subtropical climate zones in the northern hemisphere. Third, the islets have geological value. Dokdo/Takeshima is geological evidence of the evolution of the surrounding seabed terrain. Fourth, it has value as a shelter. The geographic location makes it easily accessible by fishing boats and a good place for fishermen to take a break. Fifth, it has value as an ocean-science base. The waters surrounding Dokdo/Takeshima can be used to more accurately measure the ocean's status, which can be used to make weather forecasts with greater accuracy. In addition, Dokdo/Takeshima can be used as a base for environmental research, oceanindustry research, and research into prevention of ocean pollution.

The values of Dokdo/Takeshima listed above are substantial. However, there are other factors that add more value to Dokdo/Takeshima. The first is its military value. The reason Japan was able to so easily win the Russo-Japanese War in 1905 in the East Sea/Sea of Japan was because it established an observation tower on Dokdo/Takeshima in August 1905. Today, South Korea maintains a radar system on the islets and is managing them as a strategic base. This allows it to easily detect the Russian Pacific fleet, as well as movement of the North Korean and Japanese navies. If occupied by Japan, Dokdo/Takeshima could be used in the same way by Japan to observe military activity and prevent potential threats from Russia, China, and North Korea.[9]

Next, it is important to understand Dokdo/Takeshima's seabed resources. The territorial waters of the East Sea are likely to contain gas hydrates (Ahn, 1998: 414-427). Gas hydrates are a crystalline solid consisting of gas molecules that store an immense amount of natural gas, with major implications as an energy resource as well as an "indicative resource" that can show where oil is. Gas hydrates were first discovered in the 1930s but did not gain much attention because of the availability of crude oil and natural gas. Up to now, no countries are believed to have the technology to develop gas hydrates on a commercial basis.

Nowadays, however, there is increasing interest in gas hydrates as oil depletes, and there is a greater demand for clean energy sources for environmental reasons.[10] The Korean government launched the Gas Hydrate R&D Organization (2011) in 2005 for the development of gas-hydrate technology in cooperation with the U.S. government. In 2007, the development agency of the Korean government discovered about 600 million tons of gas hydrates (an amount equivalent to 30 years of Korean natural-gas consumption) in the seabed approximately 100 kilometers south of Ulleungdo (Saegye Ilbo, June 24, 2008). The exact location of the center of this potentially rich resources (and whether it is near Dokdo-Takeshima or not) is still being debated (Energy Times, September 9, 2008; Maeil Gyeongje Sinmun, July 19, 2008).

In a world where states are worried about another oil shock, especially when the price of oil is rising, countries such as Japan, the U.S., Canada, India, and Korea are trying to develop gas-hydrate technology on a large commercial scale in the near future (Saegye Ilbo, June 24, 2008).[11]

The Dokdo/Takeshima Dispute:
A Bargaining-Model Illustration

Our discussion above shows that Dokdo/Takeshima should be viewed as a very valuable territory by informed Japanese and Koreans, which only enhances the possibility of some sort of conflict between the two countries over the issue of who owns it. The total utility each country derives out of Dokdo-Takeshima is:

$$U_{JAPAN}(Dokdo\,Takeshima) = f(U_J(T_I), U_J(T_{II}))$$
$$U_{KOREA}(Dokdo\,Takeshima) = f(U_K(T_I), U_K(T_{II}))$$

That is, the total utility each country derives would be some mixture of type I and type II utilities. The combinations for both countries will depend on both domestic and international factors, including historical memory.

In this section, we introduce a simple Nash bargaining model to illuminate the current dispute involving Dokdo/Takeshima based on the two different types of utilities described above, and by doing so, to predict the likely outcome of the dispute between the two countries.[12]

Figure 2 above portrays a general bargaining model of territorial dispute between Korea and Japan (or any two countries). The point J denotes the situation where Japan receives everything it can possibly hope for. Let us denote the utility to Korea as 0 at this point. The opposite is true at K, where Korea receives everything it can possibly hope for, and where the utility to Japan is denoted as 0. SQ denotes status quo in the absence of bargaining over Dokdo-Takeshima between the two countries or when the bargaining does not produce any agreement or negotiated settlement. In Figure 2, we assume that the SQ point is inefficient in the sense that both Korea and Japan will receive higher utility if the bargaining can produce a negotiated settlement. At the SQ point, the utility to Korea and Japan respectively becomes SQ_k and SQ_J.

We can reasonably expect that a negotiated settlement between Korea and Japan will end up somewhere on the line connecting J and K. From any point inside the triangle connecting J, K and (0,0), there will be an attempt to con-

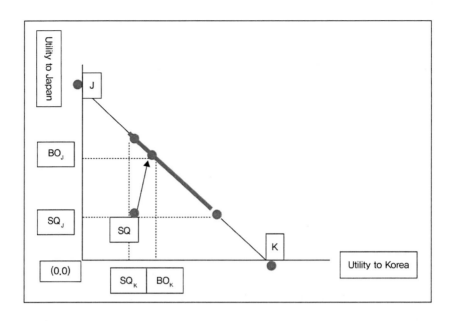

Figure 2. Territorial Bargaining Game between Korean and Japan:
A General Model.

tinue bargaining, because both countries can increase their utility by moving toward the J-K line. Among the points on the J-K line, only those on the thick portion can be the outcome of the bargaining between the two countries, because any point not on the thick portion means lower utility for either country than the status quo, and thus that country does not have any reason to agree to such an outcome. Let BOs and BOK be the final utility to Korea and Japan, respectively. The final outcome shows that the utility to both countries increases as a result of bargaining, because SQ was an inefficient point.[13]

Now let us apply the general bargaining model in Figure 2 to the specific case of the Dokdo/Takeshima dispute. Let us first consider type II utility only. That is, we assume that there is no emotional attachment to the island deriving from past colonial history (inaccurate as this assumption is). This situation is depicted in Figure 3. In this case, both countries' utility functions consist of more practical economic and military interests. In this case, the points on the bargaining line in Figure 3 represent shared fishing areas, weather forecasts, joint development of natural resources, joint geological studies, and so forth. Any point on this line provides a more efficient outcome than the status quo.

One thing we need to note, however, is that the SQ point is much closer to Korea's ideal point than Japan's in Figure 3, unlike in the more general model of territorial dispute in Figure 2. This is because Korea currently occupies the island of Dokdo/Takeshima; thus, the status quo is very advantageous to Korea (Fern, 2005: 78-89). This means that if the two countries engage in the bargaining game now, Japan will not be able to extract many concessions from Korea.

We also need to note that the bargaining game over Dokdo/Takeshima is not a single-shot, static game in which the outcome must be determined once and for all at a given time point. Instead, both countries would try to create a domestic and international environment favorable to themselves in the long run before they actually sit down for bargaining. Japan is likely to try various steps to move SQ toward its own ideal point, J. As we mentioned above, Japan has taken several aggressive steps on the Dokdo/Takeshima issue lately, which we can only interpret as an attempt to move the SQ point for a future bargaining game.

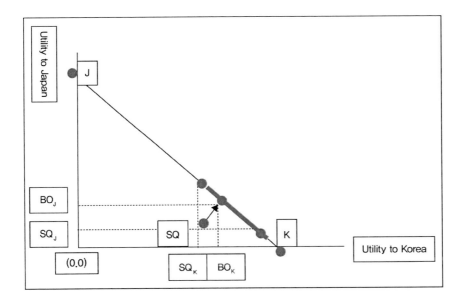

Figure 3. Dokdo/Takeshima Territorial Bargaining Game between
Korea and Japan: Scenario I

So far, we have assumed that both Japanese and Koreans have only type II utility over the disputed Dokdo/Takeshima issue. Now we will look at a more realistic scenario — one in which both Korea and Japan have some mixture of type I and type II utility with regard to the issue of the island.

As discussed above, type I utility represents the value of national sentiment associated with sovereignty and past colonial history. Although we do not have an accurate measure of national sentiment, it is reasonable to assume that type I utility dominates type II, at least in Korea, given the results of public-opinion surveys and Korean attitudestoward the Dokdo/Takeshima issue. When type I utility dominates type II, the value of potential economic and military benefits is seen as trivial. It is difficult to determine which type of utility weighs more heavily among Japanese, but it appears that type I utility is not as important for them as it is for Koreans. We can observe, though, that type I utility has been growing, due to the Dokdo/Takeshima policies of recent Liberal Democratic Party governments.

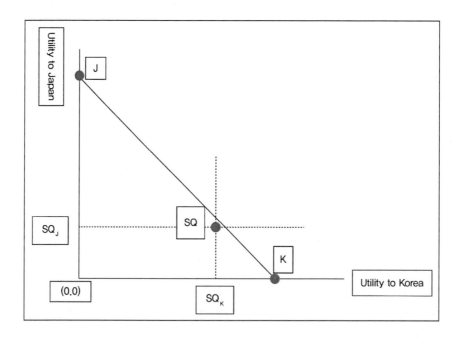

Figure 4. Dokdo/Takeshima Territorial Bargaining Game between Korea and Japan: Scenario II

Under this scenario, point K probably represents a situation where Korea completely controls the islands of Dokdo/Takeshima, the international community acknowledges that they are part of Korea, and Japan does not dare to approach the area. Given that Korea effectively occupies the island, the status quo would indicate a fairly satisfactory and efficient situation for Korea. This is represented in Figure 4, in which SQK has moved toward the (efficient) bargaining line from the situation in Figure 3. Under this scenario, Korea does not have a pressing need to engage in negotiations with Japan, because it will not bring many added benefits to Korea. So in this most realistic scenario in which both Korea and Japan have some mixture of type I and type II utility, the status quo is fairly close to the bargaining line. This means that new negotiations between the two countries about the Dokdo/Takeshima issue will not bring any new or meaningful benefits to either country; thus, the two countries will implement aggressive policies to pull the SQ point toward themselves without ever reaching a negotiated settlement. This situation will only deepen their existing hostility toward each other, resulting in an increasing weight of type I utility in the Dokdo/Takeshima dispute.

Evaluation of the Dokdo/Takeshima Strategies of Korea and Japan and the Future Prospects of the Dispute

It is not clear if the recent aggressive Dokdo/Takeshima policies of Japan are only about the disputed island. Like foreign policies of any country, Japan's Dokdo/Takeshima policies can be calculated to have particular domestic effects as well.[14] For now, however, let us look at the Dokdo/Takeshima policies of Japan in the framework of the bargaining game with Korea alone. In this light, recent attempts by Japan to sensationalize the Dokdo/Takeshima issue seem to be an effort to move SQ, which is currently located at a disadvantageous point for Japan. Japan appears to be trying to pull the SQ point as much as possible toward its most preferred point before the actual bargaining between the two countries begins.

Will this kind of strategy on the part of Japan promote a quick settlement of the issue or help it to attain a more profitable outcome? We think not. The simple reason is that the current Dokdo/Takeshima situation resembles Figure 4 rather than Figure 3. As we mentioned above, there is little room for bargaining in the case of Figure 4. Even if Japan succeeds in attracting international attention to the issue (thus, moving SQ toward its ideal point), in the end it does not gain much anyway. Korea, which in effect controls the disputed island, will refuse to respond to Japan's attempt to internationalize the issue. It will never agree to take the Dokdo/Takeshima case to the International Court of Justice. In the end, Dokdo/Takeshima will revert back to the situation in Figure 4, and the two countries will continue the same exhausting game of pulling the SQ point back and forth, unless of course they choose to go to war over the issue, which is highly unlikely at this point.[15]

The bargaining-game approach above shows why Korea and Japan have failed to even start a reasoned conversation or negotiation about the disputed islets in over half a century. It further shows that Korea and Japan will never be able to resolve the Dokdo/Takeshima dispute as long as their utility over the issue remains the same or similar. In other words, the status quoin the bargaining game between the two countries is already at or near equilibrium.[16] This means that, for a change to happen in the current circumstances, the utility functions of Korea and Japan over the value of the Dokdo/Takeshima must change first. This is especially true for Korea where the significance of type I utility is probably greater than that for Japan. The type I utility stemming from history is so great that not only is bargaining about which country Dokdo-Takeshima belongs to out of the question, but also any negotiation about sharing natural and strategic resources with Japan is, from the Korean perspective, foreclosed.

Now imagine, for whatever reason, that type I utility decreases gradually relative to type II utility for both Japanese and Koreans. Substantively, this means that Korean anti-Japan sentiment stemming from the colonial history somehow diminishes and level of trust toward Japan increases. Let us further assume that Japan follows a similar pattern. This means that bargaining over the Dokdo/Takeshima issue gradually moves from the pattern in Figure 4 to that in Figure 3. Then, the previously efficient status quo (entailing Korean physical sovereignty over Dokdo/Takeshima, but also under-development and under-utilization of surrounding resources with continuous wrangling between the two governments) suddenly looks inefficient. If this happens, both Korea and Japan have something to gain from negotiation, and there is room for compromise for the joint development of resources around the Dokdo/Takeshima region.

Conclusion

Given that most states in the international system were once ruled as colonies or dependencies of at least one foreign power, many scholars have examined the persistent effects of colonialism. We study one such topic, territorial dispute between a former colony and its former colonial ruler. In particular, we look at one such pair, Korea and Japan, and at the territorially disputed islets of Dokdo/Takeshima.

As has been shown, we are critical of past studies of the disputed islets. Until now, both policy-makers and scholars alike have emphasized the importance of history and international law in understanding/settling the dispute. These studies have formed the normative grounds for the positions taken by both Korea and Japan. As we have argued above, however, they do not explain the current deadlock or predict the outcome of the dispute, which is the main goal of social science research.

In this paper, we take an alternative route by approaching the territorial dispute as a strategic issue based on citizens' utilities/preferences regarding sovereignty over the islets. With that in mind, we introduced two different types of utility Korea and Japan have in Dokdo/Takeshima and show how the disputed islets can be valued differently depending upon the weights of these two different types of utility. Utilizing two utility functions and a bargaining model, we explain the deadlock that has existed until now and predict the most likely future outcome of the dispute, which is (very close to) the status quo.

Given the current relative importance of the two different types of utilities in Korea and Japan, any kind of negotiated settlement (i.e., the emergence of a new equilibrium) between the two countries is unlikely. Successful bargaining on the issue of the islets will only be possible when the feelings of the citizens of these countries regarding what is and is not important undergo a fundamental change. If this happens, for whatever reason, and the situation changes from that in Figure 4 to that in Figure 3, the location of the SQ point and the relative power distribution at that time will determine the outcome of a bargaining game between the two countries. In other words, for a resolution (of whatever sort) over the disputed islets to happen, change needs to be driven from below. This also implies that changes in government policies or government-funded "studies" are not likely to contribute to the resolution of the issue.

We conclude this paper by offering a few possible (but unlikely) scenarios that may change the weights the two countries place on the two different types of utility. The first possibility is a potential shock to the power balance in Northeast Asia involving a third party. If this third party is perceived to be a danger by both Korea and Japan, the two countries may approach each other with regard to stepping up strategic cooperation, resulting in a lower level of hostility and a higher level of trust between the two. This third party might be China, North Korea, or even Russia. However, whether any of them will turn out to be a big enough threat to force Korea and Japan to trust each other is simply impossible to conjecture at this point.

Second, we can imagine another oil shock. If the price of crude oil skyrockets for whatever reason when Korea and Japan have not developed (the technology for) major alternative energy sources, then both countries may turn to the gas hydrates available near Dokdo/ Takeshima. They may, out of desperation, quickly reach a negotiated solution that defines sovereignty in order to define gas-hydrate rights, knowing they simply do not have time to quibble over whose territory the gas hydrates exist on. Once again, the likelihood of this scenario is beyond our knowledge.

Finally, if political leaders in Japan and/or Korea felt that a fundamental change to the situation in Figure 4 were in the long-term national interest of their country, then they might take the political risk of trying to persuade citizens to reach consensus on a change. Given our understanding of politicians in these countries, this is unlikely, since doing so would very potentially be political suicide. This shows our paper to be of some relevance to the field of leadership studies. Leadership as an object of study in social science tends to be cyclical, and has again come into fashion. Building on a long and multi-disciplinary research program on leadership, a substantial body of work has emerged over the past two decades (Jones, 1989). However, the concept of leadership remains vague and contested, which means that the literature is incoherent. A review of the social-science literature on the topic reveals a dis-sensus on the characterization of leaders and leadership (Ahlquist and Levi, 2011: 1-24). We may here add a particular element to the term "leadership." If political leaders in a country see potential long-term national gain in a con-troversial international issue, they may try to persuade citizens to take a partic-ular position or care about that issue even at the risk of short-term political losses. In that sense, we would like to define the term "political leadership" as the ability to persuade and change citizen preferences in a legal and peaceful way, if the leaders have the strength to pursue what they see as long-term na-tional interest even at the risk of short-term political risk to themselves.

Notes

1. The ICOW Colonial History data set, available at ([http://www.icow.org]), reveals that 183 of 222 states in the modern interstate system (82.4%) have been ruled as a dependency or part of at least one foreign state at some point in the last 200 years.

2. The Korean name for the islets is "Dokdo," while the Japanese call it "Takeshima." Whenever we refer to the disputed islets, we will use the term "Dokdo/ Takeshima" to maintain neutrality.

3. The name Liancourt Rocks derives from the Liancourt, the name of the French whal-ing ship that spotted Dokdo/Takeshima in 1849. Liancourt Rocks is a third name used by the international community in place of Dokdo and Takeshima. The U.S. Congressional Library provides the standard to categorize topics in major U.S. uni-versities, research institutes, and public libraries.

4. See Figure 1 for the location of Dokdo.

5. On March 18, 2005, the Municipal Assembly of the city of Masan in Korea assed an

ordinance by unanimous vote proclaiming "Daemado (Tsushima as alled by Japanese) Day" in retaliation against "Takeshima Day" in Japan. The aemado is a much-lesser known disputed island between the two countries, nd is currently occupied by Japan.

6. Korea is currently building an East Sea-Dokdo Oceanographic Research Center, hich is expected to be completed in 2012 and will do active research on he likelihood of earthquakes and tsunamis in East Asia.

7. See Figure 1 above for the location of Oki Island.

8. A former chair of the Japanese Liberal Democratic Party and the current chair of the Diplomatic Study Meeting, a review committee of foreign policy under the Liberal Democratic Party, Daku Yamasaki, stated in an interview with a Korean daily journal, "Japan has taken steps over a long-time period in order to bring the Takeshima issue to the International Court of Justice, and ultimately the international community will judge this issue" (Joong-Ang Daily, August 14, 2008).

9. With the rapid advancement of military technology, the military value of Dokdo/Takeshima may not be as great as it used to be. For example, placing an Aegis combat system in the East Sea/Sea of Japan may have an equivalent effect.

10. Gas hydrate has an advantage over oil in that hardly any air pollution from carbon dioxide occurs in combustion.

11. Japan has a Committee on the Development of Hydrates within the Japanese Earthquake Research Center, which is a government agency. Leading Japanese oil companies, university research centers, and exploratory technician teams are all part of this committee. In addition, from Japan's point of view, there is another reason why research and the development of gas hydrates are important. Global warming and rising ocean temperatures cause the dissociation of gas hydrates, which have hitherto been safely under the sea. As a result, the main element in hydrates, methane, can be exposed to the atmosphere. If this happens, the methane will aggravate the glob-al-warming situation, sinking the hydrate grounds further and demolishing the seedbeds. Because of rising sea levels from global warming and changes in the seafloor terrain from frequent earthquakes, Japan places much importance on the research into gas hydrates for its own security (Ahn, 1998: 414-427).

12. Nash's (axiomatic) bargaining model as we introduce it here, unlike some other types of bargaining models, does not model the bargaining procedure — the sequence

of possible offers and counteroffers —but rather studies the set of outcomes consistent with some assumptions (including that of efficiency) about the characteristics of the outcome and how it depends on the players' preferences and opportunities. Also, negotiators must consider the possibility that negotiations will break down (see Nash, 1950: 155-162 and Osborne, 2004: 481 for details). As we do not need to concern ourselves with the act of bargaining or lack thereof between Korea and Japan over the issue of Dokdo/Takeshima, the Nash bargaining model serves the purpose of our analysis very well.

13. Game theorists have argued that the actual outcome of the bargaining game is determined in proportion to the relative power of the two parties involved (Nash, 1950: 155-162; Luce and Raiffa, 1957; Schott, 1984; Osborne, 2004: 481). The more powerful one party is relative to the other, the closer the final bargaining outcome will be to that party's most preferred outcome on the bargaining line. In today's world, national power includes all the resources a country can mobilize, encompassing economic resources, military might, and ability to extract the support of other countries in the region, among others.

14. For example, the recent "Northeast Project" of China may be seen as an aggressive territorial policy to Koreans, when in fact it might be more of an internal ethnic-minority policy, rather than one intended for a foreign audience. The Northeast Project, which is short for "the Northeast Borderland History and Chain of Events Research Project," was conducted by the Chinese Academy of Social Science from 2002 to 2006. The project applies the ideology of Zhonghua Minzu (Chinese nationality) to the ancient ethnic groups, states, and history of the regions of Manchuria and northern Korea. Under the Zhonghua Minzu ideology, it is assumed that there was a greater Chinese state in the ancient past. Accordingly, any pre-modern people or states that occupied any part of what is now the People's Republic of China are defined as having been part of that greater Chinese state. Similar projects have been conducted with regard to Tibet and Xinjiang, (the "Southwest Project" and the "Northwest Project," respectively). The project's claims with regard to Gojoseon, Goguryeo and Balhae, ancient kingdoms established by ethnic Koreans on land currently controlled by China, sparked disputes with Korea. In 2004, this dispute threatened to lead to diplomatic problems between the People's Republic of China and the Republic of Korea, although both governments involved exhibit no desire to see the

issue damage the relations between the two countries.

15. We do not attempt to compare the level of utility and the location of bargaining lines in Figures 3 and 4, because they are determined by factors that are too difficult to quantify or compare in the way that we have done above.

16. An interesting aspect of this (near-) equilibrium is that it looks so volatile, as it involves heated verbal provocation and exchange on the part of political leaders and citizens of both countries, which does not fit the general perception of an "equilibrium." We argue that these seemingly emotional acts are a component of a long-term steady state, of which the production of normative academic studies by scholars in both countries is another component.

13.

Educational Disadvantage and Access to the Best Universities in Korea*

Heemin Kim*, Heejin Cho** & Hyunah Lee***

* HeeMin KIM is Professor at the Department of Social Studies Education, Seoul National University. E-mail: recount01@snu.ac.kr.

** Heejin CHO is Ph.D. Candidate at the Department of Social Studies Education, Seoul National University. E-mail: puregold@snu.ac.kr.

*** Hyunah LEE is Teaching Assistant at the Department of Youth Education, Korea National Open University. E-mail: lha0816@hanmail.net.

Abstract. In Korea, the type of university that an individual student enters is largely determined by his or her performance on the national standardized aptitude test implemented by the Korean government. By investigating the factors that determine individual students' performance on this exam, we seek to identify the factors that determine their university placement. For this study, we use Korean Education and Employment Panel (KEEP) data (2004-2009). We use multivariate regression models to investigate factors affecting student performance on Korea's national standardized exam for college entrance and describe our extensive findings in this article. Our ultimate conclusion is that educational disadvantage stemming from socioeconomic factors is growing. That is, Korean education is moving in the wrong direction as far as educational equity is concerned. Based on our observations above, we make several suggestions for parents, guardians, teachers, schools, and educational policymakers to reverse this disturbing trend.

* This article is a revision of the paper presented at the 6th International Alliance of Leading Education Institutes (IALEI) Annual Conference in Melbourne, Australia, August 2012. This research was supported by a research grant from the College of Education, Seoul National University. The usual disclaimer applies.

Introduction

Factors affecting student academic performance have been studied extensively in various subfields of education research (e.g., Baker and Stevenson 1986; Campbell and Mandel 1990; Carey 1958; Crane 1996; Deslandes et al. 1997; Fan 2001; Georgiou 1999; Gordon 1996; Jeynes 2005; Hansford and Hattie 1982; Paulson 1994). This area of research can be linked to what education specialists call "educational disadvantage."[1] No matter what the factors promoting students' academic performance are, those who do not have the benefit of those factors can face significant educational disadvantages.

In this article, we examine students' academic performance in the country of Korea. The Korean educational system is perceived as high performing, partly because Korean students perform well in widely accepted international academic tests and competitions, which will be examined in detail below. Further, many believe that Korea's educational system is at least partially responsible for the country's rapid economic development. As we will see below, Korea is also unique in the sense that admission to certain types of universities can largely determine the course of one's life. Though this may be true in many countries, the situation is more extreme in Korea. Given the high stakes involved, Korean high school students endeavor to matriculate into a handful of elite universities. We investigate the factors that affect the academic performance (meaning the level of preparedness to successfully enter good universities) of Korean high school graduates. After analyzing Korean data, we discuss whether any of these factors constitute educational disadvantages, especially what we call relationship and socioeconomic factors. Based on our observations, we make several policy suggestions.

Choice of Universities and Career Consequences in Korea

Most Korean high school graduates want—and their parents want their children —to go to the best universities, rather than just any university, and for good reason. Tables 1.1 and 1.2 show the composition of Korean National Assembly members from the two most recent national elections by their respective alma maters. Looking at the current cohort, 129 out of 300, or 43 percent, of all National Assembly members received their bachelor's degrees from one of the following three schools: Seoul National University, Korea University, and Yonsei University, which are referred to by the public as "SKY," the acronym coined from the initial letters of their names. Considering that there are currently 347 four-year universities and two-year community colleges in Korea, 43 percent represents an extremely high level of concentration. This percentage was 52.9 in the previous term of the National Assembly. So, in Korean politics, nearly half of the people's representatives have graduated from the three schools.

Table 2 shows the proportion of SKY graduates among top-level bureaucrats in the national government (including ministers, deputy ministers, and so on). Again, given the number of universities in Korea, an overwhelming number of SKY graduates occupy the top-most positions in government. Nevertheless, it still pays to go to a school in or near Seoul if one cannot gain admission to a SKY school. According to a 2010 data, 80.4 percent of top bureaucrats graduated from universities in the Seoul metropolitan area. So, the message is clear: if you want to be a high-level civil servant, you have to go to a university in Seoul.

Table 1. Undergraduate Alma Maters of the 19th National Assembly Members in Korea (2012–)

	Number	Percent
Seoul National University	79	26.3
Korea University	26	8.7
Yonsei University	24	8.0
Total SKY graduates	129	43
Others	171	57

Source: Data from An, Yi, and Choi (2012)

Table 2. Undergraduate Alma Maters of the 18th National Assembly Members in Korea (2008–2012)

	Number	Percent
Seoul National University	110	36.8
Korea University	25	8.4
Yonsei University	23	7.7
Total SKY graduates	158	52.9
Others	141	47.1

Source: Data from An, Yi, and Choi (2012).

Looking at the private sector, Table 3 shows the proportion of SKY graduates among the CEOs of the 100 largest corporations in Korea. Here, the imbalance is even more severe. It is clear, therefore, why most Korean high school students want to go to a handful of top schools and why Korean parents are willing to go great lengths to ensure their children a place at the one of the most elite universities.

Table 3. Undergraduate Alma Maters of the CEOs of the 100 Largest Corporations in Korea

	Number	Percent
Seoul National University	58	38.2
Korea University	23	15.1
Yonsei University	21	13.8
Total SKY graduates	102	67.1
Others	50	32.9

Source: Data from "2012 nyeonpan 100 dae gieop CEO peuropail jeonjosa" (Profiles of CEOs of TOP 100 Companies in 2012), New Management, May 8, 2012, http://www.newmanagement.co.kr/?p=5065.

Now that such a large proportion of high school graduates go on to college[2] and aspire to attend an elite school, the logical question is "who has access to the best universities in Korea?" Are there any factors that systematically affect high school students' academic performance, which heavily impacts which college they ultimately attend? Based on these questions, therefore, our research is not about who has access to schools of higher education, but who has access to the best universities in Korea. One way to investigate this question is to survey a large and random sample of first year students at all of Korea's universities and to gather data on an individual basis. However, given the time and resources available to us, this research strategy was simply not feasible. Fortunately, there is an alternative way to investigate factors that determine high school seniors' academic performance.

The type of university that an individual student enters is largely determined by his or her performance on the national standardized aptitude test implemented by the Korean government. By investigating the factors that determine students' performance on this exam, we can understand the factors that determine which college they will attend.

Individual students can choose to be tested in subjects such as Korean language, mathematics, English language, social sciences, natural sciences, vocational education, and a second foreign language. Almost all universities require test scores from Korean language, mathematics, and English language. Thus, almost all high school seniors opt to take these three subjects, with fewer students taking tests in the other subjects. Thus, in this study, we investigate the determinants of student performance in the three subject areas: Korean language, mathematics, and English language.

Once we identify the factors that determine student performance on the national standardized test and thus access to the best universities, we will be in a position to make policy suggestions addressing how the Korean government can reduce the level of educational disadvantage faced by some students.

Hypotheses
Baseline Model

There are certain elements affecting student performance on the national standardized test that are not necessarily disadvantageous. Because they do affect test scores, however, we must control for their impact in our analysis. We discuss these elements first.

There is a common perception that female students perform better in language exams than their male counterparts, while the latter do better in math and science. Studies of gender difference in academic achievement in mathematics started as early as the 1950s by scholars like Carey (1958). Regarding the Korean situation, Ko, Do, and Song (2008) analyzed the results of the National Assessment of Education Achievement (NAEA) between 2004 and 2006. They find that although male students do significantly better than female students in all types of math questions, this gap is narrowing. They conjecture that this change is due to social and policy reasons. The NAEA data used by the above authors became available in 2003 when the Korea Institute for Curriculum and Evaluation assessed the academic achievement of students at the national level and determined the factors affecting their performance. The 2009 NAEA reports show that, among Korean high school freshmen (equivalent to 10th graders in the United States), the average score in English language was higher among female students than among their male counterparts; in math, the proportion of students who belonged to the high-performing group was higher among male students (17.0%) than female students (14.6%); and in Korean language, the average score for female students was higher than that of male students. The proportion of students who belong to the high-performing group in Korean language was also higher among female students (37.8%) than among their male counterparts (26.2%). Given the trend above, we hypothesize the following:

H1. Male students perform better in mathematics, while female students do better in Korean and English (language in general).

Breakfast has been described as the most important meal of the day, contributing substantially to daily nutrient intake and energy needs. For children, breakfast consumption has been associated with better learning and school performance (Murphy et al. 1998; Pollitt and Mathews 1988; Vaisman et al. 1996). The importance of breakfast for academic achievement is reflected in the effects of breakfast on cognitive performance (Dye and Blundell 2002; Dye, Lluch, and Blundell 2000). Research suggests that skipping breakfast detrimentally affects problem-solving ability (Pollitt et al. 1983), short-term memory (Vaisman et al. 1996), and attention and episodic memory (Wesnes et al. 2003) of children. Conversely, when children consume breakfast, performance is enhanced on measures of vigilance attention, arithmetic ability (Conners and Blouin 1983), problem-solving tasks (Pollitt, Leibel, and Greenfield 1981), and logical reasoning (Marquez Acosta et al. 2001). Among Korean studies, S. Kim (1999), Choe et al. (2003), and Park et al. (2008) all find that high school students who eat breakfast regularly tend to perform better academically than those who do not. The leading reason given by those who do not eat breakfast regularly is lack of time in the morning. Based on previous studies, we hypothesize the following:

H2. Eating breakfast regularly has a positive impact on student performance.

For the past decade or so, Korea's best students have tended to apply for pre-med programs, regardless of their interest in the subject or the reputation of the university as a whole. This is due to the stability and incomeearning potential of the medical profession, especially at a time when college graduates are finding it difficult to secure jobs for themselves. Because pre-med programs have become magnets for the best students, and these students' performance on the national test is likely to be high, we must control for their impact on our research. On the other hand, those who apply to music, art, and physical education programs tend to have lower test scores because the university admission criteria for these majors are different in nature from those of other subjects. That is, these students take their own performance tests, be they in singing, playing musical instruments, drawing, and so on. As a result, they focus much of their time on practicing for these specialized tests rather than studying traditional academic subjects, so their academic performances tend to be lower. Given the considerations above, we hypothesize the following:

H3. Those who matriculate into pre-med programs perform better in all subjects than other students, while arts, music, and physical education majors perform below average.

In his study of educational achievement in England and Wales, Gordon (1996) shows a negative relationship between the size of the student's residential community and academic achievement. This is partly due to the high level of unemployment in inner cities. This is not the case in Korea. There have been many studies showing consistent urban-rural differences in academic achievement in favor of urban areas (e.g., Na and Min 2011; Sung 2011). We believe this to be true because everything is concentrated in metropolitan areas in small countries with large populations, as is the case in many countries in Asia. Affluent people live in condos and apartments in urban centers rather than in the suburbs. Good schools and "outof-school learning" (hereafter, OSL)[3] facilities are concentrated in urban centers. Based on this observation, we expect opposite results of findings in the West:

H4. Those students living in large cities show higher academic achievement than those living in small towns and rural areas.

Relationship Disadvantages

Here we test whether having good relationships with others helps students perform better academically. Kwak (2012) finds that in Korea, good teacher-student relationships facilitate student adjustment to the school environment, which in turn raises academic performance.

In their study of Canada, Deslandes et al. (1997) find what they call "parental behavioral control" to be positively related to student performance. In his study of student achievement in the United States, Paulson (1994) finds that parental involvement significantly and positively predicts achievement above and beyond dimensions of parenting style. Jeynes (2005) performs a meta-analysis of 41 previous studies examining the relationship between parental involvement and academic achievement of urban elementary school children. His results indicate a considerable and consistent relationship between parental involvement and academic achievement among urban students.

Among Korean studies, K. Kim (2005) and Won (2009) find that social capital—defined as parental knowledge of their children's friends, school life, and so on—has a positive impact on children's academic achievement. On the other hand, Kang (2001) finds that "parental behavioral control" has little to do with the Korean elementary school students' academic performance. Byun and Kim (2008) find that parental involvement—defined as parental participation in school activities, interaction among parents, enforcing rules in the family, and so on—has selective impact on middle school students' academic achievement, primarily affecting those whose parents have attained high levels of education.

Georgiou (1999) finds that parental attribution of achievement to the child's own effort enhances the child's self-confidence and is positively related to actual achievement. Hansford and Hattie (1982) perform a metaanalysis of 128 previous studies to see the relationship between various self-measures and measures of achievement. They find 15 different self-terms in their studies. Their analysis reinforces findings from a number of studies that have reported large positive correlation between selfconcepts of ability and academic performance. Based on the works above, we hypothesize the impact of individual students' relationships with their teachers, parents, and themselves—in the form of self-confidence or self-awareness. Hypotheses 5 through 8 are:

H5. Those students having good relationships with their teachers perform better on the national standardized exam.

H6. Those students with parents who know of their children's school and social lives perform better than those whose parents are less knowledgeable.

H7. Those students whose parents are "involved" in their children's study habits and lives perform better, in general, than those students whose parents are not ("Tiger-Mom Hypothesis").

H8. Those students with self-confidence perform better than those who are less self-confident.

H8a. Those students with perceived knowledge of their own abilities perform better than those without this perception.

Socioeconomic Disadvantages

Now, we discuss factors that serve as socioeconomic (dis)advantages when high school students prepare for the national standardized test for college entrance.

Crane (1996) shows that both the father's and mother's levels of education have positive impacts on their children's mathematics achievement. Baker and Stevenson (1986) find that a mother with at least a college education knows more about her child's school performance, has more contact with her child's teachers, and is more likely to take action to manage her child's academic achievement. Several Korean studies also argue that parents' levels of education both directly and indirectly affect their children's academic performance in Korea (Park and Doh 2005; Lee and Lee 2009). Based on these earlier studies, we hypothesize:

> H9. Those students whose parents are well-educated perform better than those whose parents are not.

In Korea, a large proportion of high school students and their parents believe that a regular high school education curriculum is inadequate to prepare for the national test. Students tend to get even busier after school due to OSL activities, which is quite an odd phenomenon. These activities range from relatively inexpensive options, such as long-distance learning, to very expensive alternatives such as one-on-one tutoring with a tutor of national repute.

Using various large-scale data, Park, Sang, and Kang (2008), Kim and Lee (2011), and Lee and Kim (2005) all find that OSL experiences have positive impacts on high school students' performance in math. Lee (2007) finds that the amount of money spent on OSLs also impacts middle school students' academic performance. Based on these previous studies, we assume that extra learning activities are effective and formulate the following two hypotheses:

> H10. Those students with OSL supplements perform better on the national standardized test than those without them.

H11. Those students who take more expensive OSL supplements perform better than those who take relatively cheaper alternatives.

As we are interested in socioeconomic (dis)advantages related to test performance, we are also interested in whether children from affluent families perform better than those from less wealthy families. Many studies have shown that socioeconomic status (SES), especially family income, has positive impacts on student performance in the United States (e.g., Crane 1996). Some Korean studies have shown that family income indirectly affects student performance through increased OSL spending, family relations, self-confidence, and so on (e.g., Sohn and Kim 2006). Based on these previous findings, we hypothesize:

H12. The level of a student's household wealth makes a difference in test performance.

Finally, we add a hypothesis, which may be intuitive and universal. Despite all of the factors we have discussed so far, students must spend time studying both the material learned in school and their OSL supplements to perform well on the national standardized exam. As such, we hypothesize:

H13. The amount of time that a student actually spends on studying makes a difference in performance.

Data

To investigate the factors influencing students' performance on the national standardized test, we used data from the Korean Education and Employment Panel (KEEP) (2004-2009) collected by the Korea Research Institute for Vocational Education and Training (KRIVET), a government-created think-tank. Starting in 2004, this data was collected to study the educational experiences, college selection, and career patterns of Korean youth. Since 2004, the same sample of young people has been surveyed to develop meaningful panel data. The data was made public in 2009, the sixth year of the study.

In 2004, a random sample of 2,000 students each was selected from: (1) the graduating classes of middle schools (9th graders in the U.S. system), (2) the graduating classes of regular high schools, and (3) graduat-ing classes of vocational schools (12th graders in the U.S. system). These 6,000 students and their household members have been surveyed every year since then.

The KEEP data was collected based on one-on-one interviews using PDAs and notebooks. We chose to use the KEEP data set because it contains many survey items we can use to investigate the factors affecting student performance on the national standardized exam. Furthermore, all 12th grader survey responses were matched with the students' actual scores on the test.

We use multivariate regression models to investigate the factors affecting student performance on the national standardized exam for college entrance. We report our findings in the following section.

Findings

The individual variables we use in our models are described in detail in Appendix. We first report the findings from the baseline model. Tables 4.1 and 4.2 show findings based on the data describing students who entered college in 2005 and 2008, respectively:

There is a clear performance gap between male and female students, with girls performing better across all three main subjects. There was no clear difference in math in 2005, but a gap appeared in 2008. It is very interesting to see that those who eat breakfast perform better in all three subjects across time. Those who progressed to medical school clearly performed better across all three subjects and across time periods. Those who chose arts, music, and physical education programs clearly perform worse across all three subjects and across time periods. "The place of residence" variable is available for 2008 only. Results show that those living in large cities perform best with declining performance as the respondents move from large cities to rural areas.

Table 4.1. Baseline Model of Factors Affecting Students' Performance in the National Standardized Test (2005)

Variables	Korean		Mathematics		English	
Constant	4.204	(.155)	3.879	(.169)	4.121	(.000)
Gender	.202*	(.080)	−.027	(.085)	.255**	(.081)
Breakfast	.367***	(.057)	.409***	(.062)	.412***	(.057)
Pre−med	3.433***	(.628)	2.794***	(.638)	3.419***	(.630)
AMPE majors	−.917***	(.140)	−1.102***	(.177)	−1.388***	(.142)
N	1,733		1,578		1,729	
R^2	.069		.065		.103	

* $p < 0.05$; ** $p < 0.01$; *** $p < 0.001$

Table 4.2. Baseline Model of Factors Affecting Students' Performance in the National Standardized Test (2008)

Variables	Korean		Mathematics		English	
Constant	2.996	(.315)	3.083	(.310)	2.597	(.315)
Gender	.674***	(.123)	.358**	(.121)	.636***	(.123)
Breakfast	.210***	(.042)	.275***	(.041)	.254***	(.042)
Place of resident	.266	(.062)	.312***	(.062)	.376***	(.062)
Pre−med	2.565**	(.978)	2.156*	(.952)	.2.209*	(.973)
AMPE majors	−1.523***	(.267)	−2.100***	(.284)	−1.616***	(.268)
N	1,030		1,003		1,021	
R^2	.091		.120		.114	

* $p < 0.05$; ** $p < 0.01$; *** $p < 0.001$

Now we report the findings from expanded models containing what we call relational (dis)advantage variables. They appear in Tables 5.1 and 5.2. With the models expanded to incorporate relationship disadvantages, the gender differences in performance shrank in 2005, but not in 2008. There were clear gender differences in performance across all three subjects. The results from the pre-med, arts, music, and physical education majors are consistent with the findings of the baseline model. Eating breakfast regularly remains a very important determinant of student performance, and students living in large cities still perform better than those in rural areas.

Table 5.1. Model of Factors Affecting Students's Performance in the National Standardized Test in 2005 (baseline plus relational factors)

Variables	Korean		Mathematics		English	
(Constant)	1.596	(.374)	1.086	(.399)	.482	(.370)
Gender	.131	(.081)	−.101	(.086)	.154*	(.080)
Breakfast	.309****	(.058)	.335****	(.063)	.338****	(.057)
Pre−med	3.234****	(.619)	2.618****	(.627)	3.152****	(.611)
AMPE majors	−.903****	(.138)	−1.072****	(.174)	−1.387****	(.138)
Teachers	−.009	(.034)	−.058	(.036)	−.014	(.033)
Parental awareness	.072****	(.010)	.070****	(.011)	.086****	(.010)
Self−confidence	.032**	(.013)	.051****	(.014)	.061****	(.013)
N	1,673		1,521		1,669	
R^2	.106		.106		.167	

* $p < 0.1$; ** $p < 0.05$; *** $p < 0.01$; **** $p < 0.001$

Table 5.2. Model of Factors Affecting Students's Performance in the National Standardized Test in 2008 (baseline plus relational factors)

Variables	Korean		Mathematics		English	
(Constant)	−1.116	(.5936)	−.896	(.584)	−2.248	(.581)
Gender	.507****	(.128)	.220*	(.126)	.487****	(.126)
Breakfast	.152****	(.043)	.201****	(.043)	.193****	(.043)
Place of residence	.275****	(.067)	.282****	(.066)	.323****	(.066)
Pre−med	2.784**	(1.290)	2.291*	(1.258)	2.693**	(1.260)
AMPE majors	−1.322****	(.277)	−1.798****	(.293)	−1.530****	(.274)
Teachers	.054	(.046)	.074*	(.045)	.088**	(.045)
Parental awareness	.088****	(.017)	.077****	(.017)	.098****	(.016)

Parental involvement	.016	(.017)	.053***	(.016)	.037**	(.016)
Self–awareness	.074****	(.020)	.055****	(.020)	.078****	(.020)
N	857		834		851	
R^2	.164		.191		.221	

* $p < 0.1$; ** $p < 0.05$; *** $p < 0.01$; **** $p < 0.001$

Interestingly, a good teacher-student relationship does not seem to affect a student's performance on the national standardized test. It had zero effect in 2005 and had significant impact in English only in 2008. Our results show that when parents pay attention to their children's school and general environments, students perform better in all three subjects across different time periods. The "parental in-volvement" variable is available for 2008 only, which turns out to be an effective tool for evaluating math and English, but not Korean language. We see that the "self-confidence" variable in 2005 and the "self-awareness" variable in 2008 both have significant impacts on student performance in all three subjects.

Table 6.1. Full Model of Factor Affecting Students' Performance in the National Standardized Test in 2005

Variables	Korean		Mathematics		English	
(Constant)	1.601	(.379)	1.279	(.398)	.434	(.365)
Gender	.156*	(.081)	−.084	(.085)	.188**	(.078)
Breakfast	.250****	(.057)	.270****	(.061)	.261****	(.055)
Pre–med	2.814****	(.607)	2.420****	(.610)	2.603****	(.587)
AMPE majors	−.740****	(.138)	−.830***	(.171)	−1.160****	(.136)
Teachers	−.023	(.034)	−.062*	(.035)	−.023	(.033)
Parental awareness	.054****	(.011)	.050****	(.012)	.062****	(.011)
Self–confidence	.017	(.013)	.029**	(.014)	.036***	(.013)
Father's education	.024	(.018)	.002	(.019)	.057***	(.017)
Mother's education	.089****	(.025)	.034	(.026)	.103	(.024)
OSL experience	.151*	(.090)	.522****	(.089)	.129	(.081)
OSL expenses	.001	(.001)	3.430E–5[a]	(.001)	.001	(.001)
Household income	−4.018E–5[a]	(.000)	.000	(.000)	.000	(.000)

Amount of time studied by her/himself	.122****	(.018)	.126****	(.109)	.156****	(.018)
N		1,650		1,500		1,646
R^2		.147		.167		.236

[a]The coefficient for "household income" is−4.018E−5 (.000), which means it is an extremely small number, thus is negligible, and further, statistically insignificant for the year 2005

* $p < 0.1$; ** $p < 0.05$; *** $p < 0.01$; **** $p < 0.001$

Now we report findings from what we call "full" models containing all relevant variables whose impacts we investigate. The results are shown in Tables 6.1 and 6.2. In this full model, the gender gap appeared again. Given the pattern in all three models, it appears that female students perform better in languages (Korean and English) across time periods, with no clear differences between genders in mathematics (H1 partially supported). Eating breakfast regularly continues to have a strong impact on student performance in all three subjects across time periods (H2 sup-ported). Our full models show that, while pre-med majors clearly performed better in all subjects than other students in 2005 and that superiority declined in 2008, the poorer performance of the arts, music, and physical education majors remained consistent (H3 supported). The size of the city of the student's residence still matters as its coefficients hover around the level of significance (H4 supported).

Weak ties between a good student-teacher relationship and the student's performance remained constant (H5 not supported). According to the OECD report (2004), the level of students' attachment to regular schools in Korea is the lowest among OECD countries. At the same time, Korean students achieved top scores in the Program for International Student Assessment (PISA). We believe that this strange combination—low level of attachment to schools and high level of performance—is indirectly caused by students' OSL experiences in Korea, which we discuss extensively below. Simply put, Korean students' heavy reliance on OSLs explains both their good performance on PISA and their low level of attachment to regular schools, which in turn, explains the weak ties between (regular school) teacher-student relationship and student performance.

In this full model, "parental awareness," that is, parental knowledge of the student and his environment, made a significant difference in the student's performance in all three subjects in both 2005 and 2008. On the other hand, "parental involvement," or parental control of the student's study habits and life in general had little to no effect on the student's performance level (H6 supported; H7 not supported). However, we note that scholars have used the term "parental involvement or control" to refer to many different types of "involvement" or "control" (Deslandes et al. 1997). For example, Paulson (1994) measures "parental involvement" by including both types of survey questions we used to construct "parental attention" and "parental involvement." In the above-mentioned meta-analysis, Jeynes (2005) finds that:

Table 6.2. Full Model of Factors Affecting Students' Performance in the National Standardized Test in 2008

Variables	Korean		Mathematics		English	
(Constant)	−.385	(.590)	.116	(.580)	−1.198	(.566)
Gender	.390***	(.123)	.105	(.120)	.353***	(.117)
Breakfast	.089**	(.042)	.146****	(.041)	.126***	(.040)
Place of resident	.129*	(.067)	.114*	(.066)	.129**	(.064)
Pre−med	2.042****	(1.226)	1.554****	(1.192)	1.884	(1.170)
AMPE majors	−.950****	(.266)	−1.443****	(.279)	−1.131****	(.257)
Teachers	.047	(.043)	−.078*	(.042)	−.086**	(.041)
Parental awareness	.056****	(.016)	.043***	(.016)	.060****	(.016)
Parental involvement	−.006	(.016)	.027**	(.016)	.004	(.016)
Self−awareness	.054***	(.019)	.033**	(.019)	.053***	(.018)
Father's education	.022	(.024)	.017	(.024)	.033	(.023)
Mother's education	.097*	(.040)	.081**	(.039)	.127***	(.038)
OSL experience	.754****	(.139)	.489****	(.137)	.688****	(.134)
OSL expenses	.001	(.002)	.003*	(.002)	.004**	(.002)
Household income	.000*	(.000)	.001**	(.000)	.000	(.000)
Amount of time studied by oneself	.024****	(.004)	.028****	(.004)	.028****	(.004)

| N | 857 | 834 | 851 |
| R^2 | .256 | .285 | .338 |

* p < 0.1; ** p < 0.05; *** p < 0.01; **** p < 0.001

It was not particular actions, such as attending school functions, establishing household rules, and checking student homework that yielded the statistically significant effect sizes. Rather, variables that reflected a general atmosphere of involvement produced the strong results. Parental expectations and style may create an educationally oriented ambience, which establishes an understanding of a certain level of support and standards in the child's mind.

Campbell and Mandel (1990) also show that parental influence involves a mix of variables that cannot be understood in a variable-by-variable analysis; they must be viewed as an interrelated schema. They argue that a mix of parental factors including low levels of help, pressure, and monitoring, together with relatively high levels of psychological support, produce a high level of mathematical achievement. High levels of parental pressure, help, and monitoring were found to be dysfunctional. Fan (2001) assesses the effect of parental involvement in students' academic growth during high school years in the United States and identifies 14 items as related to parental involvement using exploratory factor analysis to examine the underlying dimensions of parental involvement. His "supervision" dimension resembles our "parental involvement" variable encompassing items such as setting limits for television watching, checking homework, and so on. His results show that the "supervision" dimension has no statistically significant effect on student academic performance, which echoes our findings about parental involvement based on similar survey items (see Appendix). In his study of student performance in Cyprus, Georgiou (1999) similarly finds that a child's school achievement is not significantly related to what he calls "parental controlling behavior," measured by such survey questions as "controlling child's TV watching time" and "approving child's friends."

The "self-confidence" (in 2005) and "self-awareness" (in 2008) variables still matter, except in the Korean language subject in 2005 (H8 supported). For some reason yet unknown, the father's education level seems to have little to no impact on the performance of the student. On the other hand, the mother's education level seems to impact the student's performance across the board, except math in 2005 (H9 partially supported).

In 2005, having OSL supplements appears to have a strong impact on performance in math, and hovers around the level of statistical significance on Korean language performance, while having no apparent impact on English language performance. Furthermore, it is the experience of OSL that mattered; the amount the household spent on OSLs, or the level of household wealth itself did not seem to make a difference in performance level (H10 partially supported; H11 not supported; and H12 not supported in 2005). However, things changed in 2008, when the OSL experience had strong impacts on performance levels in all three subjects. Furthermore, the level of money spent began to make a difference in English and, to a lesser extent, in math. It appears that more expensive tutors tracked the national standardized exam scheme better than less expensive ones. In 2008, household wealth started to matter, too. That is, all other things equal, the greater the household income, the better the student's performance on the national standardized exam. This is the case while controlling for expenses on the OSL experience. This is a troublesome trend (H10 supported; H11 partially supported; and H12 supported).[4]

One positive and intuitive finding is that, in the end, the amount of time that a student spends studying matters significantly across different subjects and time periods. Even after controlling for the impacts of all other variables in our model, it still pays to study hard (H13 supported).

Discussion

As we explained in the introduction, most Korean high school graduates want—and their parents want their children—to go to the best universities, rather than just any university. Now that such a large proportion of high school graduates go on to college and most of them want to go to a handful of elite schools, we investigated whether there are any factors that systematically affect high school students' academic performance, which heavily influence which college they ultimately attend.

As we also mentioned in the introduction, the kind of university that a student enters is largely determined by his or her performance on the national standardized test administered by the Korean government. By investigating the factors that influence individual student performance in this exam, we can understand the factors that determine which school they will attend. Thus, in this study, we investigated the determinants of student performance in the three subject areas of Korean, mathematics, and English, on which almost all high school seniors are tested.

Of all the factors identified above as relevant to student performance on the national standardized test, some of them may indeed represent "educational disadvantage" while some may not. As we have shown above, female students perform better than male students, especially in Korean and English languages. We are uncertain if this has to do with a systemic disadvantage that male students face. Rather, this disparity may have more to do with behavioral patterns of different genders in that age cohort. As we also found, eating breakfast regularly has a systematic impact on student performance. This appears to stem from lifestyle and habits rather than from economic conditions. Likewise, the performance of pre-med, arts, music, and physical education majors has more to do with the nature of their respective subjects rather than the (dis)advantages they face.

Now, we should discuss what we perceive as relational (dis)advantages. Strong family ties in the form of parental attention to a student and his environment turned out to be a definite advantage to the student. On the other hand, "parental involvement," or parental control of a student's study habits and life in general, has little to no effect on the student's performance level. "Self-confidence" and "self-awareness," which we call a relationship with self, turned out to be important determinants of student performance. As these are subjective self-assessments by students, it is important for parents and teachers to instill self-confidence and enhance self-image in children from a very young age. Finally, it is puzzling to find that a good teacher-student relationship does not lead to better performance for a student in Korea, and the current student-teacher relationship leaves something to be desired. We believe that this type of disconnect between regular school teachers and student performance is at least partially caused by extensive exposure to OSLs by Korean students.

Among socioeconomic disadvantages, we found that students living in large cities perform better than those in small towns and rural areas. Many universities already have quota-type admissions policies, which mandate admission to students from certain areas. However, it appears that the government should invest more in small towns and rural areas to alleviate this disadvantage and to enhance the quality of high school education there. Our results show that having a mother with a high level of education is a definite educational advantage. Though this is not something that can be changed in a short period time, given the high rate of college education for female students and their good academic performances, this (dis)advantage may gradually disappear.

As we have examined above, the OSL experience has had growing impacts on students' performance levels in the national standardized test. Furthermore, a comparison of the 2005 and 2008 results show that the level of money spent on OSLs makes a difference. It appears that more expensive tutors were simply better at figuring out trends in the national standardized exam scheme than less expensive ones. Our results also show that, while controlling for OSL experiences and incurred expenses, household wealth started to matter in 2008. This means that the educational disadvantage stemming from socioeconomic factors is growing. That is, Korean education is moving in the wrong direction, as far as equity is concerned. Korean educational authorities must develop inexpensive substitutes for expensive OSL options, such as private tutoring. Furthermore, they must modify regular school curricula so that high school students can go to high-caliber universities without the benefit of OSLs. Fundamentally, the Korean government must pursue redistributive policies to level the playing field.

Finally, our Korea-based study confirms a universal truth: despite all of the potential disadvantages we found above, ultimately, a student must willfully spend time studying to perform well on the college entrance exam and matriculate to a good college.

Appendix: Description of Individual Variables

Gender	This is a dummy variable with female students coded as 1 and male students as 0.
Breakfast	This is a categorical variable with a value of 1 meaning "I do not eat breakfast" and 5 meaning "I eat breakfast every day."
Place of residence	A categorical variable that shows the place of residence as either a large municipality, a city, a township, and a rural area.
Pre-med	This is a dummy variable indicating those who entered the premed program in college (including traditional medicine majors).
AMPE majors	This is a dummy variable indicating those who ended up majoring in arts, music, or physical education in college.
Teachers	This is a composite index created from four survey statements: "I have a teacher(s) that I particularly respect." "I have a teacher(s) who pays attention to my ability and future plans." "I have a teacher(s) that I particularly like." "I have a teacher(s) who understands my problems." The responding student was asked to answer "yes" or "no." We gave a score of 1 for each "yes" answer and 0 for each "no." The value of the "teachers" variable is the sum total of the scores given based on the student's responses to the four questions above.
Parental awareness	This is a composite index created from the following survey statements: "I know the student's performance at school well." "I know about the student's friends well." "I know about the parents of the student's friends well." "I know about the student's school life well." "I know the general life habits of the student well." "I know about the student's current concerns well." The responding parent (or guardian) was asked to rate the level of his or her knowledge on a five-point scale for each of the statement above. The value of the "parental awareness" variable is the sum total of the scores given by the parent.

	This is a composite index created from the following survey statements:
Parental involvement	"I check the student's homework." "I check the student's daily schedule." "I regularly communicate with the student's friends or their parents." "I regularly use Internet sources to collect educational information for the student." "I make sure that the student takes OSLs." "I check what other parents are doing for their children's education." "I forbid the student from reading anything that is not related to school work." The responding parent (or guardian) was asked to rate the level of his or her involvement on a five-point scale for each of the statements above. The value of the "parental involvement" variable is the sum total of the scores given by the parent.
Self-confidence	Due to the unavailability of the necessary survey questions, this variable exists for 2005 only. This is a composite index created from the following survey statements: "I perform very well academically." "I am good at dancing, singing, and sports." "I am a good leader." "I have high aspirations for my future." "My family is doing very well economically." "I have good relationships with my friends." "I am very diligent in my school life." The responding student was asked to rate the level of his or her confidence on a five-point scale for each of the statements above. The value of the "self-confidence" variable is a sum total of the scores given by the student. We should remember that this is the student's subjective assessment of his or her own abilities.
Self-awareness	Due to the unavailability of the necessary survey questions, this

	variable exists for 2008 only. This is a composite index created from the following survey statements:
	"I know what I am good at."
	"I know what I really like to do."
	"I understand what is really important in life."
	"I make good decisions."
	"I can perform my plans well."
	"I think I am a decent person."
	The respondent was asked to rate the level of his or her self-awareness on a five-point scale for each of the statements above. The value of the "self-awareness" variable is the sum total of the scores given by the student. We should remember that this is the student's subjective assessment of his or her own self-perception.
Father's/mother's education	A nine-point categorical variable ranging from no education (with the value of 1) to holding a Ph.D. (with the value of 9).
OSL experience	Out-of-school learning experience which includes all types of learning besides a student's regular high school curriculum in a particular subject area. This includes private tutoring, group tutoring, paid long-distance learning, and so on.
OSL expenses	The average monthly OSL expenses for the student for the previous year.
Household income	Average monthly household income for the previous year.
Amount of time spent studying by oneself	The average weekly amount of time the student spends studying by himself or herself.

Notes

1. Educational disadvantage takes many different forms, but globally is a major barrier to the well-being of individuals and communities as well as to the prosperity of nations. What represents "disadvantage" will differ from country to country (IALEI 2012).

2. According to a Korean government statistics, 81.5 percent of high school graduates went on to study in college in 2012 (http://www.schoolinfo.go.kr/index.jsp).

3. In this article, we call students' learning activities before or after regular school hours "out-of-school learning."

4. Readers may wonder if there is a high correlation between any pair of independent variables in our models. Obvious candidates are the pair of "parental awareness" and "parental involvement" and the combination of "OSL experiences," "OSL expenses," and "the household income." In our 2005 sample, the correlation coefficients are as follows: $r = .3$ between OSL experience in Korean and OSL expenses; $r = .28$ between OSL experience in math and OSL expenses; $r = .31$ between OSL experience in English and OSL expenses; $r = .231$ between OSL experience in Korean and household income; $r = .188$ between OSL experience in math and household income; $r = .237$ between OSL experience in English and household income; and $r = .507$ between OSL expenses and household income. As we can see, the correlations among these variables are low enough to give us confidence in our results. The correlation coefficients for our 2008 sample are similar, and we do not report them here due to space. The correlation coefficient between "parental awareness" and "parental involvement" is .414 for our 2008 sample (there is no "parental involvement" variable in our 2005 model). For the models reported in Tables 6.1 and 6.2, the vif values are between 1.0 and 1.6, showing no indication of multicollinearity.

14.

The Impact of Candidate's Negative Traits on Vote Choice in New Democracies: A Test Based on Presidential Elections in Korea

Heemin Kim & Jungho Roh.

Abstrcat. The impact of candidate's negative traits (CNTs) on voting behavior has received significant attention in election studies in recent decades. However, these scholarly efforts have focused on the elections in advanced Western democracies. In contrast, the relationship between candidate's personal traits and electorate's voting behaviors is rarely explored in the context of new democracies. In this study, we fill this gap by investigating the impact of CNTs on electorate's vote choice in Korean presidential elections. Our study of CNT in Korea yields a rather mixed picture. CNTs lead to a fair amount of negative voting, but they are not always powerful enough to disqualify candidates. We discuss why the candidates with negative traits won two out of the latest three elections, utilizing the impact of CNTs and those of other social cleavages.

Introduction: The Case for the Study of Candidate's Personal Traits in New Democracies

Elections entail candidates. In recent decades, the discipline has witnessed rising interest in candidate quality and characteristics. The normative concern that we want to elect high-quality candidates and an empirical concern about whether such candidates actually win continue to fuel our interest in this topic (e.g., Banks and Kiewiet, 1989; Gelman and King, 1990; Cox and Katz, 1996;

Kulisheck and Mondak, 1996; Bond, Fleisher, and Talbert, 1997; Funk, 1999; Hacker, et al., 2000; Bartels, 2002; King, 2002; Johnston and Pattie, 2006; Carson, Engstrom, and Roberts, 2007).

As a byproduct, the impact of candidate's negative traits (CNTs from here on) on voting behavior also received significant attention. CNTs include scandals in many different forms, such as marital infidelity, tax evasion, corruption, and so on (e.g., Miller, Wattenberg, and Malanchuk, 1986; Funk, 1996; Hayes, 2005). The candidate"s personal trait that can be perceived as negative, however, is a concept broader than scandals and can also include gender and race stereotypes, religion, age, education, occupation, location/residence, personality/character, and the list goes on (Terkildsen, 1993; Campbell and Cowley, 2014 Glasgow and Alvarez, 2000 Prysby, 2008 Fridkin and Kenney, 2011, among many others).

One thing that stands out is that most of these scholarly studies analyzed candidate's traits in the context of elections in the US and other Western democracies. Since the third wave of democratization began, many new democracies have practiced free and fair elections. However, we are not aware of many election studies investigating whether candidate's personal traits have affected voting behaviors in new democracies. Since those who run in the elections in new democracies have often been elites before the process of democratization, they may have skeletons in their closet regardless of whether they were on the side of the democracy movement or on the side of the previous authoritarian regime.

In this article, we study the impact of CNTs on electorate's vote choice in Korea. We use the term, "CNTs" to refer to personal issues that did the greatest damage to individual candidates. As the CNT is broader than scandals, the three main negative issues whose impact we investigate in this article include both scandals and a non-scandal, namely a candidate's family history. As readers will find out below, Korean voters apparently considered the latter case a negative trait in 2012.

We are aware of few studies of Korean elections focusing on candidate's personal traits. In this paper, we build a general model of vote choice in Korea that includes CNTs s well as the ideological, regional, and generational differences, the three main determinants of vote choice in Korea (Kang, 2002 2003 Kim, Choi, and Cho, 2008 Kim, 2011). We analyze the three latest presidential elections held in 2002, 2007, and 2012 for which we have enough survey questions to conduct meaningful research.

The remainder of the paper is organized as follows. In the next section, we briefly lay out the electoral history of Korea in the 21st century. We introduce various existing explanations of voting behavior in Korea and present a testable hypothesis regarding CNTs in Section III. After discussing the methods and data in the following section, we show the empirical results in Section V. We try to explain the actual outcomes of three elections we analyze and conclude in the last two sections of this article.

Brief Electoral History of Korea

In June 2000, the North Korean leader, Kim Jong-il, accepted South Korean President Kim Dae-jung's call for a North-South summit. The first-ever summit of the two Koreas' leaders was held in the North Korean capital of Pyongyang, followed by the visits of separated families and the flow of South Korean capital across the border. This was a dramatic and quite unexpected turn of events, since the North Korean regime (and its leader Kim Jong-il) had been known for its aggressiveness, inflexibility, and unwillingness to compromise with the outside world. These events also prompted the Clinton administration to reassess its North Korea policy, leading to US Secretary of State Madeleine Albright's visit to Pyongyang (Hankuk Ilbo, December 14, 2000 June 9, 2001).

President Kim Dae-jung's term was scheduled to end in early 2003. The opposition had been quite critical of the Kim government"s reconciliation policy and had promised to take a more conservative approach toward the North. It appeared that the opposition had an edge in the upcoming presidential election. The opposition Grand National Party (GNP) candidate, Lee Hoi-chang, had already run for the presidency against Kim Dae-jung in 1997, an election which he narrowly lost. Since then, Lee had "managed" the Party with the primary goal of taking another crack at the presidency in 2002. A succession of well-timed events led to the nomination of Roh Moo-hyun, a relative lightweight even in his own party, as the governing New Millennium Democratic Party (NMDP) candidate. Prior to the scheduled presidential election in 2002, public opinion polls had consistently shown Roh Moo-hyun trailing Lee Hoi-chang (Kim, 2011). It was not until a few days before election day that the tide of public opinion began to turn. Roh's come-from-behind win in a matter of a few days made it a bitter pill to swallow for the losing side.

Table 1. Results of the 16th presidential election in 2002

Candidate	Party	Total Number of Votes Won	Proportion of Votes Won
Lee Hoi-chang	Grand National Party	11,443,297	46.6%
Roh Moo-hyun	NMDP	12,014,277	48.9%
Others*	–		4.5%

* There were four other candidates, none of whom affected the race for all practical purposes.

As we implied above, the newly elected President Roh did not have a full control over or have a full support of his own party. His solution was to leave the party and create a new governing party comprised of politicians loyal to himself. This new governing party was called Uri Party. The 17th presidential election was scheduled for December 19, 2007. Before the election, the incumbent President Roh Moo-hyun and the governing Uri Party were unpopular among the general public for various reasons. First of all, Mr. Roh maintained the former President Kim's reconciliation policy toward the North even after it was revealed in early October 2002 that North Korea had sustained a hidden nuclear weapons program that were supposed to have been frozen under an earlier agreement. The Roh government's reconciliation policy included economic aid to the North, which many conservatives in the South argued was used to develop weapons systems rather than feeding the North Korean people. Further, when he was first elected president of the country, many Koreans found his blunt and unrefined style refreshing because he behaved so differently from his predecessors. As time passed, however, many became tired of Roh"s succession of controversial statements, some of which could be interpreted as anti-American or pro-North. By the time Roh left office, many Koreans no longer found him refreshing, but simply unpresidential (Kim, 2011).

As the election approached, members of the governing Uri Party became concerned that they would suffer a crushing defeat. They began to split from the party and attempted to form a new moderate party under an ideologically "larger tent." They also tried to distance themselves from the current president. After merging several of the new splinter groups and absorbing the remainder of the Uri Party with defectors from other parties, the United New Democratic Party (UNDP) was born. Despite its efforts to look different, the new party was essentially the governing Uri Party plus some small political groupings unaffiliated with the major opposition, i.e., the GNP. This merely created a double-edged sword for the new party, because most of the pro-Roh former Uri Party members were now members of this new party, and the Uri Party's merger with so many small but different groups created an ideological identity problem for itself. Beyond the goal of winning the presidency, it appeared that the party did not stand for anything in particular (Kim, 2011). A group of nine began vying for the party's nomination. Eventually, Chung Dong-young, a former Unification Minister, emerged as the party's nominee with a bare plurality vote.

Two very well-known and formidable individuals vied for the nomination of the opposition GNP. One was Lee Myung-bak whose career had included serving as the CEO of Hyundai Construction, a subsidiary of the now world-famous Hyundai Corporation, as a National Assemblyperson, and as the mayor of the capital city of Seoul. Lee had an extremely prestigious career, and if indeed there was anything left to do, it would be to serve as the president of the country. The other candidate was Park Geun-hye, a daughter of the former president Park Chung-hee. After grabbing power in a coup d'etat in 1961, Park Chung-hee ruled Korea until 1979 achieving rapid economic development but by ruthlessly cracking down on dissidents and forcing constitutional amendments to stay in power. By 2007, Park Geun-hye had established herself as one of the most influential leaders of the GNP. In a pairwise contest, Lee

Myung-bak barely won the nomination of the GNP and went on to face Chung Dong-young for the presidential election.

On election day in December, Lee scored a landslide victory in a multi-candidate contest by acquiring 48.7% of the total votes cast. The governing party candidate, Chung Dong-young, came in at a distant second with 26.1% of the vote.

Table 2. Results of the 17th presidential election in 2007

Candidate	Party	Total Number of Votes Won	Proportion of Votes Won
Lee Myung-bak	Grand National Party	11,492,389	48.7%
Chung Dong-young	UNDP	6,174,681	26.1%
Lee Hoi-chang	Independent	3,559,963	15.1%
Moon Kuk-hyun	Creative Korea Party	1,375,498	5.8%
Others*	–		4.3%

* There were six other candidates, none of whom affected the race for all practical purposes.

As discussed above, Park Geun-hye lost the GNP's nomination to Lee Myung-bak by an extremely narrow margin in 2007. During the next five years (that is, under Lee Myung-bak's government), no significant alternative candidate to her emerged in the GNP, and people regarded her as de facto presidential nominee of the party for 2012. With declining popularity of both the GNP and President Lee, the party changed its name to Saenuri Party.

The opposition party (by then its name had become the Democratic United Party, the DUP) nominated Moon Jae-in as its presidential candidate for the 2012 election. Moon was closely associated with the former President Roh Moo-hyun. Moon had operated a joint law firm with Roh, served as a Blue House (Presidential) Chief of Staff under Roh, and was the president of the Roh Moo-hyun Foundation until he became a presidential candidate. In an essentially pair-wise contest, Park beat Moon 51.6% to 48% and became the first female president in the history of Korea in 2012.

Table 3. Results of the 18th presidential election in 2012

Candidate	Party	Total Number of Votes Won	Proportion of Votes Won
Park Geun–hye	Saenuri Party	15,773,128	51.6%
Moon Jae–in	DUP	14,692,632	48.0%
Others*	Independents		0.4%

* There were four other candidates, none of whom affected the race for all practical purposes.

Expectations and the Hypothesis

In this section, we introduce various existing explanations of voting behavior in Korea. This group of factors includes regionalism, the left-right ideology, and generational differences. Then we develop a hypothesis regarding CNT to analyze the voting behavior of the electorate at the time of the three previously mentioned presidential elections.

Regionalism, Ideology, and Generations

With democratic opening and free elections came regionalism as the dominant cleavage in Korean politics. This was especially the case in the rivalry between the southeastern region of Youngnam and the southwestern region of Honam. Political leaders who emerged as alternatives to authoritarian rule were perceived as representing certain regions of Korea without nationwide appeal and with their party support firmly entrenched in those regions. It is widely agreed among observers of Korean politics that since the democratic opening, electoral competition has been used as an expression of regional frustration and animosity, with regionalism playing the decisive role in the choices the Korean electorate made (Chung, 1993; Park, 1993; Choi, 1995; Lee, 1998 1999). Over the years major parties have changed their names, but they essentially remain regionally-based in Honam and Youngnam. In the three elections we analyze in this study, the Honam-based party would be the NMDP, the UNDP, and the DUP chronologically, while the Youngnam-backed party would be the GNP and later Saenuri Party.

There has been a common perception among observers of Korean politics that the left-right ideology did not play an important role in the choices the electorate made, mainly because there was no meaningful ideological distinction between political parties. Essentially, all the parties formed since the democratic opening in 1987 have generally been conservative parties, reflecting Korea"s history in the war with the North and its subsequent role as the front between the East and the West during the Cold War era–establishing a basis of "anti-socialism" (Sohn, 1995; Lee, Kapyoon, 1999; Choi, 2002; Cho, 2003).

However, there has recently been a change. Some scholars have reported that ideological differences did affect the electorate's choices in a significant manner in the 2002 presidential election (Kang, 2002 2003). Kim, Choi, and Cho (2008) shows that the left-right ideology affected the vote choice of the major party supporters in the 2004 National Assembly elections.[1] Based on the observation that the impact of the left-right ideology has been growing since 2002, we expect that ideology had a significant impact on the choice of the voters at the time of the presidential elections in 2002, 2007, and 2012.

The presidential election of 2002 is viewed as the first national-level election in the history of Korea in which generational differences played a critical role in the election outcome - the old primarily supported Lee Hoi-chang, the GNP candidate, while the young preferred Roh Moo-hyun, representing the then governing party, the NMDP (Kim, 2011). Furthermore, Kim, Choi, and Cho (2008) showed that generational differences played an important role in the National Assembly elections in 2004. Because a new cleavage of generational differences clearly played an important role since the 2002 presidential election and there is no reason to believe that it has since dissipated, we expect that generational differences continued to have a significant impact on voters' choices in the presidential elections of 2007 and 2012.

Candidate's Negative Traits - Morality/Corruption/Association with the Past

Lee Hoi-chang ran for the presidency and lost in 1997. During the campaign, an accusation was made that Lee's son avoided mandatory military service by losing weight to the point that he was declared unfit to serve. In Korea, where every young man is required to serve in the military for over two years, voters are quite sensitive to this type of issue. It would be quite damaging to Lee politically, especially if it was done with Lee's knowledge or influence. It would be impossible to assess the impact of this allegation in 1997 because the candidate morality question was never asked in the survey. However, we may be able to see the impact of this accusation in 2002 as Lee ran again as an opposition party candidate. Needless to say, the same accusation was repeated in 2002.

Moving ahead to 2007, the opposition GNP candidate Lee Myung-bak seemed to have had an extremely prestigious career as we discussed above. At the same time, however, Lee had many encounters with the law throughout his career. By our count, he has been investigated or indicted over 20 times for bribery, violations of construction law, city-park laws, labor laws, election laws, and stock-trading laws. He was found innocent of many of these charges, and the most severe punishment he ever received was fines. By this time, however, many felt that he had established a pattern of careless attitude toward the law.

Just a few months before the presidential election, the so-called BBK scandal broke out. The BBK was a company that engaged in stock price fixing and money laundering, which resulted in the loss of hundreds of millions of dollars for small-scale investors. The CEO of the company had fled the country, but rumor had it that the real owner of the BBK was Lee. He was also implicated in a land speculation scandal in an area of Seoul where land prices were among the highest in the nation. Given the serious nature of the charge, a special prosecutor was appointed to investigate Lee's involvement in these cases shortly before the presidential election (Kim, 2011).

In 2012 the governing party's presidential candidate was Park Geun-hye. As we mentioned above, she was a daughter of the former president Park Chung-hee, who engaged in a coup d"etat in 1961 and ruled Korea until 1979 when he was assassinated by his own Korean CIA director. Being a daughter of Park Chung-hee had a mixed effect on her candidacy. First, Park Chung-hee ruled the country by ruthlessly cracking down on dissidents and forced constitutional amendments to stay in power for life by avoiding direct popular election of the president, i.e., the so-called Yushin constitution. Many dissidents were tortured, and some were probably killed. Second, to gain legitimacy after the coup, Park consistently pushed for economic development plans under his reign, which most Korean people believe to have moved Korea from one of the world's poorest countries after the Korean War to its current position as one of the 15 largest economies in the world. The Korean people were thus split in their evaluation of the Park Chung-hee era. His daughter Park Geun-hye's run for the presidency would show this split more clearly. To some, being associated with the nation's most notorious dictator would work like a "semi-scandal" for Park Geun-hye, although she herself had nothing to do with her father's reign. Based on our discussion of CNT above, we propose the following hypothesis:

Hypothesis : The CNT causes negative vote choice on the part of the electorate in presidential elections in Korea.

Data, Methods, and the Model

In order to test the hypothesis proffered in the previous section, we employ binary logistic models for the 2002 and 2012 presidential elections and multinomial logistic models for the 2007 election. The latter is appropriate when the dependent variable is nominal and has more than two categories (more than two viable candidates running in our case). Relying on these methods, we analyze the factors affecting the vote choices in the presidential elections in Korea. The data for the elections are based on presidential election surveys conducted by the Korean Social Science Data Center (KSDC).[2] Our benchmark model is as follows:

$$V_i = \alpha_1 CNT_i + R_i'\beta + \gamma_1 Ideology_i + \gamma_2 Age_i + Z_i'\lambda + \varepsilon_i \quad \text{.............. (1)}$$

The dependent variable, V, has either two or multiple discrete categories: the electorate's choices of candidates. In the binary logit for the 2002 presidential election, the vote choice is coded 1 for Lee Hoi-chang and 0 for Roh Moo-hyun. Likewise, it is coded 1 for Park Geun-hye and 0 for Moon Jae-in in the model for the 2012 election. In the multinomial logistic model for the

17th presidential election held in 2007, it is coded 0 for Lee Myung-bak (the base outcome), 1 for Chung Dong-yung, 2 for Lee Hoi-chang, and 3 for Moon Kook-hyun. The multinomial logistic regression allows us to estimate the effects of the independent variables for all possible pairs among the categories (candidates in our study) of the dependent variable. Because Lee Myung-bak was such a clear winner, we did not find a pair-wise comparison between any two losing candidates meaningful. This is the reason why voting for Lee Myung-bak is set to zero as the base outcome. Below, we will present the effects of the independent variables for the pairs involving Lee Myung-bak and the next three top vote-getters. We drop respondents who voted for minor candidates as well as those who refused to answer.

CNT is our key independent variable of interest for which we use different survey items for different elections. We use the variable, Morality, in the 2002 survey, which is coded 1 for those who considered candidate morality important in deciding for whom they voted and 0 otherwise. This variable is the only relevant variable involving a CNT available in the 2002 survey. Beside Lee's son, there was no mentionable "moral" issue in the 2002 election. That is, Roh Moo-hyun was considered a "clean" candidate. There were only two major candidates, and Lee's son issue was so controversial in 2002 that any expert in Korean politics would agree that the respondent was thinking this issue when s/he answered the morality was important (see Kim, 2011, and Kim, Choi, and Cho, 2008 for similar arguments).

The 2007 survey contains a question that asks the respondent specifically about the BBK. It is a dummy coded 1 for those who considered the BBK scandal the most important in terms of how they voted and 0 otherwise, and this variable is appropriate to test our hypothesis. We choose to use Yushin variable based on the respondent"s placement of score 1 "not important at all" to 10 "very important" for the legacy of Yushin in deciding for whom they voted in the 2012 presidential election. It is appropriate to test our hypothesis as it is related to Park Geun-hye's ill association with the past.

Numerous studies have pointed to three dominant factors that determine the vote choice of Korean electorate: regional, ideological, and generational differences. R in equation 1 above is a vector of regional dummy variables based on the hometown of a respondent. The regional dummies include Youngnam, Honam, Choongchung, and Other regions. The Seoul-Incheon-Gyeonggi metropolitan region is used as a base category (excluded). The Ideology variable is based on the responses to the self-ideological tendency item, which is measured on an 11-point scale ranging from 0 for "extremely left" to 10 for "extremely right."[3] The Age variable is included to account for the effect of the generational differences. In addition to these fundamental determinants, we include the usual control variables of Gender, Education, and Income in Z vector.[4]

Findings

Table 4 presents results from our logit regressions for the 2002, 2007, and 2012 presidential elections. Instead of reporting coefficients, we report the average marginal effects (dF/dx), which can be interpreted as the change in the probability of voting for the candidate in the column, associated with a unit change in the independent variable.

Table 4. Determinants of vote choice in South Korean presidential elections

	2002	2007			2012
	Lee_HC	Chung_DY	Lee_HC	Moon_KH	Park_GH
Morality	−0.139***				
	(0.033)				
BBK		0.176***	0.053**	0.007	
		(0.032)	(0.025)	(0.015)	
Yushin					−0.055***
					(0.009)
Youngnam	0.218***	−0.083***	−0.026	−0.025	0.106**
	(0.039)	(0.030)	(0.027)	(0.018)	(0.045)
Honam	−0.337***	0.411***	−0.081***	0.024	−0.442***
	(0.034)	(0.053)	(0.028)	(0.026)	(0.049)

Choongchung	−0.024	−0.033	0.109**	−0.010	−0.110*
	(0.052)	(0.039)	(0.047)	(0.025)	(0.063)
Others	0.028	0.015	0.064	−0.016	−0.078
	(0.069)	(0.064)	(0.060)	(0.031)	(0.086)
Ideology	0.167***	−0.033***	0.005	−0.016***	0.119***
	(0.018)	(0.007)	(0.006)	(0.004)	(0.013)
Age	0.005***	0.001	−0.002*	−0.002***	0.008***
	(0.001)	(0.001)	(0.001)	(0.001)	(0.002)
Gender	0.005	−0.022	0.029	−0.007	0.006
	(0.032)	(0.028)	(0.023)	(0.016)	(0.042)
Income	0.022**	0.012**	−0.008*	0.004	−0.002
	(0.009)	(0.006)	(0.005)	(0.003)	(0.007)
Education	0.008	−0.034	0.016	0.020	−0.072*
	(0.023)	(0.025)	(0.023)	(0.017)	(0.041)
Observations	1,176	828	828	828	978

Entries are dF/dx and robust standard errors in parentheses obtained from binary logit regressions for the 2002 and 2012 presidential elections and multinomial logit regressions for the 2007 election. For the multinomial logit regression, the base outcome is voting for Lee Myung-bak. * $p < 0.1$, ** $p < 0.05$, *** $p < 0.01$.

The results for the variables we put in our model based on previous studies of Korean elections are generally consistent with expectations. We see the Honam-Youngnam split in their support of political parties. Candidates of the left (the NMDP, the UNDP, and the DUP) and right (the GNP and the Saenuri) received their respective ideologically oriented support, statistically speaking. Therefore, ideology, whose impact had been growing at the turn of the millennium, continued to play a significant role in the presidential elections in 2002, 2007, and 2012. As Kim, Choi, and Cho (2008) showed for the presidential election in 2002 and the National Assembly elections in 2004, our results also support the generational differences that the old supported conservative party candidates and the young were on the side of the left in all three elections.

We now report the results of the test for our main hypothesis regarding CNT. We found strong support for our hypothesis. Those voters who found morality as the most important criterion for their choice voted against Lee Hoi-chang in 2002. Those who thought that the BBK was an important issue heavily voted against Lee Myung-bak in 2007. Those who thought the legacy of Yushin was relevant voted against Park Geun-hye in 2012. Overall, our results show that the individual CNTs significantly affect the vote choices of Korean electorate. Furthermore, the relationship between CNT and voting against the candidate with a negative trait is statistically very strong in all three presidential elections (p-values smaller than .00001).

The 2007 and 2012 surveys contain an interesting question that asks the respondent to choose from the following options: 1 = "s/he voted for her/his favorite candidate hoping that the person would be elected"; 2 = "s/he voted against a particular candidate s/he disliked"; and 3 = "s/he did not particularly care for who would get elected." In a way, this question directly asks whether the respondent cast a negative vote. We utilize this survey question to establish the causal link for the story we tell in this study.

Table 5. Determinants of negative voting

Variables	2007	2012
	Vote_Against	Vote_Against
BBK	0.080***	
	(0.029)	
Yushin		0.020***
		(0.005)
Youngnam	−0.063*	−0.053*
	(0.035)	(0.030)
Honam	−0.048	0.038
	(0.041)	(0.040)

Choongchung	−0.097***	−0.022
	(0.040)	(0.041)
Others	0.065	0.121*
	(0.069)	(0.067)
Ideology	−0.003	−0.010
	(0.006)	(0.006)
Age	−0.000	−0.002**
	(0.001)	(0.001)
Gender	0.024	−0.023
	(0.027)	(0.026)
Income	0.006	0.009**
	(0.006)	(0.004)
Education	0.024	0.054**
	(0.026)	(0.027)
Observations	854	979

Entries are dF/dx and robust standard errors in parentheses obtained from binary logit regressions. * $p < 0.1$, ** $p < 0.05$, *** $p < 0.01$.

First, we analyze who the negative voters are, i.e., who chose the option 2 in the abovementioned survey item. The results reported in Table 3 shows that, after holding other variables constant, those who thought the BBK and the legacy of Yushin important were strongly more likely to be negative voters in the 2007 and 2012 Korean presidential elections.[5] In other words, in both elections voters voted negatively because of their aversion for CNTs. Given this tendency, we conjecture that the military service issue of Lee Hoi-chang's son also caused the negative voting back in 2002, although we do not have data to back it up. Second, we analyze the impact of negative voting on vote choice. We generated three dummy variables from the responses to the abovementioned survey question. We used option 1 as a reference category (excluded) and show the impact of options 2 (Vote Against) in Table 6. The results clearly indicate that negative voters voted against candidates with negative traits.

Table 6. Negative voting against candidates with negative traits.

	2007			2012
	Chung_DY	Lee_HC	Moon_KH	Park_GH
Vote_Against	0.250***	0.071**	0.006	−0.189***
	(0.045)	(0.031)	(0.021)	(0.046)
Vote_None	0.022	0.129***	−0.007	0.014
	(0.036)	(0.038)	(0.019)	(0.067)
Youngnam	−0.059**	−0.012	−0.028	0.128***
	(0.029)	(0.026)	(0.018)	(0.044)
Honam	0.457***	−0.072***	0.015	−0.428***
	(0.050)	(0.024)	(0.025)	(0.049)
Choongchung	0.002	0.133***	−0.012	−0.097
	(0.042)	(0.048)	(0.025)	(0.061)
Others	−0.004	0.050	−0.020	−0.037
	(0.053)	(0.054)	(0.031)	(0.087)
Ideology	−0.037***	0.007	−0.016***	0.120***
	(0.007)	(0.005)	(0.004)	(0.012)
Age	−0.000	−0.001	−0.002***	0.008***
	(0.001)	(0.001)	(0.001)	(0.002)
Gender	−0.023	0.040*	−0.012	0.026
	(0.029)	(0.022)	(0.016)	(0.041)
Income	0.011*	−0.007*	0.004	−0.002
	(0.006)	(0.004)	(0.003)	(0.007)
Education	−0.052**	0.015	0.020	−0.064
	(0.026)	(0.021)	(0.017)	(0.041)
Observations	829	829	829	991

Entries are dF/dx and robust standard errors in parentheses obtained from multinomial logit regressions for the 2007 presidential election and binomial logit regressions for the 2012 election. For the multinomial logit regression, the base outcome is voting for Lee Myung-bak. * $p < 0.1$, ** $p < 0.05$, *** $p < 0.01$.

Taken together, the results reported in Tables 3 and 4 show that the electorate's aversion for CNTs was closely associated with negative voting which is directed against candidates with negative traits. This analysis allows us to establish a probable direction of causal relationship between CNTs and vote choice in Korean presidential elections.

Interactions betwee CNTs and dominant determinants of vote choice

We have provided evidence that CNTs significantly impact the vote choice in presidential elections in Korea. We also have confirmed that the three dominant determinants of vote choice — regional attachment, ideology, and generation — continue to play significant roles. In this section, we explore the interactions between CNTs and these dominant factors. Do the effects of negative traits differ across important individual charactieristics?

We use the multiplicative interaction framework to investigate how the effects of the CNT variables are conditioned by regional, ideological, and generational differences. In addition to Model 1, we include the interactive terms between CNT and the regional dummies, between CNT and Ideology, and between CNT and Age.[13] The interaction model is as follows:

$$V_i = a_1 CNT_i + R_i'\beta + \gamma_1 Ideology_i + \gamma_2 Age_i + [CNT \times R]_i^1 \delta$$
$$+ \theta_1 [CNT \times Ideology]_i + \theta_2 [CNT \times Age]_i = Z_i^1 \lambda + \epsilon_i \quad (2)$$

Instead of reporting coefficients, we calculate the marginal effects of the CNT variables for each of the different voter groups — that is, voters from different regions, voters with different ideologies, and voters from different generations — and plot them in Figure 1. The dot plots represent the marginal effects of CNTs conditional on regional attachment, ideology, and age. The pointwise 95% confidence intervals obtained using the delta method are indicated by capped spikes. The left, middle, and right graphs present the marginal effects of CNTs on the probabilities of voting for Lee Hoi-chang in 2002, Lee Myung-bak in 2007, and Park Geun-hye in 2012, respectively.13.

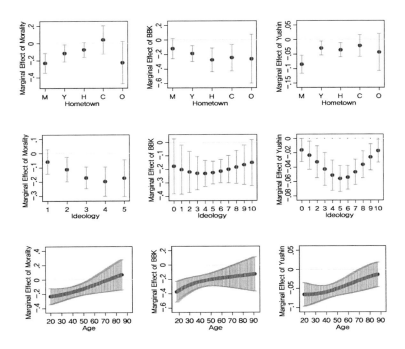

Figure 1. Marginal effects of CNTs by regional attachment, ideology, and age, the 2002, 2007, and 2012 presidential elections.

Note: The dot plots represent the marginal effects of CNTs on the probabilities of voting for Lee Hoi–chang (left panel), Lee Myung–bak (middle panel), and Park Geun–hye (right panel). The capped spikes indicate .95 confidence intervals obtained using the delta method. In the top graphs, M, Y, H, C, and O indicate the Seoul–Incheon–Gyeonggi Metropolitan area, Youngnam, Honam, Choongchung, and Other regions, respectively.

Figure 1 clearly suggests that the effects of negative traits differ across different conditions. However, the three dominant factors do not always systematically moderate the effects of CNTs in a consistent way across elections. First, it is clear from the bottom graphs that generation is an interesting moderating variable. The marginal effects of CNTs are significant among younger voters, and the effects grow smaller as voters grow older. Among the oldest voters, the effects are not significantly different from zero. This finding is consistent with a recent study by Choi et al.(2017) showing that older South Koreans are highly likely to become "ritual partisans" – a type of voters who rely heavily on their partisan cues when they vote (Dalton, 1984, 2000, 2013). Ritual partisans rarely deternine their stances on issues important when choosing how to vote.

Second, ideology also seems to moderate the effects of CNTs, though its pattern is less clear compared to the case of generation. From the middle graphs, we can see that the effects of CNTs tend to be stronger among voters with moderate ideologies and weaker among those with extreme ideologies. Voter with extreme ideologies may support for candidates and parties based strongly on their ideolgical preferences, whereas voters with moderate ideologies may not be loyal supporters. Therfore, the effects of CNTs on vote choice may be conditional on voters' ideologies.

The two abovementioned findings suggest that voters who are more deterministic are less likely to be affected by CNT issues. Older voters and voter with extreme ideologies tend to be more certain about their voting intentions. If we apply this to the case of the interadtion between CNT issues and regional attachment, we sould expect the effects of CNTs to be the smallest among voters from Youngnam or Honam. However, the top graphs conditadict this expectation. In 2002 and 2012, the effects of CNTs were greater among the voters from the Seoul-Incheon-Gyeonggi metropolitan area than among those from Youngnam and Honam. In 2007, however, the effects were greater among voters fromf Youngnam, Honam and Choongcheong than among those from the metropolitan area. One possible reason for this descrepancy may be that Lee Myungf-bak was a former mayor of the capital city of Seoul until 2006, one year before the presidential election.

Conclusion

In this article, we investigated the impact of CNT in South Korea. We noted that most scholarly studies analyzing CNTs deal with elections in advanced Western democracies, resulting in a gap related to the knowledge of third-wave countries. We analyzed the three latest presidential elections held in 2002, 2007, and 2012 because there were important CNT issues and relevant survey questions. Our study of CNT in Korea shows that CNTs, be they in the form of personal morality issue, a corruption issue, or a bad personal association issue, have statistically significant and negative effects on the vote choices of the electorate.

We also investigated the interactions between CNTs and the three dominant determinants of South Korean vote choice, namely, regional attachment, ideology, and generation. Though the patterns are not strikingly persistent over the three elections, we found that deterministic voters, such as older voters who are more likely to be "ritual partisans," and voters with extreme ideologies, are less likely to be affected by CNT issues. Thus, our findings suggest that the effects of CNT issues are conditioned by important individual characteristics.

We understand that our study has room for improvement. In this study, we designed the empirical models such that voters' responses to CNT issues affect their vote choices, following the specifications used in the literature on issue voting (Alvarez and Nagler, 1995; Ansolabehere et al., 2008; Erikson and Tedin, 2015). However, we cannot entirely exclude the possibility that voters' vote choices affect their responses to CNT issues. Thus, controlling for this possibility of reverse csusality would have improved the research. Unfortunately, it is almost impossible to control for such a possibility, especially given the cross-sectional data used in this study. It is important to note that we raise this possible limitaion, not to abandon what we have argued, bu to precisely specify the limitations of our analysis.

Finally, we argue that this study is an important step in filling the gap between the developed and developing democracies. We think that this is the most important contribution of this study because our findings can potentially be generalized to other developing democracies. This is especially important given that more new democracies are now implementing fair and free elections in which the elites left over from authoritarian rule are running. Extending the scope of inquiry to other new democracies, such as countries in Asia and Latin America, will enhance our understanding of CNTs in general.

Notes

1. The KSDC maintains all post-democratization presidential and National Assembly election studies run jointly by the National Election Commission (NEC). Those who are not familiar with Korean surveys can simply consider these studies as equivalent to the NES in the U.S. or the BES in the U.K.. The KSDC election surveys are the most frequently used data for analyzing Korean elections.

2. Note that in the 2002 presidential election survey, the Ideology variable is measured on a 5-point scale, with 1 being "very liberal" and 5 being "very conservative."

3. For Gender, a 1 is assigned if a respondent is female while 0 is assigned if a respondent is male. The level of Education was categorized into three groups: 1 = "less than middle school," 2 = "high school graduate," and 3 = "more than some college education." Income variable is measured differently in different surveys. It is an 8-, 10-, and 12-point scaled variables in the 2002, 2007, and 2012 surveys, respectively. Higher values represent higher income.

4. The dependent variable is coded 1 for those who chose option 2; and 0 otherwise. We repeated the analysis after excluding the respondents who chose option 3 (not reported). The results were essentially the same.

5. Dobratz and Whitfield (1992) found a similar result in Greek elections.

6. The entries reported in the seventh to last rows were excerpted from the National Election Commission (2003, 2008, 2013). On every presidential election, NEC has sampled about 10% of total eligible voters and documented the voter turnouts broken down by sex, age cohorts, and places of residence.

◈ Reference

본 QR 코드를 스캔하시면 '김희민 교수의 정치학 연구'의
참고문헌을 확인하실 수 있습니다.

챕터별 학술지

○●○

[1] Voter Ideology in Western Democracies, 1946–1989.
* *HeeMin Kim and Richard C. Fording. 1998.*
* *European Journal of Political Research 33: 73—97.*

[2] Voter Ideology, the Economy, and the International Environment in Western Democracies, 1952–1989.
* *HeeMin Kim and Richard C. Fording. 2001.*
* *Political Behavior 23(Special Issue on Comparative Political Behavior Guest Edited by Richard Johnston): 53—73.*

[3] Does Tactical Voting Matter?:
The Political Impact of Tactical Voting in Recent British Elections.
* *HeeMin Kim and Richard C. Fording. 2001.*
* *Comparative Political Studies 34: 294—311.*

[4] Government Partisanship in Western Democracies, 1945–1998.
* *HeeMin Kim and Richard C. Fording. 2002.*
* *European Journal of Political Research 41: 165—184.*

[5] Voter Ideology in Western Democracies: An Update.
* *HeeMin Kim and Richard C. Fording. 2003.*
* *European Journal of Political Research 42: 95—105.*

[6] Electoral Systems, Party Systems, and Ideological Representation:
An Analysis of Distortion in Western Democracies.
* *HeeMin Kim, G. Bingham Powell, Jr., and Richard C. Fording. 2010.*
* *Comparative Politics 42:167—185*

[7] Does Tactical Voting Matter?:
The Political Impact of Tactical Voting in Canadian Elections.
* *HeeMin Kim and Tatiana Kostadinova. 2011.*
* *International Area Studies Review 14: 49−71*

[8] The Role of Media in the Repression−Protest Nexus:
A Game−Theoretic Model.
* *HeeMin Kim, Jenifer Whitten−Woodring, and Patrick James. 2015.*
* *Journal of Conflict Resolution 59: 1017−1042.*

[9] When Meritocracies Fail
* *HeeMin Kim and Glenn R. Parker. 1995.*
* *Journal of Economic Behavior and Organization 28: 1−9.*

[10] Signalling and Tariff Policy:
The Strategic Multi−Stage Rent Reduction Game.
* *Mike Lustzig, Patrick James, and HeeMin Kim. 2003.*
* *Canadian Journal of Political Science, 36: 765−790.*

[11] Changing Cleavage Structure in New Democracies:
An Empirical Analysis of Political Cleavages in Korea.
* *HeeMin Kim, Jun Y. Choi, and Jinman Cho. 2008.*
* *Electoral Studies 27: 136−150.*

[12] A New Approach to the Territorial Dispute Involving a Former
Colonizer−Colony Pair: The Case of the Dokdo−Takeshima Dispute be-
tween Japan and Korea.
* *HeeMin Kim and Jinman Cho. 2011.*
* *Korea Observer 42: 431−459.*

[13] Educational Disadvantage and Access to the Best Universities in Korea.
* *HeeMin Kim, Heejin Cho, and Hyunah Lee. 2014.*
* *Korea Journal 54: 30−59.*

[14] The Impact of Candidates' Negative Traits on Vote Choice in New
Democracies: A Test Based on Presidential Elections in South Korea.

* HeeMin Kim and Jungho Roh. 2019.

* Journal of Asian and African Studies 54: 211−228.

▌김희민

　　1981년 미국에 유학하여 1983년 미네소타 대학교(University of Minnesota)에서 정치학 학사 학위를 받았다. 1990년에는 워싱턴대학교(Washington University in St.Louis)에서 정치학 박사학위를 받았다. 1989년에 플로리다 주립대학교(Florida State University)에 조교수로 임용이 되었고, 그곳에서 22년을 근무하였다. 2011년 귀국, 서울대학교 사회교육학과에서 정치교육을 가르쳤다. 플로리다 주립대학교에서는 명예교수직을 수여받으며 계속 연을 이어가고 있다. 2015년에는 중국 길림대학교에서 객좌교수로 임명을 받아 정기적으로 방문하여 강의를 하고 있다. 연구관심 분야는 합리적 선택이론, 민주주의 성취도 비교연구, 미래 가버넌스 연구 등이다. Rationality and Politics in the Korean Peninsula(1995), Mapping Policy Preferences: Estimates for Parties, Electors, and Governments, 1945–1998(2001), 매니페스토의 올바른 이해와 사용: 서구 24개국의 정당 매니페스토 연구(2007), Korean Democracy in Transition: A Rational Blueprint for Developing Societies(2011), 게임이론으로 푸는 한국의 민주주의(2013), 민주주의와 리더십 이야기(2016), 한국 보수정부의 부침 2008–2017(2019) 등의 저서를 출판하였고, 그 외에도 약 40편의 해외 학술지 논문이 있다. 북미한국정치연구회의 회장을 역임하였고, 학술활동을 통한 국위선양을 인정받아 김대중 대통령으로부터 대통령 훈포장을 받았다.

김희민 교수의 정치학 연구

초판발행   2022년 6월 20일

지은이   김희민
펴낸이   안종만 · 안상준

편 집   양수정
기획/마케팅   손준호
표지디자인   이영경
제 작   고철민 · 조영환

펴낸곳   (주) **박영사**
                    서울특별시 금천구 가산디지털2로 53, 210호(가산동, 한라시그마밸리)
                    등록 1959. 3. 11. 제300-1959-1호(倫)

전 화   02)733-6771
f a x   02)736-4818
e-mail   pys@pybook.co.kr
homepage   www.pybook.co.kr
ISBN   979-11-303-1540-9 93340

정 가   24,000원